World
of Reading

A Thematic Approach
to Reading Comprehension

3

Joan Baker-González
University of Puerto Rico, Mayagüez (retired)

Eileen K. Blau
University of Puerto Rico, Mayagüez

PEARSON
Longman

World of Reading 3
A Thematic Approach to Reading Comprehension

Pearson Education, 10 Bank Street, White Plains, NY 10606

Acknowledgments: There are many to be thanked for helping us in the process of developing the *World of Reading* series. First and foremost is the University of Puerto Rico at Mayagüez (UPRM) for granting Dr. Blau a sabbatical leave that enabled her to give this project the attention it needed. We are also grateful to the English Department at UPRM, in particular Dr. Betsy Morales, Director, who has supported us in every way possible. We would like to thank the following colleagues, former colleagues, friends, and family members who have generously supported us in the process of developing these books. Those who have helped us in locating appropriate reading selections to use in the series are: Dorothy Blau, John Green, Emily Graesser, Leonora Hamilton, Anthony Hunt, Jeannette Lugo, Rosita Rivera, and Prisca Rodríguez. We would also like to thank the following people for sharing their expertise with us: Claudia Acevedo, Eric Blau, Dr. Gary Breckon, Dr. William Frey, Kenneth Lewis, Aliette Marcelin, Susan Niemeyer, Patricia Payne, Dr. Aixa Rodríguez, Dr. Robert W. Smith, and Dr. Christa Von Hilldebrandt. We are especially grateful to Steven Neufeld and Ali Billuroglu for helping us use their valuable vocabulary profiler at the Compleat Lexical Tutor website. And of course we are grateful to the staff at Pearson Education who have helped us along the way: Pietro Alongi, Danielle Belfiore, Rosa Chapinal, Paula Van Ells, and our development editors, Stacey Hunter, Gosia Jaros-White, and Martha McGaughey. And finally, we wish to thank the writers whose work constitutes the core of these books, as well as all the students we have had over the years who have helped us learn about teaching English language learners to be good readers.

Staff credits: The people who made up the *World of Reading 3* team, representing editorial, production, design, and manufacturing, are Pietro Alongi, Danielle Belfiore, Rosa Chapinal, Dave Dickey, Christine Edmonds, Oliva Fernandez, Stacey Hunter, Martha McGaughey, Paula Van Ells, and Pat Wosczyk.

Text composition: ElectraGraphics, Inc.
Text font: 11.5/13 Minion
Illustrations and tech art: Dan Rosandich and Kenneth Batelman
Text and photo credits: See page 210.

Library of Congress Cataloging-in-Publication Data
Baker-González, Joan.
 World of reading/Joan Baker-González, Eileen K. Blau.
  p. cm.
  Rev. ed. of two previous publications: Building on basics, 1999 and Building understanding, 1995.
  ISBN 978-0-13-600244-4 (student book 1)—ISBN 978-0-13-600210-9 (teacher's ed. 1)—
ISBN 978-0-13-600211-6 (student book 2)—ISBN 978-0-13-600212-3 (teacher's ed. 2)—
ISBN 978-0-13-600214-7 (student book 3)—ISBN 978-0-13-600215-4 (teacher's ed. 3) 1. English language—Textbooks for foreign speakers. 2. Reading comprehension—Problems, exercises, etc. 3. Readers. I. Blau, Eileen K. II. Baker-González, Joan. Building on basics. III. Baker-González, Joan. Building understanding. IV. Title.
  PE1128.B274 2009
  428.0076—dc22

2008034098

ISBN-13: 978-0-13-600214-7
ISBN-10: 0-13-600214-5

PEARSON LONGMAN ON THE WEB

Pearsonlongman.com offers online resources for teachers and students. Access our Companion Websites, our online catalog, and our local offices around the world.

Visit us at **www.pearsonlongman.com**.

Printed in the United States of America
6 7 8 9 10 11 12—V064—17 16 15 14

Contents

Scope and Sequence

UNIT	CHAPTER	TITLE AND GENRE	READING AND STUDY SKILLS*
	Student's Introduction		Previewing Highlighting important information
1 **Friendship**	1	All Kinds of Friends *book excerpt*	Note-taking Interpreting the author's ideas Main ideas
	2	Online Friendships *Internet article*	Awareness of voice Note-taking
	3	How Do I Like Thee . . . *textbook excerpt*	Understanding how sources are cited in academic writing
	4	The First Day of School *short story*	Finding supporting details Point of view
Unit Wrap-Up			
2 **Parents and Children**	5	Mother Was Really Somebody *magazine article; personal essay*	Introduction to less structured/ more independent previewing
	6	The Problems of Fathers and Sons *personal essay*	Note-taking Distinguishing between reasonable and unreasonable inferences
	7	Greener Grass *magazine article; essay*	
	8	Love, Your Only Mother *short story*	Noticing details
Unit Wrap-Up			

*All chapters practice the following skills which are not repeated in the Scope and Sequence: **Activating background knowledge, Previewing, Determining a purpose for reading, Inferring meaning of vocabulary while reading,** and **Supporting answers with evidence from the reading.**

Scope and Sequence

VOCABULARY SKILLS	FOUNDATIONS FOR WRITING
Multiword expressions Participial adjectives	Paragraph contribution Paraphrasing
	Paragraph contribution
Definitions of scientific terms in text	Citing sources in magazines
Using paraphrases to learn vocabulary	
Word families Polysemous words	Personal and academic writing
Using paraphrases to learn vocabulary	Paragraph contribution Word order
Using paraphrases to learn vocabulary	Supporting general statements
	Characteristics of essays
Synonyms	
Word families Collocations	Personal and academic writing

Scope and Sequence

VOCABULARY SKILLS	FOUNDATIONS FOR WRITING*
Multiword expressions	Providing transitions
Synonyms Multiword expressions	Paraphrasing Supporting general statements Author's purpose
	Text organization (introduction, body, conclusion)
Using paraphrases to learn vocabulary	Careful selection of details
Word families Collocations	Personal and academic writing
Word analysis	Using an analogy to illustrate a concept
Multiword expressions	Applying knowledge of text organization, format, and writer's purpose
	Lists
Word families Polysemous words Unit glossary	Personal, academic, and creative writing

Teacher's Introduction

World of Reading, a multi-genre thematic reading series, is a revision and expansion of the successful *Building on Basics* and *Building Understanding* books. The new, more streamlined three-book series has updated reading selections that are engaging and varied, and a vocabulary program built on current research and the results of vocabulary profiler analysis. The careful selection of complementary thematic readings and the research-based focus on vocabulary building give students a solid foundation for academic reading.

The Readings

Central to the increased academic focus is the variety of texts in the new series.

- Texts are authentic, written for native speakers of English, moving from adapted to non-adapted.
- Texts cover a broad spectrum of topics common in college level courses including science, social science, business, and literature.
- Each book has at least one selection from a textbook.
- Each book has readings that report on research.
- Some selections are contemporary and some are older, encouraging students to develop historical perspective.

Vocabulary Building

To select vocabulary for the stronger vocabulary component, every reading was analyzed using tools at the Compleat Lexical Tutor website. Reading selections were submitted to the vocabulary profiler developed by Billuroglu and Neufeld, the BNL, as well as the Classic version of the British National Corpus vocabulary profiler, to reveal the words on the Academic Word List—the AWL (Coxhead 2000).[*] In all cases we began with authentic readings, but in Book 1, we adapted most of them so that 90–95% of the vocabulary can be found on the list of the 2,000 most frequent words. Book 2 has minimally adapted texts while texts in Book 3 are unadapted and thus entirely authentic.

Facts concerning vocabulary and reading length are summarized as follows:

World of Reading 1: Targeted vocabulary is generally chosen from words that are less common than the first 2,000 words of English, selected AWL words and multiword expressions. Selections are approximately 400–800 words.

World of Reading 2: Most targeted vocabulary also comes from words that are less common than the first 2,000 words, but since these readings are minimally adapted, there is a heavier vocabulary load. Again, selected AWL words and multiword expressions are targeted. Selections are approximately 500–1,200 words.

[*]Coxhead, Averil (2000). A New Academic Word List. *TESOL Quarterly* 34:2 (213–238).

World of Reading 3: Targeted vocabulary is generally chosen from words that are less frequent than the 2,500 most frequent words, selected AWL words, and multiword expressions. Selections are usually 800 words or longer.

World of Reading serves as a foundation for academic work and presents teachers with various opportunities to foster an academic mindset in their students. Thus, exercises in this series encourage students to:

- support answers to questions with evidence from the text
- develop the ability to distinguish a writer's ideas from one's personal opinions of them
- give writers and researchers credit for their ideas
- be curious about the world, its problems and their solutions

Description of the Books

Each book consists of six units that focus on a topic of personal or world interest. The units have four chapters, almost all with one reading plus exercises. The first three chapters of each unit are non-fiction—usually magazine, newspaper or Internet articles, or excerpts from non-fiction books, such as content area textbooks. The fourth selection is a piece of literature—a short story, a poem, a personal essay, or an excerpt from an autobiography or memoir. The literature selections are not adapted.

To benefit from a thematic reader, students must read several selections on a single topic. When determining what to include in a reading program, it's important to think in terms of whole units rather than individual reading selections. Omitting a single selection from a unit would probably leave enough material for students to benefit from related readings, but choosing a single reading from a unit would not. Also, when choosing selections remember that the non-fiction selections tend to build background knowledge that facilitates the comprehension and enjoyment of the literature selections.

Each book begins with a Student's Introductory Chapter that is designed to introduce students to important features of the book. It should not be omitted. In the back of the book, you will find maps of the world and North America. It has been our experience that a teacher can't count on students knowing geography, and we suggest you use this series to improve students' knowledge of the world. Talk with them about the many places mentioned in *World of Reading* and find out what they know about them.

Organization of the Units

Units and chapters of *World of Reading* follow a consistent format, making it easier for students and teachers to use the series.

The title, picture(s), questions, and quote(s) on the **Unit Opener** can all be used to activate students' background knowledge of the unit topic as well as to make predictions about its content. However, do not expect students to have more than partial answers to the questions until they have completed the unit.

The material in **About the Reading** varies in length and content depending on the reading; it contains information about the source of the reading, occasionally background information on the topic, and especially in the case of literary selections, information about the author. We suggest that you talk to students about the fact that the source of material is of interest and value in the academic world.

Before You Read usually includes two parts: **Thinking about the Topic** and **Previewing**. These are designed to activate students' background knowledge for the chapter. Sometimes vocabulary that is essential for comprehension of the reading is introduced before students read; in this case, it is italicized. You may find these words in the Vocabulary Review exercise described below.

Good readers generally preview non-fiction material. Therefore, we provide practice of this skill for non-fiction selections. Previewing gives readers an idea of what to expect and, consequently, a better chance to understand. In most cases the whole class should do these parts together.

Another important reading skill that comes before reading is **having a purpose for reading**. Students are regularly instructed to turn to the questions in Comprehension Check—First Reading. Being able to answer the two or three questions in that exercise provides a purpose for the first reading.

A new feature of this series is what we call **marginal multiple choice (MMC)**. It provides help in inferring at least partial meanings of words while reading. In the margin next to a word or expression that is likely to be unfamiliar but which is partially inferable, students will see two choices, only one of which makes sense in the context. Encourage students to take advantage of this unique feature so they can continue reading more fluently when the vocabulary load is heavy for them.

Another feature that helps students to continue reading is **glossing**. The following types of items are typically glossed: culturally specific and technical terms, proper names, foreign words and phrases, acronyms and abbreviations, slang terms, archaic vocabulary, and occasionally some difficult vocabulary that is not important for students to learn at their current level. For the poems, difficult vocabulary is glossed so students can read them easily and with maximum enjoyment.

Students will read each selection twice; **Comprehension Check—First Reading** is a short set of questions that students should be able to answer after finishing the first reading of a selection. The questions are text-bound and require a basic comprehension of the whole text; they cannot be answered simply by reading the beginning of the selection.

Comprehension Check—Second Reading requires more thorough understanding but still focuses on the text and its meaning as opposed to students' opinions of it. Formats include true/false, multiple choice, matching, listing, filling in charts, sorting, and the more traditional *wh*-questions. When responding to this exercise, students should always be required to support their answers with evidence from the text. There are good reasons for doing this:

- Having students explain how they arrived at an answer or a conclusion can help teachers see where comprehension is weak, and enables them to guide students onto the right track if necessary.
- Sometimes students see things in the text that we may have overlooked. For example, teachers may not notice ambiguities that students do notice, and what appears to be an "incorrect" answer might actually be supported by evidence from the text.

Starting in Book 2, you will sometimes find a note-taking icon in **Comprehension Check—Second Reading** when there are *wh*-questions. When this icon appears, students are instructed to highlight or jot down facts, words and phrases, but not complete sentences (at least not without using quotation marks). The purpose is to develop an important academic skill, note-taking, and the instruction not to copy whole sentences is an opportunity to begin teaching students to be careful about plagiarism. Whatever the form of the comprehension check, its primary purpose is to help students develop the ability to read and learn from authentic texts on their own, not to test their comprehension.

Vocabulary exercises follow all readings except poems. Target vocabulary includes words that are pre-taught in Thinking about the Topic, that have marginal multiple choices, and that appear in Vocabulary Building exercises. These are listed by chapter at the back of the book. The vocabulary exercises in this program are intended to give students help in learning the meanings of the numerous words and expressions that they will encounter in authentic texts. Given that it takes multiple exposures to learn new words and expressions, and the fact that there are so many polysemous words in the language, we strongly recommend that vocabulary exercises be seen as an opportunity for teaching rather than testing. We also hope you will encourage your students to keep a word bank as described in the Student's Introductory Chapter of each book.

The first vocabulary exercise in each chapter is marginal multiple choice. The key goal in this exercise is for students to get partial meaning and to be able to continue reading. The first after-reading vocabulary exercise is Vocabulary Building, in which words and expressions are presented in the exact context in which they are used in the selection. The second exercise, provided in nearly half the chapters, helps students use the steps described in the Student's Introductory Chapter to Book 1: recognizing and skipping non-essential vocabulary; noticing and learning multiword expressions as single units; locating definitions in the text; inferring from context and using prefixes, suffixes, and the parts of compound words to figure out their meaning; and practicing dictionary use.

The last vocabulary exercise, **Vocabulary Review**, is a cloze exercise that draws on vocabulary in the previous exercises, multiple choice vocabulary checks from the margins next to the readings, and words introduced in the **Before You Read** section. This exercise gives additional exposure to some of the targeted vocabulary, an important factor in vocabulary acquisition. It also provides a summary of the selection, which can help improve comprehension and can serve as a model for summarizing, if you choose to use it that way.

Please note that several units in the series include a glossary of technical terms related to the unit topic. This new academic feature mirrors content area textbooks and helps students expand their vocabularies.

Text Analysis exercises help students derive meaning from a selection, notice elements that can aid their reading comprehension, and learn some things that will help them with their own writing. Many of the exercises in this section involve looking at overall organization of texts, revealing ways in which texts are commonly organized by North American and British writers. Other exercises focus on smaller segments of text down to the word level. Elements of literature and conventions of academic writing are the focus of a few Text Analysis exercises.

Responding to Reading offers discussion questions that relate closely to the text but extend to broader, related issues, allowing students to talk about their own personal experience and opinions. These questions allow students to engage in the academic practice of developing and discussing ideas on a topic they now know something about. When doing this section, you can foster vocabulary acquisition by listing vocabulary items on the chalkboard and encouraging students to use them in their discussion.

The **Unit Wrap-Up** has two major components: **Extending Your Vocabulary** and **Writing**. Extending Your Vocabulary recycles vocabulary from the unit and has two parts. The first part is **Word Families**, which extends vocabulary knowledge by teaching related words; it also sensitizes students to parts of speech and derivational suffixes. The second is either **Polysemous Words** or **Collocations**. The former calls attention to other meanings of words seen in the unit; the latter focuses attention on how native speakers combine words and thus leads learners to speak and write more like native English speakers. These exercises provide additional exposure to reinforce vocabulary acquisition while helping to refine and deepen word knowledge.

The **Writing** section offers further opportunity for thinking about the topic and issues raised in the unit. It allows students to express themselves, to try to use new vocabulary, and to learn some of the fundamentals of clear writing for both test-taking situations and success in future writing courses.

Flexibility in Ordering Exercises and Grouping Students

Varying the order of exercises for a selection might be advantageous for your students. For example, it might be beneficial to do Vocabulary Building exercises between the first and second readings. In this way students can benefit from a stronger awareness of vocabulary and sensitivity to context during their second reading. The Vocabulary Review, however, should be done later because it serves the dual purpose of reviewing vocabulary and summarizing the selection itself. It may also be helpful to do a Text Analysis exercise before the second reading, especially when the exercise provides an overview of how the entire selection is organized. Final decisions about ordering of exercises are best made by you, the teacher.

With regard to grouping your students for doing the exercises, use your judgment concerning whether it would be best to have students work in pairs, small groups, as a whole class, or individually.

Teacher's Manual with Tests

There is a Teacher's Manual to accompany each book. It includes answer keys, a few tips for teachers, recommended readings and websites and a unit test. Unit tests have two sections: Reviewing, which focuses on the vocabulary and content of the unit and Exploring, which consists of a new authentic reading on the unit topic with vocabulary and comprehension questions. The new reading in the test can also be used as instructional material if you prefer.

* * *

We hope that both you and your students find this series a helpful and enjoyable way for students to increase their ability to read authentic texts and ultimately to succeed in their academic endeavors.

GETTING STARTED WITH *WORLD OF READING 3*

Welcome to the third book of the *World of Reading* series, a reading program designed to develop your general reading skills, enlarge your English vocabulary, and increase your enjoyment of reading, all to prepare you for the challenge of post-secondary education in English.

Reading for the purpose of learning is important not only to earn a diploma, but also as a foundation for adapting to change in any career and in dealing with many of life's problems. It is going to be necessary, whether online or on paper, to keep you up to date and to solve problems in a changing world no matter what career you pursue.

The general review of the reading process which follows should help you handle not only the longer readings in this book, but also those you will meet when you do academic work in English.

Before You Read

Before you begin to read, **preview** your reading assignment to get a general idea of the topic and how the reading is organized. This will make reading easier and your comprehension better. Previewing includes doing one or more of the following:

- reading the title and section titles, called headings, to help you see what's coming and how it is organized
- reading the first paragraph or two and the last paragraph or two (for longer readings)
- reading the first sentence of the other paragraphs
- studying the pictures, charts, graphs, and tables and reading their captions

Then think about what you already know about the topic. Efficient readers use what they know about a topic to help them understand new ideas and information in the text. In this book, you will sometimes find information to read in the section Thinking about the Topic, which should help you understand the topic better. Finally, use the questions in Comprehension Check—First Reading to give you an initial purpose for reading. Those questions give you an idea of what you can reasonably expect to understand on a first reading.

While You Read

When you have longer reading assignments, as you will in *World of Reading 3*, you may want to read them in shorter, more manageable pieces. Some of the longer readings in this book have suggestions for where to divide them, and sometimes comprehension questions are divided in the same way.

Handle Unfamiliar Vocabulary

While reading, you will be dealing with unfamiliar vocabulary. As in *World of Reading 1* and *World of Reading 2*, help in improving your ability to infer at least partial meanings of unfamiliar words and expressions is provided in the multiple choices in the margin. In addition, use the five steps listed below to help figure out the meaning of other unfamiliar words, especially while doing the first reading, so you do not have to stop to use your dictionary.

Step 1: Locate the problem. (Is the problem a single word or a multiword expression? Does it look like a word in your own language?)

Step 2: Decide if the word or phrase is important or not. If you can understand the sentence without it, you can continue reading.

Step 3: Look for a definition in the text.

Step 4: Check the parts of the word and the context.

Step 5: Get help: use your dictionary.

It might be a good idea to do Vocabulary Building and the second vocabulary exercise, when there is one, right after your first reading. Save the Vocabulary Review for later.

Using your new knowledge from the vocabulary exercises, reread the article or the parts of it that you need to answer the Comprehension Check—Second Reading.

Especially when the topic of the reading is more technical or academic, highlighting important words in the text or jotting down notes while you are reading to answer the comprehension questions will give you practice in a skill you will use often in doing college reading.

After You Read

In order to learn more vocabulary, you should keep some kind of record of the new words and expressions that you need or want to learn. We recommend making a vocabulary card, like the examples below, for important words and multiword expressions. On the front, write the word or expression and its part of speech (*noun, verb, adjective,* or *adverb*). On the back, write: 1) the context you read it in, 2) the definition, and, if it helps you, 3) the equivalent in your language. The most important of these three things is the context. You learn how to use words and expressions in English by noticing how English speakers and writers use them.

mentor n.	1) *The older instructs the younger. (The older person is the mentor.)* 2) *Advisor (an experienced person who advises and helps an inexperienced person)* 3) *[Equivalent in your language]*
FRONT OF CARD	BACK OF CARD

```
┌─────────────────────────┐        ┌─────────────────────────────────┐
│                         │        │ 1) Friends broaden our horizons. │
│                         │        │                                 │
│                         │        │ 2) Help us understand new       │
│                         │        │    things                       │
│  broaden your horizons  v. │     │                                 │
│                         │        │ 3) [Equivalent in your language] │
│                         │        │                                 │
│                         │        │                                 │
└─────────────────────────┘        └─────────────────────────────────┘

       FRONT OF CARD                          BACK OF CARD
```

One last suggestion about vocabulary: the fact that using the dictionary is the final step in handling unfamiliar vocabulary does not mean it's not important. A learner's dictionary is an invaluable tool and a worthwhile investment. Learner's dictionaries have two features that are crucial for second language learners: they provide example sentences that show how native speakers use words, and they define many multiword expressions that dictionaries for native speakers do not.

In addition to taking full advantage of this book, we encourage you to read whatever is around you: ads, signs, labels, instructions, newspaper and magazine articles—whatever interests you. You have already put in a lot of work to become a proficient reader, and you have come a long way. Keep up the good work as you make this important transition to authentic reading material.

Friendship

Discuss

1. What are friends?
2. What function do friendships serve? Do all friendships serve the same function?
3. How do we make friends? Where do we meet the people who become our friends?

> *A friend is a person with whom I may be sincere.*
> *Before him I may think aloud.*
>
> Ralph Waldo Emerson

> *A friend is someone who walks in when the whole world has walked out.*
>
> author unknown

CHAPTER 1

ABOUT THE READING

"All Kinds of Friends" by Judith Viorst is from her book, *Necessary Losses: The Loves, Illusions, Dependencies and Impossible Expectations That All of Us Have to Give Up in Order to Grow.* After becoming known as a writer for both children and adults, Viorst studied psychology, the study of the human mind and human behavior. Her nonfiction books for adults, such as *Necessary Losses*, reflect her interest in psychology.

BEFORE YOU READ

Thinking about the Topic

Discuss these questions in a small group.

1. Consider the definitions of a friend on the introductory page; think about your friends and write your own definition of a friend. Share your definition with your group. What are the two or three most common definitions that the group came up with?
2. Answer the questions in the chart below about three of your friends.

	Friend 1	Friend 2	Friend 3
1. Are you the same age?			
2. How long have you known each other?			
3. How much face-to-face time do you spend together?			
4. What do you do together?			
5. What do you do for each other?			
6. Why do you like this person?			

3. Share what you discovered about friends. Are your relationships with your various friends the same or different? Are they all the same kind of friend?

Previewing

Review the suggestions for previewing on page xvii if necessary. Preview the selection appropriately. Tell your classmates what you looked at in your preview and why. Then answer these questions.

1. What kinds of friends do you expect to read about?
2. What do you think each category of friend might be?

Before you read, turn to Comprehension Check, First Reading, on page 4. Your purpose for the first reading is to be able to answer those questions.

All Kinds of Friends *By Judith Viorst*

1   Friends broaden our horizons.[1] They serve as new models with whom we can identify. They allow us to be ourself—and accept us that way. They enhance our self-esteem because they think we're OK, because we matter to them. And because they matter to us—for various reasons, at various levels of intensity—they enrich the quality of our emotional life.

[. . .]

2   In my discussions with several people about the people we call our friends, we established the following categories of friendship:

CONVENIENCE FRIENDS

3   These are the neighbor or office mate or member of our car pool[2] whose lives **routinely intersect with** ours. These are the people with whom we exchange small favors. They lend us their cups and silverware for a party. They drive our children to soccer when we are sick. They keep our cat for a week when we go on vacation. And, when we need a lift, they give us a ride to the garage to pick up the Honda. As we do for them.

4   But we don't, with convenience friends, ever come too close or tell too much: We maintain our public face and emotional distance. "Which means," says Elaine, "that I'll talk about being overweight but not about being depressed. Which means I'll admit being mad but not **blind with rage**. And which means I might say that we're **pinched** this month but never that I'm worried sick over money."

5   But which doesn't mean that there isn't sufficient value to be found in these friendships of mutual aid, in convenience friends.

SPECIAL-INTEREST FRIENDS

6   These friendships depend on the sharing of some activity or concern. These are sports friends, work friends, yoga friends, nuclear-freeze friends.[3] We meet to participate jointly in knocking a ball across a net, or saving the world.

7   "I'd say that what we're doing together is *doing* together, not being together," Suzanne says of her Tuesday-doubles friends. "It's mainly a tennis relationship but we play together well." And as with convenience friends, we can, with special-interest friends, be regularly involved without being **intimate**.

[. . .]

CROSS-GENERATIONAL FRIENDS

8   A tender intimacy—tender but unequal—exists in the friendships that form across generations, the friendships that one woman calls her daughter-mother and her mother-daughter relationships. Across the generations the younger enlivens the older, the older instructs the younger. Each role, as mentor or quester,[4] as adult or child, offers gratifications of its own. And because we are unconnected by blood, our words of advice are accepted as wise, not intrusive. . . . We enjoy the rich **disparities** to be found among our cross-generational friends.

(continued)

---

[1] **broaden our horizons** *help us understand new things*
[2] **car pool** *system where people take turns driving so each person uses his or her car less*
[3] **nuclear-freeze friends** *people who work together in the movement to stop the spread of nuclear weapons*
[4] **quester** *person who wants to learn*

routinely intersect with
a. regularly cross with
b. never come together

blind with rage
a. with bad eyesight
b. extremely angry

pinched
a. short of money
b. relaxed about money

intimate
a. very close
b. very weak

disparities
a. mistakes
b. differences

CLOSE FRIENDS

9   Emotionally and physically (by seeing each other, by mail, by talks on the phone) we maintain some ongoing friendships of deep intimacy. And although we may not expose as much—or the same kinds of things—to each of our closest friends, close friendships involve revealing aspects of our private self—of our private feelings and thoughts, of our private wishes and fears and fantasies and dreams.
[...]

10   Close friends contribute to our personal growth. They also contribute to our personal pleasure, making the music sound sweeter, the wine taste richer, the laughter ring louder because they are there. Friends **furthermore** take care—they come if we call them at two in the morning; they lend us their car, their bed, their money, their ear; and although no contracts are written, it is clear that intimate friendships involve important rights and obligations. Indeed, we will frequently turn—for reassurance, for comfort, for come-and-save-me help—not to our blood relations but to friends
[...]

furthermore
a. more distantly
b. in addition

COMPREHENSION CHECK

First Reading

Answer these questions.

1. What type of research, if any, did Viorst conduct to determine her categories of friendship?
2. What are some of the general benefits of friends according to Viorst?
3. Which categories of friends are not usually very close?

Second Reading

Reread parts of the selection as needed to do the tasks below.

1. As you read, highlight or jot down on a separate paper words or phrases that define each category of friendship. Put Viorst's words in quotation marks. Then paraphrase the definition, that is, explain the meaning in your own words. Follow the example given.

Convenience friends: *"we exchange small favors," "friendships of*

mutual aid"

Paraphrase: _Convenience friends are people who help each other._

_____

Special-interest friends: _____

Paraphrase: _____

Cross-generational friends: _____

Paraphrase: _____

Close friends: _____

Paraphrase: _____

2. Do you think the author would agree (A) or disagree (D) with the following statements? Jot down a phrase from the reading that supports your answer.

_A_ a. Convenience friends benefit from each other, but are not close friends.

"But we don't, with convenience friends, ever come too close or tell too much"

____ b. There is a high degree of intimacy between special-interest friends.

_____

____ c. We sometimes get along better with cross-generational friends than with our parents.

_____

____ d. We confide equally in all our close friends.

_____

____ e. Close friends are sometimes more important than family.

_____

3.

MAIN IDEA
You will sometimes be asked, "What is the main idea of what you read?"
Be sure your statement is neither too specific nor too general.
Be sure your statement does not add anything that was not in the reading itself.

Which is the best statement of the main idea in this selection? Circle the letter of the correct answer. What is wrong with the statements that you did not choose?

a. All friends serve the same purpose in our lives.
b. Different friends serve different purposes in our lives.
c. Special-interest friends are people who do things together.
d. For younger people, older friends are the most important for personal growth.
e. Friends are important to us.

Vocabulary Building

Read the underlined word or expression in its context and match it with the correct meaning. The paragraph number is in parentheses. Use a dictionary if necessary.

____ 1. They (friends) <u>enhance</u> our self-esteem . . . (¶1)

____ 2. . . . at various levels of <u>intensity</u> . . . (¶1)

____ 3. . . . I'll talk about being overweight but not about being <u>depressed</u>. (¶4)

____ 4. . . . friendships of <u>mutual aid</u> . . . (¶5)

____ 5. Each role, as <u>mentor</u> or quester, as adult or child . . . (¶8)

____ 6. Each role . . . offers <u>gratifications</u> of its own. (¶8)

____ 7. . . . our words of advice are accepted as wise, not <u>intrusive</u> . . . (¶8)

____ 8. And although we may not <u>expose</u> as much . . . to each of our closest friends . . . (¶9)

____ 9. . . . intimate friendships involve important rights and <u>obligations</u>. (¶10)

____ 10. . . . we will frequently turn—for <u>reassurance</u> . . . not to our blood relations but to friends . . . (¶10)

a. advisor

b. helping each other

c. duties, things you have to do

d. show, reveal

e. improve, make better

f. interfering

g. pleasures, rewards, satisfaction

h. support, comfort

i. very sad

j. strength

Word Analysis

Words can have several parts. Analyzing words and thinking about the meanings of their parts can help you figure out the meanings of unfamiliar words.

A **prefix** comes at the beginning of a word and changes the meaning of the basic word. For example, *un-* in the word *unconnected* means *not;* therefore *unconnected* means not connected.

A **suffix** comes at the end of a word and changes its meaning or grammatical function. For example, the suffix *-ly* in *regularly* changes the adjective *regular* to an adverb.

The suffix *-ship* changes the noun *friend* into another word with a related meaning: *Friendship* is the state or condition of being friends. Other words with the same suffix include: *companionship, leadership, membership,* and *ownership.*

A **compound word** is made of two words. For example, homework (home + work), is school work that you do at home.

Divide the following words into their meaningful parts: basic word(s), prefix, suffix. How does the prefix or suffix change the meaning of the basic word? Write definitions on the lines. Use a dictionary only if necessary.

1. broad/en (¶1) _-en means make, broaden means make broad or wide_
2. enrich (¶1) _____
3. silverware (¶3) _____
4. overweight (¶4) _____
5. unequal (¶8) _____
6. enlivens (¶8) _____
7. ongoing (¶9) _____
8. reassurance (¶10) _____

Vocabulary Review

Complete the following statements about the reading selection with the correct word from the list below. Use each word only once.

broaden	intersect	intrusive	obligations
enhance	intimate	mentor	reassurance

1. With cross-generational friends, the older friend may be a/(an) _____ to the younger. Or the older may play the role of parent, but without his or her advice seeming to be _____, which may be the case with real parents.

2. Convenience friends and special-interest friends, although not close friends, are valuable to us, and our lives routinely _____.

3. Friendship involves _____—responsibilities we have toward our friends—but the _____ we get from them when we need it is a worthy reward.

4. According to Viorst, friends _____ our lives in many ways. They _____ our horizons and generally contribute to our personal growth.

5. There are different categories of friends, but we probably have only a few close or _____ friends to whom we reveal our most private thoughts.

Lists

The order of items in a list should have some logic, for example, from most important to least important or vice versa. How has Viorst ordered her list of different kinds of friends?

Making Definitions Clearer with Specific Examples

To say "Convenience friends do each other favors" is not a very lively definition. Viorst enlivens or enhances her definitions of convenience friends and special-interest friends by providing numerous examples.

List examples of things convenience friends do for each other and things special-interest friends do together.

Convenience Friends	*Special-Interest Friends*
_____	_____
_____	_____
_____	_____
_____	_____

Discuss these questions.

1. Do you agree or disagree with the statements below? Support your opinion with examples from your own experience.
   a. Convenience and special-interest friends may become close friends.
   b. We confide equally in all our close friends.
   c. We sometimes get along better with cross-generational friends than with our parents.
   d. Close friends are sometimes more important than family.

2. What "rights and obligations" of close friends could Viorst be referring to in paragraph 10? What do you consider the "rights and obligations" of close friends?

3. If you have left your country, how would you categorize friends that you left behind? Do they fit into any of the four categories in this selection? If not, what category would you invent?

4. Since Viorst is a woman, do you think her description of different types of friends is equally true for men as well as women? Explain.

"Online Friendships" appeared in *Current Health 2*, an Internet magazine for high school students.

BEFORE YOU READ

Thinking about the Topic

Discuss these questions.

1. How do you stay in contact with your friends?
2. How are friendships made online similar to or different from other types of friendships? Do they form a special category of friends? Are they close friends or not?
3. Do you have a Facebook® or MySpace® page? Why? Do you look at other people's social networking pages? If so, whose profiles do you look at and why?

Previewing

Preview the selection appropriately. Then answer these questions.

1. Do you think the author's attitude toward online friendships will be mostly positive or mostly negative? Explain.
2. How common is online social networking among teenagers in the United States?

Before you read, turn to Comprehension Check, First Reading, on page 12. Your purpose for the first reading is to be able to answer those questions.

READ

Online Friendships *By Jan Farrington*

How They Touch Your Real-Life World

1   Did you know that MySpace has more than 100 million users? Okay, you're not shocked. Ninety percent of U.S. 12- to 17-year-olds say they go online. Whether they use MySpace or Xanga, instant messaging (IM) or e-mail (how last century is that?), teens spend a lot of time **linked** in cyberspace.

(continued)

linked
a. eating
b. connected

2   What do social-networking sites really do for American teens? Does the online world affect face-to-face friendships—or is it just as good as the "real thing"? You might be surprised at what *Current Health* found out!

3   Marcus R., a 14-year-old from Springfield, Ill., loves online role-playing games—where he operates in "realms" populated by thousands of other players. But, he says, he likes to take some of his real-world friends along with him. "It isn't as much fun unless you can talk to someone you know," says Marcus.

4   Lauren B., 17, from Arlington, Texas, attends a high school "so big my friends and I never see each other during the day. So we IM everybody after school."

5   "It's so easy for teens to stay connected—and that's a great thing," says Patricia Hersch, the author of *A Tribe Apart.* She is currently working on a book about teens' strong need for connection with others. With busy schedules and long distances making face-to-face time rare, Hersch says, "young people desperately need community, and a community in cyberspace can be a **tremendous** help and outlet."

tremendous
a. terrible
b. big

HANGING (ONLINE) WITH FRIENDS: IT CAN BE GOOD FOR YOU!

6   If it all disappeared one day—IM and Facebook, MySpace and e-mail—would you care? "It would be a pretty big deal to me," says Mike L., a 13-year-old from Elmhurst, Ill. He uses IM to keep in touch with local pals and friends from his old school in England.

7   Mike is pretty typical, say researchers at Carnegie Mellon University. They found that most teens spend **the bulk** of their time online keeping up with real-life friends, not talking to strangers in chat rooms (which many think are "a waste of time," the study found).

the bulk
a. most
b. none

8   Researchers say IM is an especially useful tool. It gives teens an easy way to keep in touch with a small group of "core" friends while letting them hang out with a wider social circle. Teens seem to need both types of friendships.

9   Two years ago, Lauren J., 16, moved from Texas to Severna Park, Md., leaving behind her best friend and a big circle of buddies. Now she's moving back to Texas and says that because of "IM and MySpace and Yahoo Messenger,® it's like I never really was gone." Without online communication, she says, "I wouldn't have felt as happy and connected, and it would have been way harder to be away from my friends. But my best friend back home is still my best friend—and now I have friends in Maryland to IM too!"

10 Still, life online isn't always friendly. "There's a lot of gossip," says Lauren B. "One of my friends was looking at somebody else's MySpace [profile] and found comments about her. [That person] **denied it**, but the words were there, and [my friend] was really upset."

denied it
a. said it was true
b. said it wasn't true

quarrels
a. fights
b. games

11 Problems or **quarrels** that begin in the real world are often "kept up" online, she adds and it can be easy to get excited and "sound too mean" about somebody in an IM or a MySpace comment. Lauren B. thinks if there's trouble with real-life friends, teens should try to handle it face-to-face: "It's more sincere to break up with a guy or apologize for something important in person, not with an IM."

12 Still, Hersch says that in tough situations the Internet becomes a place where teens can explore their feelings and talk honestly about events in the world and in their lives. "Young people often express a level of emotion that they never would have expressed face-to-face with each other," she told *Current Health.*

13 Parry Aftab, the executive director of WiredSafety.org, also believes that the online world has a lot to offer. "This is a place where teens can really be who they

are," she says. "Online, kids are judged by their ideas," not by who has the hottest body or the coolest car.

14   "One of the fabulous things about the Internet is that no matter where you live, it can put you together with people who share your special interests or situation. . . . It **enlarges** your community and lets you know you're not alone," Aftab notes.

WHEN TO BE CAREFUL

15   Still, says Aftab, teens need to be **cautious** even when they think they're talking to their real-life friends. "You can't ever know for sure who you're talking to online," agrees Lauren J. "It might be some other person pretending to be your friend. So you try not to say things you wouldn't want other people to [know]."

16   She and her friends are quick to take action when something doesn't seem right. "One time, a girl who wasn't really a friend of mine told me in an IM that she was going to have somebody beat up one of my best friends," says Lauren. "That was a big deal! I printed off the instant message and turned it in at the school office—and that stopped it."

17   Never be afraid to back out of a situation online, block unwanted communications, or report bullying or hurtful comments.

YOU'VE GOT CONNECTIONS

18   Parents say they worry that the online world is taking over teen social life. But here's the reality: A 2005 Pew Research Center survey found that though 12- to 17-year-olds spent 7.8 hours a week connecting to friends online, they spent even more time face-to-face. That's an average of 10.3 hours of social activity with friends (outside school) per week!

19   What's more, teens plan to stay connected to their friends through college—and maybe forever. Unlike your parents and grandparents, you will have a much easier time keeping in touch with a lifetime's worth of people you know and care about, no matter where you go. If you avoid trouble spots, the online world gives you a real opportunity to spend even more time, now and in the years ahead, with some very important people in your life: your friends!

CAUGHT IN THE NET?

Keeping Yourself Safe Online

However fun and interesting the online world can seem, you need to be safe. Parry Aftab, the executive director of WiredSafety.org, says there's a lot you can do to protect yourself. She calls it learning to use "the filter between your ears," your brain! Here's her best advice.

- "Have fun, learn things, talk to people—but understand that people you meet online are not real-life friends."
- "Don't tell secrets to someone you met online."
- "Recognize that there are many adults online posing as teens—more of them than teens like to think."
- "Don't tell your personal stuff. You can't really know who that online person really is."
- "Have a cyberbuddy—a good friend who will look over your online communications and tell you when something doesn't feel right, or who can look at your profile on MySpace and say, 'Change that.'"

First Reading

Answer these questions.

1. What two groups of people are the sources of information for this article? What kind of information does each provide?
2. What is the main purpose of this article?
   a. to examine the role of online friendships in the lives of teenagers
   b. to persuade the reader of the advantages of online friendships
   c. to warn teenagers of the dangers of cyber life

Second Reading

Reread parts of the selection as needed to answer these questions. As you read, highlight or jot down helpful words or phrases.

1. What is Marcus's opinion of online role-playing games?
2. Why does Lauren B. IM friends that go to the same high school?
3. Who does Mike keep in touch with online?
4. How did keeping in touch online help Lauren J.?
5. What do these students' uses of the Internet have in common?
6. What do adults quoted in this article say about the social needs of teens and the benefits of socializing online?
7. What are some of the negative aspects and dangers of online socializing? What are some of the precautions you can take?
8. What does the article predict about the maintenance of friendships in the future?

Vocabulary Building

Read the underlined word or expression in its context and match it with the correct meaning. Use a dictionary if necessary.

____ 1. . . . he operates in "realms" populated by thousands of other players. (¶3)

____ 2. . . . young people desperately need community . . . (¶5)

____ 3. " . . . community in cyberspace can be a tremendous help and outlet." (¶5)

____ 4. . . . an easy way to keep in touch with a small group of "core" friends . . . (¶8)

____ 5. "There's a lot of gossip," says Lauren B. (¶10)

____ 6. . . . looking at somebody else's MySpace [profile] . . . (¶10)

____ 7. "It's more sincere to break up with a guy or apologize for something important in person . . . (¶11)

____ 8. "One of the fabulous things about the Internet . . ." (¶14)

____ 9. Never be afraid to back out of a situation online . . . or report bullying or hurtful comments. (¶17)

____ 10. . . . teens plan to stay connected to their friends through college— and maybe forever. (¶19)

____ 11. . . . there are many adults online posing as teens . . . (box)

a. central, most important

b. for all time

c. great, wonderful

d. areas

e. way to express yourself or satisfy a need

f. strongly, very much

g. pretending to be (in order to deceive)

h. say you are sorry

i. talk about other people, often not true

j. short description with important details

k. cruel or frightening

Multiword Expressions

Being able to recognize multiword expressions as units is an important reading skill. For each definition below, scan the indicated paragraph to find the equivalent multiword expression and write it on the line.

1. equal to (¶2)_____

2. communicate with (¶6)_____

3. very important (¶19)_____

4. staying informed about (¶7)_____

5. spend time with (¶8)_____

6. continued (¶11)_____

7. end a relationship with (¶11)_____

(continued)

8. hit, hurt (¶16) _____

9. remove yourself from (¶17)_____

10. dominating, becoming too important, controlling (¶18) _____

11. an amount accumulated over your whole life (¶19)_____

12. examine (last bullet in box) _____

Vocabulary Review

Complete the following statements about the reading selection with the correct word or expression from the list below. Use each word or expression only once.

bulk	enlarging	keep in touch
cautious	forever	posing
core	hanging out	taking over

1. Some people think social networking and IMing are primarily a way of meeting people and broadening or _____ our circle of friends. But actually the _____ of the communication that takes place online is to _____ with our real-world friends.

2. Although online friendships give us a wider circle of friends, our _____ of close friends is still most important to us.

3. Parents fear that the online world is _____ the social lives of their children. However, that is not accurate since teens spend more time _____ with friends in the real world than in the cyberworld.

4. Experts warn that everyone needs to be _____ when socializing online. Don't reveal too much. Block unwanted communication and be careful about adults _____ as teenagers.

5. Electronic communication makes it easy to keep up with old friends. You won't have to lose contact; you can keep in touch _____.

TEXT ANALYSIS ## *Awareness of Voice*

The writer considers that both experts and teens have important ideas to contribute to the discussion of online friendships. She presents ideas from these two sources, as well as her own ideas. Thus, there are three voices in this article: the voice of the author of this article, Jan Farrington; the voice of teens; and the voice of experts.

Write the name of the person whose voice is presented in each paragraph or group of paragraphs. The first five paragraphs are done as examples.

¶1–2   *Jan Farrington citing statistics to introduce the topic, capture the reader's interest, and present the question that the article will answer*

¶3–4   *teens talking about what the Internet offers them*

¶5   *expert author Patricia Hersch talking about benefits of cyberspace for teens*

Hanging (Online) with Friends: It Can Be Good for You!

¶6   _____

¶7–8   _____

¶9   _____

¶10–11   _____

¶12   _____

¶13–14   _____

When to Be Careful

¶15   _____

¶16   _____

¶17   _____

You've Got Connections

¶18–19   _____

box   _____

RESPONDING TO READING

Discuss these questions.

1. If you have left your homeland, how do you keep in touch with friends there?

2. What is your opinion of online communication as opposed to face-to-face communication?

3. Do you agree with the experts cited in this article that people judge each other differently when they get acquainted online rather than in person? Which do you prefer? Explain. If you communicate online, are you more open and sincere online than face-to-face? Explain.

4. How has online communication affected use of the telephone?

CHAPTER 3

ABOUT THE READING

"How Do I Like Thee? Let Me Count the Ways" is from a psychology textbook, *Essentials of Understanding Psychology,* by Robert S. Feldman. This excerpt focuses on the factors or conditions that research has shown bring adults together as friends.

BEFORE YOU READ

Thinking about the Topic

Think about the friends you have now or have had in the past. Then answer these questions.

1. Where did you meet most of your friends?
2. Why did/do you like them?

Previewing

Read the first two sentences of each section (including relevant glosses), and look at the graph at the end. Then answer these questions.

1. What does *proximity* mean?

   a. being friendly   b. being near

2. What does *exposure* mean?

   a. coming into contact   b. staying out in the sun too long

3. What does *similarity* mean?

   a. quality of being alike or almost the same

   b. being familiar with

4. In ¶4, what do you think the boldfaced word *reciprocity* means?

   a. differences   b. giving and receiving mutually

5. *Physical attractiveness* in ¶5 refers to being _____.

   a. popular   b. good-looking

6. What do the words on the left of the graph on page 18 refer to?

   _____

Before you read, turn to Comprehension Check, First Reading on page 18. Your purpose for the first reading is to be able to answer those questions.

READ

How Do I Like Thee?[1] Let Me Count the Ways *By Robert S. Feldman*

a good deal of
a. a lot of
b. incorrect

chances are
a. it's impossible that
b. it's probable that

stemming from
a. coming from
b. disappearing into

folk wisdom
a. an ethnic group
b. common knowledge

promotes
a. helps, advances
b. reduces

critical
a. negative
b. important

1   Research has given us **a good deal of** knowledge about the factors that initially attract two people to each other (Harvey & Weber, 2002). The important factors considered by social psychologists are the following:

2   *Proximity.* If you live in a dormitory[2] or an apartment, consider the friends you made when you first moved in. **Chances are**, you became friendliest with those who lived geographically closest to you. In fact, this is one of the more firmly established findings in the literature on interpersonal attraction: *Proximity* leads to liking (Festinger, Schachter, & Back, 1950; Burgoon et al., 2002).

3   *Mere exposure.* Repeated exposure to a person is often sufficient to produce attraction. Interestingly, repeated exposure to any stimulus—a person, picture, compact disc, or virtually anything—usually makes us like the stimulus more. Becoming familiar with a person can evoke positive feelings; we then transfer the positive feelings **stemming from** familiarity to the person himself or herself. There are exceptions, though. In cases of strongly negative initial interactions, repeated exposure is unlikely to cause us to like a person more. Instead, the more we are exposed to him or her, the more we may dislike the individual (Kruglanski, Freund, & Bar Tal, 1996; Zajonc, 2001).

4   *Similarity.* **Folk wisdom** tells us that birds of a feather flock together.[3] However, it also maintains that opposites attract. Social psychologists have come up with a clear verdict regarding which of the two statements is correct: we tend to like those who are similar to us. Discovering that others have similar attitudes, values, or traits **promotes** our liking for them. Furthermore, the more similar others are, the more we like them. One reason similarity increases the likelihood of interpersonal attraction is that we assume that people with similar attitudes will evaluate us positively. Because we experience a strong **reciprocity-of-liking effect** (a tendency to like those who like us), knowing that someone evaluates us positively promotes our attraction to that person. In addition, we assume that when we like someone else, that person likes us in return (Metee & Aronson, 1974; Bates, 2002).

5   *Physical attractiveness.* For most people, the equation *beautiful = good* is quite true. As a result, physically attractive people are more popular than are physically unattractive ones, if all other factors are equal. This finding, which contradicts the values that most people say they hold, is apparent even in childhood—with nursery-school-age children[4] rating their peers' popularity on the basis of attractiveness—and continues into adulthood.

6   These factors alone, of course, do not account for liking. For example, surveys have sought[5] to identify the factors **critical** in friendships. In a questionnaire answered by some 40,000 respondents, people identified the qualities most valued

(continued)

---

[1]**thee** *old-fashioned word for you; title refers to a poem by Elizabeth Barrett Browning (1806–1861)*
[2]**dormitory** *housing for students on university campuses*
[3]**birds of a feather flock together** *similarity attracts; people who are alike come together*
[4]**nursery-school-age children** *preschool children*
[5]**sought** *past tense of seek (look for)*

in a friend as the ability to keep confidences, loyalty, and warmth and affection, followed closely by supportiveness, frankness, and a sense of humor (Parlee, 1979). The results are summarized in the following graph.

Qualities Most Valued in a Friend

- keeping confidences
- loyalty
- warmth, affection
- supportiveness
- frankness
- sense of humor
- willingness to make time
- independence
- good conversationalist
- intelligence

The list of references cited in this selection appears on page 21.

COMPREHENSION CHECK

First Reading

Answer these questions.

1. What are the factors shown by research to bring people together as friends?
2. What other factors do participants in surveys rank as very important in a friend?

Second Reading

Reread parts of the selection as needed to answer these questions. Mark the statements *T* (true) or *F* (false). Write the paragraph number(s) where you found evidence for each answer.

1. T F We tend to become friends with people we live near and see frequently. ¶___

2. T F Seeing someone frequently usually changes negative initial interactions into more positive feelings. ¶___

3. T F People usually like people who like them. ¶___

4. T F Good-looking children tend to be more popular than unattractive children. ¶___

5. T F Most people believe physical attractiveness is an important quality in choosing friends. ¶___

6. T F According to the survey, intelligence is among the five most important qualities in choosing a friend.

Vocabulary Building

Read the underlined word or expression in its context and then match it with the correct meaning. Use a dictionary if necessary.

____ 1. . . . repeated exposure to . . . <u>virtually</u> anything usually makes us like the stimulus more. (¶3)

____ 2. Becoming familiar with a person can <u>evoke</u> positive feelings . . . (¶3)

____ 3. Social psychologists have come up with a clear <u>verdict</u> regarding which of the two statements is correct . . . (¶4)

____ 4. Discovering that others have similar attitudes, values, or <u>traits</u> promotes our liking for them. (¶4)

____ 5. This finding, which <u>contradicts</u> the values that most people say they hold . . . (¶5)

____ 6. . . . with nursery-school-age children rating their <u>peers'</u> popularity on the basis of attractiveness . . . (¶5)

____ 7. In a questionnaire answered by some 40,000 <u>respondents</u> . . . (¶6)

____ 8. . . . people identified the qualities most valued in a friend as the ability to <u>keep confidences</u> . . . (¶6)

____ 9. . . . followed closely by supportiveness, <u>frankness</u> . . . (¶6)

____ 10. . . . followed closely by supportiveness, frankness, and a <u>sense of humor</u> . . . (¶6)

a. ability to make people laugh

b. almost

c. characteristics, qualities

d. children (people) of the same age

e. produce, bring out

f. disagrees with, states the opposite of

g. not tell secrets

h. honesty, directness

i. decision

j. people who answer something (like a questionnaire)

Vocabulary Review

Complete the following statements about the reading selection with the correct word from the list below. Use each word only once.

attractive	critical	promote	reciprocity
contradicts	exposure	proximity	traits

1. Research has shown that several _____ factors lead people to form friendships.

2. People become friends because they find themselves in the same place. In other words, _____ is often the first step in making friends.

(continued)

3. Repeated contact over time is also a factor. People need to have _____ to each other in order to become friends.

4. Psychologists have found that people who share a variety of attitudes, values, and _____ tend to become friends.

5. It is also true that we like people who like us; this is called the _____-of-liking effect.

6. And, although it _____ what most people say they believe, people also tend to choose friends who are physically _____.

7. Clearly, a variety of factors work together to _____ the positive interpersonal relationships that are so important in our lives.

TEXT ANALYSIS   *Academic Writing: Citing Sources*

Academic writers cite their sources, that is, they tell you where their information comes from. Different fields have different conventions for citing sources. In psychology, writers indicate partial information about the source in parentheses in the text, for example, (Bates, 2002), and give a complete reference list or bibliography at the end of the article, chapter, or book. The purpose of these citations is to give the reader enough information to be able to find and check the material.

The information in each entry has to be in the following order:

Book: author, date of publication, book title, city, and publisher

Magazine or journal article: author, date of publication, article title, magazine or journal title, volume number (issue number if available), page numbers

Article or chapter in a book: author, date of publication, title of article or chapter, book's editor, book title, page numbers, city, and publisher

Although this reading did not include Internet sources, academic writers also report their online sources.

Online periodical: Author, A.A. & Author, B.B. (Date of publication). Title of article. *Title of Online Periodical, volume number* (issue number if available). Retrieved month, day, year, from http://www.someaddress.com

Nonperiodical Web document, webpage, or report: Author, A.A. & Author, B.B. (Date of publication). Title of document. Retrieved month, day, year, from http://www.someaddress.com

1. For each entry in the references on page 21, indicate whether the source is a book, an article in a magazine or journal, or an article or chapter in a book. Pay attention to the use of italics, punctuation, and capitalization in each example.

REFERENCES

Bates, R. (2002). Liking and similarity as predictors of multi-source ratings. *Personnel Review, 31,* 540–552.

Burgoon, J.K., Ramirez, A. J. R., Dunbar, N.E., Kam, K., & Fisher, J. (2002). Testing the interactivity principle: Effects of mediation, propinquity, and verbal and non-verbal modalities in interpersonal interaction. *Journal of Communication, Special Issue: Research on the relationship between verbal and nonverbal communication: Emerging integrations, 52,* 657–677.

Festinger, L., Schachter, S., & Back, K.W. (1950). *Social pressure in informal groups.* NY: Harper.

Harvey, J.H. & Weber, A.L. (2002). *Odyssey of the heart: Close relationships in the 21st Century,* (2nd ed.). Mahwah, NJ: Erlbaum.

Kruglanski, A.W., Freund, T., & Bar Tal, D. (1996). Motivational effects in the mere-exposure paradigm. *European Journal of Social Psychology, 26,* 479–499.

Metee, D.R. & Aronson, E. (1974). Affective reactions to appraisal from others. In T.L. Huston (Ed.) *Foundations of interpersonal attraction,* 235–283. NY: Academic Press.

Parlee, M.B. (1979, October). The friendship bond. *Psychology Today,* 43–45.

Zajonc, R.B.J. (2001). Mere exposure: A gateway to the subliminal. *Current Directions in Psychological Science, 10,* 224–228.

2. Scan the text and match each topic on the left with the sources on the right that most likely would give you further information about that topic.

____ Proximity leading to liking	a. Bates; Metee and Aronson
____ The role of exposure in interpersonal attraction	b. Festinger et al.; Burgoon et al.
____ Reciprocity-of-liking	c. Kruglanski et al.; Zajonc
____ Results of survey on friendship	d. Parlee

RESPONDING TO READING

Discuss these questions.

1. Which of the factors involved in liking other people seem to be common sense? Which do you find more surprising? Which play the biggest role in the formation of your friendships?

2. Have you ever developed a long-distance friendship over the Internet? Did it develop in the same way as a friendship that started because of proximity? How was it similar? How was it different?

3. If you were one of the respondents to the *Psychology Today* survey (results in the graph on page 18), which qualities would you consider very important? Which of these would you consider less important? Why?

4. Which aspects of friendship below do you think are important? Explain.

having fun together	having similar political views
being the same age	being of the same ethnicity
having similar educational and professional level	

"The First Day of School" is a short story by William Saroyan (1908–1981), a prolific writer of novels, short stories, and plays, many based on his experience growing up as the son of Armenian immigrants in California. He is known for his insight into human nature.

BEFORE YOU READ

Thinking about the Topic

Discuss these questions.

1. How do children make friends? Do children make friends in the same ways as adults?
2. What did you have in common with your earliest friends? What did you do together?

Previewing

People do not usually preview literature that they read for pleasure. In school, teachers sometimes help students get started reading a story. Read the title and first eleven lines of this story. Then answer these questions.

1. Who are the three people mentioned in lines 1–5?
2. In lines 9–11 there is a conversation, but no quotation marks. Who are the two people talking in this conversation?
3. What do you think might happen in this story?

READ

The First Day of School

By William Saroyan

1   He was a little boy named Jim, the first and only child of Dr. Louis Davy, 717 Mattei Building, and it was his first day at school. His father was French, a small heavy-set man of forty whose boyhood had been full of poverty and unhappiness and ambition. His mother was dead; she died when Jim was born, and the only
5 woman he **knew intimately** was Amy, the Swedish housekeeper.

    It was Amy who dressed him in his Sunday clothes, and took him to school. Jim liked Amy, but he didn't like her for taking him to school. He told her so. **All the way** to school he told her so.

    I don't like you, he said. I don't like you any more.
10   I like you, the housekeeper said.

    Then why are you taking me to school? he said.

    He had taken walks with Amy before, once all the way to the Court House Park for the Sunday afternoon band concert, but this walk to school was different.

    What for? he said.
15   Everybody must go to school, the housekeeper said.

    Did you go to school? he said.

    No, said Amy.

    Then why do I have to go? he said.

knew intimately
a. had a close relationship with
b. knew as a relative

all the way
a. during the whole trip
b. always

You will like it, said the housekeeper.

20   He walked on with her in silence, holding her hand. I don't like you, he said. I don't like you any more.

I like you, said Amy.

Then why are you taking me to school? he said again.

Why?

25   The housekeeper knew how frightened a little boy could be about going to school.

You will like it, she said. I think you will sing songs and play games.

I don't want to, he said.

I will come and get you every afternoon, she said.

30   I don't like you, he told her again.

She felt very unhappy about the little boy going to school, but she knew that he would have to go.

The school building was very ugly to her and to the boy. She didn't like the way it made her feel, and going up the steps with him she wished he didn't have to go

35 to school. The halls and rooms **scared her**, and him, and the smell of the place too. And he didn't like Mr. Barber, the principal.

Amy despised Mr. Barber.

What is the name of your son? Mr. Barber said.

This is Dr. Louis Davy's son, said Amy. His name is Jim. I am Dr. Davy's

40 housekeeper.

James? said Mr. Barber.

Not James, said Amy, just Jim.

All right, said Mr. Barber. Any middle name?

No, said Amy. He is too small for a middle name. Just Jim Davy. All right, said

45 Mr. Barber. We'll **try him out** in the first grade. If he doesn't **get along all right** we'll try him out in kindergarten.

Dr. Davy said to start him in the first grade, said Amy. Not kindergarten.

All right, said Mr. Barber.

The housekeeper knew how frightened the little boy was, sitting on the chair,

50 and she tried to let him know how much she loved him and how sorry she was about everything. She wanted to say something fine to him about everything, but she couldn't say anything, and she was very proud of the nice way he got down from the chair and stood beside Mr. Barber, waiting to go with him to a classroom.

On the way home she was so proud of him she began to cry.

55   Miss Binney, the teacher of the first grade, was an old lady who was all dried out. The room was full of little boys and girls. School smelled strange and sad. He sat at a desk and listened carefully.

He heard some of the names: Charles, Ernest, Alvin, Norman, Betty, Hannah, Juliet, Viola, Polly.

60   He listened carefully and heard Miss Binney say, Hannah Winter, what are you chewing? And he saw Hannah Winter **blush**. He liked Hannah Winter right from the beginning.

Gum, said Hannah.

Put it in the wastebasket, said Miss Binney.

65   He saw the little girl walk to the front of the class, take the gum from her mouth, and drop it into the wastebasket.

And he heard Miss Binney say, Ernest Gaskin, what are *you* chewing?

Gum, said Ernest.

And he liked Ernest Gaskin too.

(continued)

scared her
a. made her comfortable
b. made her fearful, frightened her

try him out
a. treat him well
b. give him a chance

get along all right
a. go away
b. do OK

on the way home
a. while going home
b. coming from home

blush
a. fall asleep
b. turn red from embarrassment

70   They met in the schoolyard, and Ernest taught him a few jokes.
      Amy was in the hall when school ended. She was sullen and angry at everybody
until she saw the little boy. She was amazed that he wasn't changed, that he wasn't
hurt, or perhaps utterly unalive, murdered. The school and everything about it
frightened her very much. She took his hand and walked out of the building with
75   him, feeling angry and proud.
      Jim said. What comes after twenty-nine?
      Thirty, said Amy.
      Your face is dirty, he said.
      His father was very quiet at the supper table.
80   What comes after twenty-nine? the boy said.
      Thirty, said his father.
      Your face is dirty, he said.
      In the morning he asked his father for a nickel.
      What do you want a nickel for? his father said.
85   Gum, he said.
      His father gave him a nickel and on the way to school he stopped at Mrs. Riley's
store and bought a package of Spearmint.
      Do you want a piece? he asked Amy.
      Do you want to give me a piece? the housekeeper said.
90   Jim thought about it a moment, and then he said, Yes.
      Do you like me? said the housekeeper.
      I like you, said Jim. Do you like me?
      Yes, said the housekeeper.
      Do you like school?
95   Jim didn't know for sure, but he knew he liked the part about gum. And
Hannah Winter. And Ernest Gaskin.
      I don't know, he said.
      Do you sing? asked the housekeeper.
      No, we don't sing, he said.
100   Do you play games? she said.
      Not in the school, he said. In the yard we do.
      He liked the part about gum very much.
      Miss Binney said, Jim Davy, what are you chewing?
      Ha ha ha, he thought.
105   Gum, he said.
      He walked to the waste-paper basket and back to his seat, and Hannah Winter
saw him, and Ernest Gaskin too. That was the best part of school.
      It began to grow too.
      Ernest Gaskin, he shouted in the schoolyard, *what* are you *chewing*?
110   Raw elephant meat, said Ernest Gaskin. Jim Davy, what are *you* chewing?
      Jim tried to think of something very funny to be chewing, but he couldn't.
      Gum, he said, and Ernest Gaskin laughed louder than Jim laughed when Ernest
Gaskin said raw elephant meat.
      It was funny no matter what you said.
115   Going back to the classroom Jim saw Hannah Winter in the hall.
      Hannah Winter, he said, *what in the world* are you *chewing*?
      The little girl was startled. She wanted to say something nice that would
honestly show how nice she felt about having Jim say her name and ask her the
funny question, making fun of school, but she couldn't think of anything that nice
120 to say because they were almost in the room and there wasn't time enough.

Tutti-frutti,[1] she said **with desperate haste.**

It seemed to Jim he had never before heard such a glorious word, and he kept repeating the word to himself all day.

Tutti-frutti, he said to Amy on the way home.

125   Amy Larson, he said, *what, are, you, chewing*?

He told his father all about it at the supper table.

He said, Once there was a hill. On the hill there was a mill. Under the mill there was a walk. Under the walk there was a key. What is it?

I don't know, his father said. What is it?

130   Milwaukee, said the boy.

The housekeeper was delighted.

Mill. Walk. Key,[2] Jim said.

Tutti-frutti.

What's that? said his father.

135   Gum, he said. The kind Hannah Winter chews.

Who's Hannah Winter? said his father.

She's in my room, he said.

Oh, said his father.

After supper he sat on the floor with the small red and blue and yellow top[3]
140   that hummed while it spinned. It was all right, he guessed. It was still very sad, but the gum part of it was very funny and the Hannah Winter part very nice. Raw elephant meat, he thought with great inward delight.

Raw elephant meat, he said aloud to his father who was reading the evening paper. His father folded the paper and sat on the floor beside him. The housekeeper
145   saw them together on the floor and for some reason tears came to her eyes.

---

[1]**tutti-frutti** *mixed fruit flavor (Italian for all fruits)*
[2]**Milwaukee** *largest city in the state of Wisconsin in the north central part of the United States (pronounced* mill + walk + key*)*
[3]**top** *(see picture at right)*

COMPREHENSION CHECK

Answer these questions.

1. What do you learn about Jim's family?
2. How does Jim really feel about Amy?
3. How does Jim feel about starting school? How do you know?
4. How does Amy feel about Jim's starting school? How do you know?
5. How does Jim make friends at school?
6. What happens at the end of the story? What is Amy's reaction?
7. Which of the characters in the story change? How do they change?

Vocabulary Building: Synonyms

Read the underlined word in its context. Mark the *two* choices that are similar in meaning to the underlined word. Use a dictionary if necessary.

1. The housekeeper knew how <u>frightened</u> a little boy could be about going to school. (line 25)

   a. afraid   b. brave   c. scared

2. Amy <u>despised</u> Mr. Barber. (line 37)

   a. admired   b. detested   c. hated

3. She was <u>sullen</u> and angry at everybody until she saw the little boy. (line 71)

   a. glad   b. quiet   c. silently angry

4. She was <u>amazed</u> that he wasn't changed, that he wasn't hurt . . . (line 72)

   a. happy   b. shocked   c. very surprised

5. . . . or perhaps <u>utterly</u> unalive, murdered. (line 73)

   a. completely   b. partially   c. totally

6. Jim tried to think of something very <u>funny</u> to be chewing, but he couldn't. (line 111)

   a. amusing   b. comical   c. unhealthy

7. The little girl was <u>startled</u>. (line 117)

   a. started   b. taken aback   c. surprised

8. The housekeeper was <u>delighted</u> (by the jokes). (line 131)

   a. disappointed   b. happy   c. pleased

Vocabulary Review

Complete the following statements about the reading selection with the correct word or expression from the list below. Use each word or expression only once.

delighted	got along	scared
funny	on the way	

1. Jim was only five when Amy, the housekeeper, took him to school the first day. Amy never went to school herself; therefore, the halls, the rooms, and the smell of the place _____ her.

2. Mr. Barber, the principal, decided to try Jim out in first grade. If he _____ OK, he could stay there. If not, he would go into kindergarten.

3. It didn't take Jim long to begin to make friends. When he asked Hannah what she was chewing, she was startled but came up with a(an) _____ answer—tutti-frutti.

4. To become part of the group, Jim stopped at Mrs. Riley's store

   _____ to school and bought a package of chewing gum

   which Miss Binney didn't allow the children to chew in class.

5. Amy felt better at the end of the story and was _____

   when Dr. Davy started to pay more attention to his son.

TEXT ANALYSIS

Chronological Order

The events in this story are narrated in chronological order, that is, in the order in which they happened. Each section could have a heading.

Write the number of the line in the story that each suggested heading should come before.

Suggested Heading	*Where It Belongs in the Story*
a. Before arriving at school	before line _6_
b. Registering Jim for school	before line ___
c. In school, the 1st day	before line ___
d. The end of the 1st day	before line ___
e. Before school the next morning	before line ___
f. The 2nd day at school	before line ___
g. At home that evening	before line ___

Point of View

Stories can be told from different points of view; the point of view depends on who is telling the story. If the narrator is a character in the story, you notice the pronoun *I* in the text; the point of view is that of a first-person narrator. If the narrator is a voice that appears to know everything about the story and characters, the point of view is often called that of an omniscient, or all-knowing, author.

Answer the questions about point of view.

a. What is the point of view in this story? Support your answer with evidence from the story.

b. Talk about how the story would be different if told from the point of view of Dr. Davy, Amy, or Jim.

RESPONDING TO READING

Discuss these questions.

1. Which of the factors that bring friends together played a role in Jim's experience when he started school? Which, if any, of the types of friends described by Viorst might children like those in Saroyan's story have?

2. How did you feel when you started school?

3. How are your current reasons for forming friendships similar to or different from the reasons you made friends as a young child?

Extending Your Vocabulary

Word Families

Study the chart below to learn other forms of some of the words in this unit. If a box is blank, either there is no word to fill it, or the word is missing because it is not one you need to know now.

	NOUNS	VERBS	ADJECTIVES	ADVERBS
1.	apology	apologize	apologetic	apologetically
2.	caution	caution	cautious	cautiously
3.	contradiction	contradict	contradictory	—
4.	exposure exposition	expose	expository	—
5.	intensity	intensify	intense intensive	intensely intensively
6.	intrusion	intrude	intrusive	intrusively
7.	obligation	obligate	obligatory	obligatorily
8.	support supportiveness	support	supportive	—

For each item, look at the row in the chart above with the same number. Choose the word that correctly completes the sentence; be sure it is in the correct form.

1. Miriam felt bad about forgetting our appointment; she was very _____.

2. The sign warned drivers: "Slippery when wet, proceed with _____." So we drove very _____.

3. The two experiments gave different and _____ results.

4. Repeated _____ to new vocabulary is necessary before you can learn it well.

5. As the date of the exam approached, the pressure _____.

6. I needed to talk to my boss, but she was in a meeting and I couldn't _____.

7. Taking the College Board Examination is an _____ part of the process of applying to most colleges.

8. My parents were very _____ of my decision to study music.

Polysemous Words

In all languages, some words have more than one meaning; technically they are called *polysemous words*. Polysemous words have several numbered definitions in a dictionary. The following exercise will help you extend your vocabulary by recognizing different meanings for some of the words in this unit.

Read each sentence. Match the underlined word with the correct meaning. In some cases, you will use the same answer twice. An asterisk indicates a meaning that was used in this unit.

1. ___ Do you feel <u>depressed</u>* during the winter months?

   ___ It's hard to find a job when the economy is <u>depressed</u>.

   a. at a low level
   b. very sad

2. ___ Judith Viorst <u>established</u>* various categories of friendship.

   ___ That proximity leads to friendship is one of the most firmly <u>established</u>* findings in the literature on interpersonal attraction.

   ___ They <u>established</u> the publishing company in 1959.

   a. began
   b. determined, identified

3. ___ We <u>identify</u>* with our friends.

   ___ The survey <u>identified</u>* the critical factors in friendships.

   ___ The witness <u>identified</u> the thief.

   a. selected, picked out
   b. found, revealed, indicated
   c. feel connected to, share or understand the feelings of

4. ___ Friendships <u>involve</u>* rights and obligations.

   ___ In the 1960s many young people were <u>involved</u> in the Civil Rights Movement.

   ___ How many people were <u>involved</u> in the crime?

   a. connected to, had a part in
   b. include

5. ___ Psychologists <u>maintain</u>* that people who are similar become friends.

   ___ It is wonderful to <u>maintain</u>* old friendships.

   ___ It takes a lot of money to <u>maintain</u> a family.

   ___ It can cost a lot to <u>maintain</u> a house or apartment.

   a. support financially
   b. keep in good condition
   c. state, say
   d. keep, not lose

(continued)

6. ___ Familiarity promotes* liking.

   ___ The supervisor promotes employees who work hard.

   ___ Advertising promotes consumerism.

   a. helps, increases

   b. raises to a higher position

WRITING

Choose one of the suggestions for writing below. Talk about what you plan to say in your writing with a classmate who chose the same topic. Then follow the instructions for writing.

Personal Writing

1. The quote on the introductory page reads: *A friend is someone who walks in when the whole world has walked out.* Write about a situation when you had a serious problem and felt like "the whole world walked out." Whom did you turn to? How did this person help you? If you prefer, write about a time when a friend turned to you for help.

Academic Writing

2. A summary of a piece of writing presents the most important ideas and examples in a shortened form in the writer's own words. By summarizing something you read, you can check your understanding of it, and your summary can then help you study for a test on the material. Summarize one of the reading selections from this unit.

Creative Writing

3. Write a brief version of "The First Day of School" from the point of view of one of the characters. For example, if you were telling this story from Dr. Davy's point of view, you might begin: "My little son started school today. I wanted him in the first grade even though he is only five . . . "

Try to use some of the following vocabulary in writing about the topic you choose: *apologize, back out of, broaden, (the) bulk of, cautious, contradict, depressed, enrich, fabulous, face-to-face, forever, furthermore, gossip, hang out with, just as good as, keep in touch with, mentor, obligation, reassure/reassurance, sense of humor, supportive, traits.*

Parents and Children

Discuss

1. What do the pictures suggest about families? Who is responsible for raising children today?
2. How do parents influence their children's lives, both as children and as adults? Consider both positive and negative influences.
3. How do parents react as their children mature and become more independent?

> *Oh, to be half as wonderful as my child thought I was when he was small, and only half as stupid as my teenager now thinks I am.*
>
> Rebecca Richards

> *Bear in mind that children of all ages have one thing in common—they close their eyes to advice and open their eyes to example.*
>
> anonymous parent

CHAPTER 5

ABOUT THE READING

"Mother Was Really Somebody" is a story about a real family, which appeared in *Reader's Digest* in a regular section called "My Most Unforgettable Character."

BEFORE YOU READ

Thinking about the Topic

Read about parenting styles and discuss the questions that follow.

PARENTING STYLES*

There are four main styles of parenting, and although no parent follows only one style all the time, parents and caregivers have a prevailing, or usual, style when dealing with children.

Authoritarian Parents
Authoritarian parents expect complete obedience from the child. They also expect the child to accept the family beliefs and principles without question. They are strict disciplinarians, often using physical punishment and the removal of affection to make their children obey rules.

Authoritative Parents
Authoritative parents show respect for their children by allowing them to be different. They set rules and have final authority, but they allow discussion and compromise. They discipline with love and affection rather than power.

Permissive Parents
Permissive parents, parents who permit their children a maximum amount of freedom, have little or no control over the behavior of their children. If there are rules, the children decide whether they will follow them or not. They learn that they can usually get away with any behavior. Although permissive parents love their children, they are not strict and discipline may be inconsistent.

Disengaged Parents
Finally, disengaged (detached) parents are uninvolved in their children's lives. They do not pay attention to their children's needs for affection and discipline.

*Based on Baumrind, D. (1991) as cited in "Parenting Style and Its Correlates."
http://www.athealth.com/Practitioner/ceduc/parentingstyles.html. *Accessed February 14, 2008.*

1. What are typical goals that parents you know have for their children?
2. Which parenting styles are most likely to achieve these goals?
3. Which style do you think most children would prefer? Why?

Review the suggestions for previewing on page xvii if necessary. Preview the selection appropriately. Tell your classmates what you looked at in your preview and why. Then answer these questions.

1. What kind of influence did the author's mother have on him?
2. Is the point of view in this article that of a young child or an adult child?

Before you read, turn to Comprehension Check, First Reading on page 36. Your purpose for the first reading is to answer those questions.

READ

Mother Was Really Somebody

By Joseph N. Michelotti, M.D.

She challenged us to succeed—and then showed us the way.

1   In June 1976, I graduated from Northwestern University Medical School in Chicago. When my name was called, I walked quickly across the stage and reached for my diploma. But before the medical-school dean handed me the certificate, he asked my parents, Anna and Carlo Michelotti, to stand. Surprised, they rose from their seats in the audience. They looked at each other and seemed **puzzled**.

puzzled
a. unable to understand
b. ready to act

2   The dean told the crowd that my parents, an immigrant Italian couple from a farm outside Chicago, had managed to send their six children to top colleges and graduate schools. (Three of us would become doctors, two were already lawyers and one was a physicist.) "It's remarkable," the dean said. Everyone **cheered** loudly.

cheered
a. shouted approval
b. shouted "boo!"

3   Mama's face was **radiant** with pride. I knew that everything we had achieved or would achieve was because of my parents. When we were young children, my mother, especially, was our mentor. Not until I became an adult did I realize how special she was.

radiant
a. sad
b. happy-looking

4   ***Delight in Devotion***   My mother was born in a small town in northern Italy. She was three when her parents immigrated to this country in 1926. They lived on Chicago's South Side, where my grandfather worked making ice cream.

5   Mama thrived in the hectic urban environment. At 16, she graduated first in her high-school class, went on to secretarial school, and finally worked as an executive secretary for a railroad company.

6   She was beautiful too. When a local photographer used her pictures in his monthly window display, she was **flattered**. Her favorite portrait showed her sitting by Lake Michigan, her hair windblown, her gaze reaching toward the horizon. My mother always used to say that when you died, God gave you back your "best self." She'd show us that picture and say, "This is what I'm going to look like in heaven."

flattered
a. pleased
b. disappointed

7   My parents were married in 1944. Dad was a quiet and intelligent man who was 17 when he left Italy. Soon after, a hit-and-run accident left him with a permanent limp. Dad worked hard selling candy to Chicago office workers on their break. He had little formal schooling. His English was self-taught. Yet he **eventually** built a small, successful wholesale candy business. Dad was generous, handsome, and deeply religious. Mama was devoted to him.

eventually
a. after a long time
b. never

8   After she married, my mother quit her job and gave herself to her family. In 1950, with three small children, Dad moved the family to a farm 40 miles from

Chicago. He worked the land and commuted to the city to run his business. Mama said good-bye to her parents and friends and traded her busy city neighborhood for a more isolated life. But she never complained. By 1958, our modest white farmhouse was filled with six children, and Mama was delighted.

9   ***"Think Big"***   My mother never studied books on parenting. Yet she knew how to raise children. She heightened our self-esteem and helped us reach our potential.

10   One fall day, I sat at the kitchen table while Mama peeled potatoes. She spied Dad out the window on his tractor and smiled. "Your father has accomplished so much," she said proudly. "He really is somebody."

11   My mother wanted each of us to be somebody too. "Your challenge is to be everything you can. Mine is to help," she always said.

12   She read to us every day and used homemade flash cards to teach us phonics.[1] She **bolstered** our confidence, praising even our most ordinary accomplishments. When I was ten, I painted a stack of wooden crates and nailed them together to make a **wobbly** bookcase. "It's wonderful!" Mama exclaimed. "Just what we need." She used it for many years.

13   In the dining room are two paint-by-number pictures that my sister Gloria and brother Leo did as kids. Several years ago, Leo commented that the pictures weren't very good and offered to take them down. But Mama wouldn't hear of it. "They are there to remind you how much you could accomplish even as children," she said.

14   From the very beginning, she urged us to think big. One day, after visiting our grandparents on the South Side, she made Dad detour past the Prudential Building construction site. Mama explained that when finished, the 41-story building would be Chicago's tallest. "Maybe someday one of you can design a building like this," she said.

15   Her confidence in us was infectious. When my sister Carla was 12, she announced she was going to be a lawyer.

16   "You can do that," Mama said. "You can do anything you put your mind to."

17   ***Tour Guide***   To Mama, education was a key part of her blueprint[2] for success. Four of us went to a nearby, one-room schoolhouse. My mother made up for its shortcomings by getting us educational toys, talking to us about history, politics and current events, and helping with homework. The best part of getting a good report card[3] was her unstinting praise.

18   When I was in third grade, she urged our teacher to organize a field trip to Chicago museums. My mother helped the teacher rent a bus and plan the trip. She even served as tour guide, pointing out landmarks and recounting local history.

19   When it came time to think about college, there was never a question that we'd all go. Inspired by our parents' sacrifice, we studied hard to earn scholarships, and applied for grants and financial aid.[4] We also took jobs to earn money for school. Working in a grocery store, I learned the value of a dollar. "Work is a blessing," Mama always reminded us.

20   She never asked for anything for herself. "You don't have to buy me a birthday present," she said one time. "Instead write me a letter about yourself. Tell me about your life. Is anything worrying you? Are you happy?"

21   ***"You Honor Us All"***   My mother made family values and pride tangible. One time when I was a high-school junior, our school put on a production of *The*

bolstered
a. increased, built up
b. destroyed

wobbly
a. expensive
b. weak, unstable

---

[1]**phonics** *system for teaching children the relationship between sounds and letters when learning to read*
[2]**blueprint** *architect's plan, used here to mean* plan
[3]**report card** *report of child's grades in school sent to parents*
[4]**financial aid** *money that is given or lent to help pay for educational expenses*

insignificant
a. unimportant
b. large

reflects on
a. thinks carefully
  about
b. shows something
  about

with a jolt
a. gradually
b. suddenly

indomitable
a. strong
b. weak

Music Man. My role was totally **insignificant**. I played bass in the orchestra. "You don't have to come and see me," I told Mama. "I'm not doing anything important."

22 "Nonsense," she said. "Of course we're coming, and we're coming because you're in the program." The whole family showed up.

23 The next year when I was elected president of my high school's National Honor Society, my mother pulled Michael and Maria, my younger brother and sister, out of grade school and brought them to the ceremony. Other students' parents came to the event. But I was the only one with a brother and sister there.

24 "Everything you do **reflects on** the family," Mama explained. "If you succeed, you honor us all."

25 In the same way, she crowded us all around the kitchen table for breakfast and supper. She made sure we shared chores. She nurtured our religious faith, which kept our family close. Every Sunday, we filled a pew at church. At night, we knelt together in the living room and prayed.

26 My mother suggested games everyone could play and often joined in. I remember laughing as she marched around the dining-room table one evening, while John Philip Sousa[5] boomed from the record player. "Keep in step now," she called out to her parading children. "If you're gonna march or do anything else, you always want to do it the best you can."

27 ***Time for Everyone*** Success wasn't just making money, Mama always said. Success was doing something positive for others.

28 In 1977, when Leo received his Ph.D. in physics from the University of California at Irvine, my mother wrote him a long, warm letter. She praised his years of hard work and, typically, reminded him to use his education to help others. "To think, you have the knowledge to work for the betterment of mankind!" she stressed. "There is much good for you to accomplish."

29 Mama took time for everyone. One cold day, she saw the neighbors' three young children playing in our yard. They were shivering in thin, worn sweaters. Mama called the youngsters to our door, where they stared greedily at a pot of steaming homemade soup she was making for supper. She hustled them in, fed them and rummaged through our closets for extra coats.

30 From that day, until the family moved a year later, Mama often brought stew, soup and pasta to their home. She telephoned the children in the morning to make sure they got up for school. Often, she walked them down the lane and waited with them for the bus. At Christmas, she even bought the children gifts.

31 My mother was the driving influence in my decision to become a physician. "Do good" she always said—and be there for others. I recall a long, difficult night when I was a resident[6] at Northwestern Memorial Hospital. I hadn't slept much for days. Finally, one morning at around four o'clock, I dropped into a restless slumber. An hour later, I awoke **with a jolt**. I had dreamed my father died. Confused and exhausted, I called home in tears. "Everything is all right," my mother assured me. "Don't worry."

32 At six o'clock, the hospital security buzzed my room. I had visitors. Stumbling into the elevator, I wondered who had come to see me at that hour. There stood my parents. They had gotten up and driven into the city in the predawn darkness. "I just wanted to make sure you were okay," Mama said, sleepy-eyed and anxious.

33 ***View from Above*** While my mother's spirit remained **indomitable**, her health turned poor. Early last year, she had major surgery. Complications developed. Eight days later, on January 31, 1990, Mama died suddenly. She was 66.

(continued)

---

[5]**John Philip Sousa** *(1854–1932) American bandmaster and composer of music for bands, primarily marches*
[6]**resident** *a doctor in his or her last year of training*

34 　 More than 200 people came to her funeral service. In his eulogy, Leo said, "Mama poured her life out for us, reserving nothing for herself, thinking of us always, of herself never."

35 　 Sitting in church, I could picture my mother in heaven, looking young and beautiful just as she did in her favorite photograph. But instead of gazing out over Lake Michigan, she would be looking down at us, her six children. And she would be **bursting** with pride.

36 　 But we're the proud ones—proud of her and all she accomplished. More than any of us, Mama was really somebody.

bursting
a. exploding
b. falling

COMPREHENSION CHECK

First Reading

Answer these questions.

1. What are the important facts in the early lives of Anna and Carlo Michelotti? What were their early successes?
2. What kind of person was each parent?
3. How did Anna feel about her husband? What kind of marriage did they have?
4. What adjectives would you use to describe life in the Michelotti family?
5. As an adult, how does Joseph Michelotti feel about his mother and her influence on him?

Second Reading

On a separate piece of paper, list the specific examples that Joseph Michelotti uses to support the statements below. Reread parts of the selection as needed.

1. [She urged us] to think big. She heightened our self-esteem and helped us reach our potential. (¶9)
2. Education was a key part of her blueprint for success. (¶17)
3. She never asked for anything for herself. (¶20)
4. She made family values and pride tangible. (¶21)
5. Success was doing something positive for others. (¶27)

Vocabulary Building

Read the underlined word or expression in its context and match it with the correct meaning. Use a dictionary if necessary.

PART 1

_____ 1. ... my parents, an immigrant Italian couple ... had <u>managed to</u> send their six children to top colleges and graduate schools. (¶2)

_____ 2. Mama <u>thrived in</u> the hectic urban environment. (¶5)

_____ 3. Mama thrived in the <u>hectic</u> urban environment. (¶5)

_____ 4. Mama ... traded her busy city neighborhood for a more <u>isolated</u> life. (¶8)

_____ 5. She heightened our self-esteem and helped us reach our <u>potential</u>. (¶9)

_____ 6. ... she <u>urged</u> us to think big. (¶14)

_____ 7. Her confidence in us was <u>infectious</u>. (¶15)

a. did well, was successful

b. alone, away from others

c. the best a person is capable of

d. busy, hurried

e. easily passed from one person to another

f. succeeded in doing something difficult

g. encouraged, strongly advised

PART 2

_____ 8. "You can do anything you <u>put your mind to</u>." (¶16)

_____ 9. My mother made up for (the school's) <u>shortcomings</u> ... (¶17)

_____ 10. (Mama) even served as tour guide, pointing out <u>landmarks</u> ... (¶18)

_____ 11. <u>Inspired</u> by our parents' sacrifice ... (¶19)

_____ 12. My mother made family values and pride <u>tangible</u>. (¶21)

_____ 13. She made sure we shared <u>chores</u>. (¶25)

_____ 14. She <u>nurtured</u> our religious faith ... (¶25)

h. encouraged to do well

i. helped to grow

j. jobs you have to do regularly, especially at home or on a farm

k. decide you want and really work hard at

l. important places

m. limitations

n. real, touchable

Using a Dictionary

SYNONYMS: GENERAL COMPARED TO MORE DETAILED MEANING

Synonyms are rarely identical in meaning. One word in a set of synonyms will usually have general meaning and the other(s) will have more vivid or detailed meaning. Other times synonyms will differ in level of formality or the words they collocate with.

Example:

General word: *do*

More specific words *accomplish, achieve* (do successfully, usually with great effort)

In order to keep reading, efficient readers accept partial meaning for words when the exact meaning is not essential. So when you meet new words like *accomplish* and *achieve*, don't stop reading if you understand the general meaning (*do something*). If you are curious, look up the more specific meaning when you have time.

In the sets below, the boldfaced word has the most general meaning. Work with a partner and use your dictionaries to find the more specific meaning of the underlined word(s). Write them on a separate piece of paper. In some cases, one word may be more formal than another.

1. **picture**, <u>portrait</u> (¶6) *portrait = painting or photograph of a person*
2. **walk**, <u>limp</u> (¶7), <u>stumble</u> (¶32)
3. **loved**, <u>was devoted to</u> (¶7)
   love (n.) <u>devotion</u> (¶4)
4. **travel** to, <u>commuted</u> to (¶8)
5. **look**, <u>spy</u> (¶10), <u>stare</u> (¶29), <u>gaze</u> (out) (¶35)
6. **show**, <u>point out</u> (¶18)
7. **tell**, <u>recount</u> (¶18)
8. **brought** them into the house, <u>hustled</u> them into the house (¶29)
9. **look** through closets, <u>rummage</u> through closets (¶29)
10. **tired**, <u>exhausted</u> (¶31)

Vocabulary Review

Complete the following statements about the reading selection with the correct word from the list below. Use each word only once.

accomplishments	hectic	nurtured
chores	isolated	potential

1. As a young girl, Anna Michelotti thrived in the _____ urban environment of Chicago.

2. After getting married, she traded big city life for a more _____ life in the country, where she raised six children.

3. Though she never read books about parenting, she knew she should praise her children's _____, big or small.

4. She taught them the value of work and cooperation by giving them
_____ to do; she taught them the importance of helping
others through her example.

5. Anna _____ her children in many ways, helping them
with schoolwork, guiding their religious development, opening their lives to
the world, and helping them reach their _____.

TEXT ANALYSIS Text Organization

> Writing is often organized according to the Introduction–Body–Conclusion
> (IBC) pattern. Each part has specific functions.
>
> **Introduction**
> - gets the reader's interest
> - states the topic
> - states or suggests the writer's purpose for writing
> - states or suggests the main idea
>
> **Body**
> - presents ideas with supporting information, examples, and explanations to
>   develop the main idea in detail, as you saw in Comprehension Check,
>   Second Reading.
>
> **Conclusion**
> - provides a closing, or completion, to the article
> - often summarizes or reviews important ideas in the body

Answer these questions.

1. Which paragraphs serve as an introduction to the article? How does the writer
   get the readers' interest? Which sentences state or suggest the reason Joseph
   Michelotti wrote this article?
2. Which paragraphs form the body? What does the writer do in these paragraphs?
3. Which paragraphs serve as the conclusion? How does the conclusion provide a
   closing or completion to the article?

RESPONDING TO READING Discuss these questions.

1. Describe Mrs. Michelotti as a parent. Which of the four parenting styles do you
   think Mrs. Michelotti best exemplifies? What characteristics of the style are
   either mentioned or inferable in the reading?

2. While you were growing up, what is one specific thing that a parent or
   caregiver did that is similar to the types of things that Mrs. Michelotti did for
   her children? What effect did this have on you?

3. What were Mrs. Michelotti's values, especially with regard to work and success?
   Are these values still important today? Explain.

4. What do "success" and "being somebody" mean to you?

CHAPTER 6

ABOUT THE READING

"The Problems of Fathers and Sons" was written by Enrique Hank López (1920–1985). López is the second son of Mexican immigrants, and is believed to be the first Hispanic-American to graduate from Harvard Law School. He published a Hispanic literary journal and wrote several books, including *The Harvard Mystique*.

BEFORE YOU READ

Thinking about the Topic

Some of the vocabulary necessary to understand this reading selection expresses negative emotions. Read the definitions and example sentences below.

Words that Describe Anger

annoyance: the feeling of being slightly angry

> *I was annoyed that my sister didn't answer my email.*

frustration: the feeling of being annoyed or angry because you are unable to do or have what you want

> *I was really frustrated when my computer crashed before I could save my work.*

fury: state or feeling of extreme anger

> *My parents were furious when they found out I had lied to them.*

resentment: a feeling of anger about something that someone has done to you

> *For years I resented the fact that my father didn't come to my wedding.*

Words that Describe Embarrassment

humiliation: a feeling of shame or embarrassment including feeling stupid or weak

> *I felt humiliated when my teacher criticized me in front of the class.*

guilt: a feeling of shame and sadness when you have done something wrong

> *I felt guilty that I cheated on the exam.*

shame: the feeling you have of being guilty or embarrassed after doing something that is wrong

> *I feel ashamed that I cheated. I knew better than to do that.*

One Other Negative Emotion

hatred (formal), hate: extreme dislike

> *A feeling of hatred comes over me whenever I think of how my stepfather treated my mother.*

Think about these questions.

1. When do children sometimes feel angry with their parents?
2. When do children sometimes feel frustrated?
3. When do children feel embarrassed by or ashamed of their parents?

Preview the selection appropriately. Then answer these questions.

1. Is the point of view one of a young child or an adult child?
2. What bothers the writer about his father?

Before you read, turn to Comprehension Check, First Reading on page 43. Your purpose for the first reading is to be able to answer those questions.

READ

The Problems of Fathers and Sons *By Enrique Hank López*

1   My father was an articulate, fascinating storyteller, but totally illiterate.

2   By the time I entered fourth grade, in Denver, Colorado, I was a proud, **proficient** reader—and painfully aware of my father's inability to read a single word in either Spanish or English. Although I'd been told there were no schools in his native village of Bachimba, Chihuahua,[1] I found it hard to accept the fact that he didn't even know the alphabet.

proficient
a. good
b. bad

consequently
a. as a result
b. sometimes

dumb
a. smart
b. stupid

3   **Consequently**, every night as I watched my mother read to him I would feel a surge of resentment and shame. Together they bent over *La Prensa* from San Antonio, Texas—the only available Spanish-language newspaper. "How can he be so **dumb**?" I would ask myself. "Even a little kid can read a damned[2] newspaper."

4   Of course, there were many adults in our barrio[3] who couldn't read or write, but that was no comfort to me. Nor did it console me that my hero Pancho Villa[4] was also illiterate. After all, this was my own father, the man I considered to be

---

[1]**Chihuahua** *state in northern Mexico*
[2]**damned** *strong word showing anger*
[3]**barrio** *neighborhood (Spanish)*
[4]**Pancho Villa** *one of the leaders of the Mexican Revolution of 1910, considered by some to be a champion of the people*

smarter than anyone else, who could answer questions not even my mother could answer, who would take me around the ice factory where he worked and show me how all the machinery operated, who could make huge cakes of ice without any air bubbles, who could fix any machine or electrical appliance, who could tell me all those wonderful stories about Pancho Villa.

5 But he couldn't read. Not one damned word!

6 His ignorance was almost too much for me to bear. In fact, whenever I saw my mother reading to him—his head thrust forward like a dog waiting for a bone—I would walk out of the kitchen and sit on the back porch, my stomach churning with a **swelling** anger that could easily have turned to hatred. So bitter was my disappointment, so deep my embarrassment, that I never invited my friends into the house during that after-dinner hour when my mother habitually read to him. And if one of my friends had supped[5] with us—which happened quite frequently—I would hastily herd them out of the kitchen when my mother reached for *La Prensa*.

7 Once, during a period of deepening frustration, I told my mother that we ought to teach him how to read and write. And when she said it was probably too late to teach him—that it might hurt his pride—I stomped out of the house and ran furiously down the back alley, finally staggering behind a trash can to vomit everything I'd eaten for supper.

8 Standing there in the dark, my hand still **clutching** the rim of the can, I simply couldn't believe that anyone as smart as my dad couldn't learn to read, couldn't learn to write "cat" or "dog" or even "it." Even I, who could barely understand the big words he used when he talked about Pancho Villa (*revolución, cacique, libertad, sabotaje, terreno*), even I, at the mere age of 10, could write big words in both English and Spanish. So why couldn't he?

9 Eventually, he did learn to write two words—his name and surname. Believing that he would feel less humble if he could sign his full name rather than a mere "X" on his weekly paycheck, my mother wrote "José López" on his Social Security card and taught him to copy it letter by letter. It was a slow, painstaking process and usually required two or three minutes as he drew each separate letter with **solemn** tight-lipped determination, pausing now and then as if to make sure they were in the proper sequence. Then he would carefully connect the letters with short hyphen-like lines, sometimes failing to close the gaps or overlapping the letters.

10 I was with him one Friday evening when he tried to cash his paycheck at a local furniture store owned by Frank Fenner, a red-faced German with a bulbous nose and squinty eyes. My father usually cashed his check at Alfredo Pacheco's corner grocery store, but that night Pacheco had closed the store to attend a cousin's funeral, so we had crossed the street to Fenner's place. "You *cambiar* this?" asked my father, showing him the check. "He wants you to cash it," I added, annoyed by my father's use of the word *cambiar*. "Sure, Joe," said Fenner, "just sign your moniker[6] on the back of it." "*Firme su nombre atrás*," I told my father, indicating that Fenner wanted him to sign it. "Okay, I put my name," said my father, placing his Social Security card on the counter so he could copy the "José López" my mother had written for him.

---

[5]**had supped** *(old use) had eaten supper, the evening meal*
[6]**moniker** *name*

swelling
a. growing
b. diminishing

clutching
a. cutting
b. holding

solemn
a. serious
b. happy

Glossary

scribbles
a. written marks
b. musical notes

yelled
a. wrote
b. shouted

restrain
a. hold
b. teach

blurred
a. made clear
b. made unclear

throbbing
a. thinking
b. beating, pulsing

wistful
a. beautiful
b. sad

11 With Fenner looking on, a smirk building on his face, my father began the ever-so-slow copying of each letter as I literally squirmed with shame and hot resentment. Halfway through "López," my father paused, nervously licked his lips, and glanced sheepishly at Fenner's leering face. "No write too good," he said. "My wife teach me."

12 Then, concentrating harder than before, he wrote the final *e* and *z* and slowly connected the nine letters with his jabby little **scribbles**. But Fenner was not satisfied. Glancing from the Social Security card to the check, he said, "I'm sorry, Joe, that ain't[7] the same signature. I can't cash it." "You bastard!"[8] I **yelled**. "You know who he is! And you just saw him signing it."

13 Then suddenly grabbing a can of furniture polish, I threw it at Fenner's head, but missed by at least 6 inches. As my father tried to **restrain** me, I twisted away and screamed at him, "Why don't you learn to write, goddamn it! Learn to write!"

14 He was trying to say something, his face **blurred** by my angry tears, but I couldn't hear him, for I was now backing and stumbling out of the store, my temples[9] **throbbing** with the most awful humiliation I had ever felt. My throat dry and sour, I kept running and running down Larimer St. and then north on 30th St. toward Curtis Park, where I finally flung myself on the recently watered lawn and wept into a state of complete exhaustion.

15 Hours later, now guilt-ridden by what I had yelled at my dad, I came home and found him and my mother sitting at the kitchen table, a writing tablet between them, with the alphabet neatly penciled at the top of the page. "Your mother's teaching me how to write," he said in Spanish, his voice so **wistful** that I could hardly bear to listen to him. "Then maybe you won't be so ashamed of me."

16 But for reasons too complex for me to understand at that time, he never learned to read or write. Somehow, the multisyllabic words he had always known and accurately used seemed confusing and totally beyond his grasp when they appeared in print or in my mother's handwriting. So after a while, he quit trying.

---

[7]**ain't** *is not (nonstandard)*
[8]**bastard** *literally, an illegitimate child; insult used for males*
[9]**temples** *(see picture at right)*

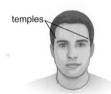
temples

COMPREHENSION CHECK

First Reading

Answer these questions.

1. What are the father's strengths and weaknesses in the child's eyes?
2. How does the wife help her husband get along in the world without being able to read?
3. What happened at the furniture store?
4. How did the boy feel later that evening?
5. How successful is the mother in teaching her husband to read and write?

Second Reading

Reread parts of the selection as needed to answer these questions. As you read, highlight or jot down helpful words or phrases.

1. How did Hank López feel in the following situations? Use the vocabulary of emotions introduced on page 40.

   a. when he watched his mother read to his father (¶3–6)

   b. when his mother said it was probably too late to teach his father to read and write (¶7–8)

   c. during the incident at Fenner's store (¶10–14)

   d. hours after the incident at Fenner's store (¶15)

2. Read each statement. If it is a reasonable inference, circle *R*; if unreasonable, circle *U*. Write any evidence you can find for your choice on the line. For some items, the inference could be either reasonable or unreasonable.

   a. (R) U Mrs. Lopéz was a patient person.

   read to husband every night, taught him to copy his signature,

   tried to teach him to read again (¶15)

   b. R U Hank hates his father.

   _____

   c. R U He wanted his father to be perfect.

   _____

   d. R U He had no respect for his father.

   _____

   e. R U Fenner is a mean person.

   _____

   f. R U Hank wanted to hurt Fenner with the furniture polish.

   _____

   g. R U The father understood how his son felt.

   _____

VOCABULARY

Vocabulary Building

USING PARAPHRASES

Reading material written for native speakers sometimes includes sentences with difficult words. If you ask native speakers for help, they may paraphrase the whole idea, not specific words.

This exercise, which gives you a paraphrase for complete sentences, shows you synonyms for several words at a time.

Work with a partner. Study the sentence on the left. Underline the difficult words in the sentence and find their meanings in the paraphrase on the right. Use a dictionary if necessary.

Sentence from the Text	Paraphrase
1. My father was an articulate, fascinating storyteller, but totally illiterate. (¶1)	My father could express ideas clearly and tell very interesting stories, but he couldn't read or write.
2. Consequently, every night as I watched my mother read to him I would feel a surge of resentment and shame. (¶3)	As a result, every night I felt waves of anger and embarrassment when my mother read to him.
3. Nor did it console me that my hero Pancho Villa was also illiterate. (¶4)	It didn't make me feel better that a person I really admired couldn't read either.
4. His ignorance was almost too much for me to bear. (¶6)	It was almost impossible for me to tolerate the fact that he didn't know certain things.
5. Believing that he would feel less humble if he could sign his full name . . . my mother . . . taught him to copy (his name) letter by letter. (¶9)	Thinking that he would not feel so lowly and simple if he could sign his complete name . . . my mother . . . taught him to copy his name letter by letter.
6. It was a slow, painstaking process . . . (¶9)	Making the letters required very careful effort.
7. . . . my father . . . glanced sheepishly at Fenner's leering face. (¶11)	My father looked quickly with an embarrassed look at Fenner who was giving him a look of superiority.
8. . . . I finally flung myself on the recently watered lawn and wept into a state of complete exhaustion. (¶14)	Finally I threw myself on the grass and cried until I was extremely tired and had no more energy left.
9. . . . the multisyllabic words he had always known and accurately used seemed confusing and totally beyond his grasp when they appeared in print or in my mother's handwriting. (¶16)	My father could use long words correctly when he talked, but he couldn't understand them when they were written.

Using a Dictionary: Words that Paint Pictures

Work with a partner to find the specific meanings of these colorful words that help you understand how strong the boy's emotions were. The first one is done for you.

Word	Partial Meaning (enough to keep reading)	Specific Meaning and the Picture Created
1. . . . I would hastily <u>herd</u> them out of the kitchen . . . (¶6)	move	*move or push like a herd (group) of animals*
2. . . . I <u>stomped</u> out of the house . . . (¶7)	walked	
3. . . . finally <u>staggering</u> behind a trash can . . . (¶7)	walking	
4. . . . Fenner, a red-faced German with a <u>bulbous</u> nose and <u>squinty</u> eyes . . . (¶10)	probably something negative because the child is angry	
5. With Fenner looking on, a <u>smirk</u> building on his face . . . (¶11)	some facial expression	
6. . . . I literally <u>squirmed</u> with shame . . . (¶11)	moved	
7. . . . <u>grabbing</u> a can of furniture polish, I threw it at Fenner's head . . . (¶13)	taking	
8. As my father tried to restrain me, I <u>twisted</u> away . . . (¶13)	moved	

Vocabulary Review

Complete the following statements about the reading selection with the correct word or expression from the list below. Use each word or expression only once.

beyond his grasp	humble	illiterate
fascinating	ignorance	painstaking

1. Hank López's father was a(an) _____ storyteller and an articulate man.

2. Hank, however, was painfully aware that his father was _____. To him, not being able to read and write was a sign of _____ that the child could not bear.

3. Mrs. López thought her husband would feel less _____ if he could at least write his name. He learned to do so, but it was a(an) _____ process.

4. Even though his wife tried to teach him to read and write, he could never learn. Somehow reading and writing were _____.

TEXT ANALYSIS

Text Organization

Match each paragraph or set of paragraphs with its contribution to the whole piece of writing. Then answer the question.

Paragraphs	*Contribution*
___ ¶1–8	a. presents the major anecdote or story and its results
___ ¶9	b. gives a final comment on the situation
___ ¶10–15	c. presents the problem and child's feelings about it
___ ¶16	d. provides a transition or link between problem and anecdote

How is the reading selection organized? Does it have IBC organization or not? Explain.

RESPONDING TO READING

Discuss these questions.

1. Why do you think that the father's illiteracy upset the boy so much? Would he have felt the same if his mother were illiterate? Consider his comments in paragraph 4.

2. What would you do to help this boy understand his father and his own feelings better?

3. How do you think the wife felt about her husband's illiteracy and the son's embarrassment?

4. How do you think López's father may have influenced him? Use the information about Hank López in About the Reading on page 40.

5. Why do you think Enrique Hank López wrote this selection?

CHAPTER 7

ABOUT THE READING

The essay, "Greener Grass," appeared in the July 22, 2007 *New York Times Magazine* in a section called "Lives."

BEFORE YOU READ

Thinking about the Topic

Discuss these questions.

1. What do parents want for their children?
2. How do parents react when their children grow up and begin to make their own major life decisions?
3. What often happens in the parent-child relationship as parents raise children in a culture other than their own?

Previewing

Preview the selection appropriately. Then answer these questions.

1. What do you learn about the author from your preview?
2. What do you learn about José from your preview?
3. How do they happen to know each other?

Before you read, turn to Comprehension Check, First Reading on page 50. Your purpose on the first reading is to answer those questions.

READ

prune
a. cut
b. dry

Greener Grass[1] *By Susan Straight*

1   When I was divorced 10 years ago, the one thing I couldn't take care of was the lawn. I could **prune** trees and roses. But the grass was wide, and my ex-husband, the son of a landscaper, took the lawn mower. For five years, my friend Terri cut the grass for me. She was a landscaper in business for herself, with her second husband, but he left. She married again and moved away. She sold her business to a young American guy who lasted one month. I had no one until I saw a truck with two lawn mowers and two men on a nearby street.

2   José was from Guatemala. I spoke some Spanish, and he spoke some English. He had a green card.[2] I had never hired anyone for anything, despite my residence in Southern California, where everyone hires immigrant labor. He and his brother came faithfully every week. José told me that his wife was back in Guatemala with their four children, a teenage girl, two teenage boys, and a very young daughter; he'd come to California because school fees, gas and food were so expensive that he couldn't support his family in Guatemala.

---

[1]**Greener Grass** *from the saying, "The grass is always greener on the other side of the fence," which means that what others have looks better from our point of view than it really is.*
[2]**green card** *card showing permanent residence status and allowing the person to live and work in the United States*

day off
a. work day
b. free day

3   He came on Tuesdays, which was my **day off**, so we've talked a lot over the past five years. José said he missed his youngest daughter, who is very smart and attends private school because there is no public school where they live. About two years ago, José's son Henry, who was 18, arrived with a visa, and then Freddy, who was 16, got a visa and joined him, too. José and his sons formed their own landscaping company, with two trucks. Henry had his father's wide pale face, delicate mustache and thinning hair, and Freddy, who had dark brown skin and thick black hair, was always joking and laughing. He wanted me to call him Freddy Krueger, after the horror-movie character.

4   This spring, taking burritos³ to the three of them at the picnic table, I found myself envying José's easy laughter with his sons. My oldest daughter had applied to colleges far from Southern California, stating unequivocally that she wanted to be anywhere but here. Ohio was her first choice. Even though I'd defended her right to go away to family and friends who were against it, I couldn't believe she wanted to be thousands of miles away from me, from our house and this life.

show up
a. go back to Guatemala
b. appear, come

5   Then, in May, José and his sons didn't **show up** for two weeks. Two strangers came to cut the grass. I asked in Spanish where José was, and they said, "He's not here."

drawn
a. relaxed and happy-looking
b. thin and pale because of worry

6   The following Tuesday, I met José in the driveway. His face was **drawn**, and he kept his hat and dark sunglasses on while we talked. "They go away," he began. "They don't like to do what I do." In English and Spanish, he told me that his sons hated gardening. Henry had gone to New York to work construction. Freddy was in—Memphis, Missouri, Nashville? He didn't know, at first. He knew Freddy was doing electrical assembly work, but he had trouble remembering the state. When I said, "Memphis is in Tennessee," I saw that behind the dark glasses he was crying.

7   "Now they go somewhere else," he said, "I have to find workers." He pointed, and I realized he was hiring men off the street, just like an American.

(continued)

---

³**burritos** *Mexican food, usually beans or meat and cheese rolled in a tortilla (flat round bread)*

handle

machete

8   A few days later, I found under a pile of leaves the machete Freddy left behind. It was long and heavy, with a red handle. When José came, I gave it to him. We stood near the trash cans, and his eyes filled with tears again. "Yes," he said, nodding slowly. "Freddy leave his machete. Yes. He don't want to work with me. I think I will go back to Guatemala now. I have nothing here."

frowning
a. looking unhappy
b. looking happy

9   I told him about my daughter. We'd gotten the acceptance letter. She's going to college in Ohio, leaving later this summer.

10   "Ohio?" he said, **frowning**. "That is near Memphis?"

11   "They're both far away," I said.

12   He shook his head. "I miss my wife," he said. "I miss my daughter. In two months, maybe I go back."

13   I tried to convince him that this was really what we wanted: We wanted our children to do something better than we did, to have more than we have, and that meant we had to let them go. I said these things even though I knew full well how different our situations really were. I would see my daughter over Christmas vacation. José might not see his sons again.

14   "It's the American dream," I finally heard myself say. José smiled with one side of his mouth.

15   "Yes," he said. "Yes. That is the American dream. I think I go home to Guatemala."

16   But he came the next week, with two different workers.

17   When I went outside with cold drinks, he shrugged and held up his hands, as if he hadn't quite made up his mind about whose dream it was.

COMPREHENSION CHECK

First Reading

Mark the statements *T* (true) or *F* (false) Write the paragraph number(s) where you found evidence for each answer.

1. T F   José is the first immigrant the author has ever employed. ¶___

2. T F   José and his sons are illegal immigrants. ¶___

3. T F   José's whole family is with him in California. ¶___

4. T F   José is an entrepreneur. ¶___

5. T F   The author's daughter doesn't want to stay in California. ¶___

Second Reading

Reread parts of the selection as needed to answer these questions. As you read, highlight or jot down helpful answers or phrases.

1. Why did José leave Guatemala?
2. What details show that José is responsible with his clients?

3. What details in the essay show that Freddy and Henry probably want to become more American?
4. What is José's reaction to his sons' decision to leave California?
5. How does the author feel about her daughter's going to college in Ohio?
6. How well does the author understand José's situation?
7. What is the American dream and how does it affect each person in this essay?

VOCABULARY

Vocabulary Building

Read the underlined word or expression in its context and match it with the correct meaning. Use a dictionary if necessary.

_____ 1. I had never <u>hired</u> anyone for anything . . . (¶2)

_____ 2. . . . José's son Henry . . . arrived with a <u>visa</u> . . . (¶3)

_____ 3. . . . I found myself <u>envying</u> José's easy laughter with his sons. (¶4)

_____ 4. . . . stating <u>unequivocally</u> that she wanted to be anywhere but here. (¶4)

_____ 5. "Yes," he said, <u>nodding</u> slowly. (¶8)

_____ 6. I tried to <u>convince</u> him that this was really what we wanted . . . (¶13)

_____ 7. . . . he <u>shrugged</u> and held up his hands . . . (¶17)

_____ 8. . . . as if he hadn't quite <u>made up his mind</u> about whose dream it was. (¶17)

a. clearly, without doubt

b. persuade, make someone feel certain that something is true

c. document permitting a citizen of another country to enter a foreign country

d. employed to work

e. raised and lowered the shoulders to show you don't know (or care) about something

f. wanting what someone else has

g. decided

h. moving head up and down to show you agree

Vocabulary Review

Complete the following statements about the reading selection with the correct word or expression from the list below. Use each word or expression only once.

convince	hired	visas
envied	made up his mind	

1. The author _____ José, a Guatemalan immigrant, to take care of her lawn.

2. After a while José's two sons obtained _____ and came to California to work with their father.

3. The author _____ the easy relationship between José and his sons and thought about her relationship with her daughter, who wanted to leave Southern California.

(continued)

4. When Henry and Freddy took other jobs in far away parts of the United States, she realized that José's situation with his children was more difficult than hers. Nevertheless, she tried to _____ him that parents are supposed to let go of their children as they search for a better life.

5. José apparently wasn't so sure he agreed and though he hadn't _____ yet, he was thinking about going back to Guatemala.

TEXT ANALYSIS   *Essays*

An essay is usually a fairly short piece of literary or journalistic writing in which authors explain their personal ideas about a social or personal topic. Writers are often prompted to write an essay because of something that touches their lives. The word *essay* comes from the French verb, *essayer,* which means *to attempt* or *try.* In writing an essay, writers try out their ideas and come to understand them better through writing.

Answer these questions about the essay.

1. What event in Susan Straight's life do you think prompted her to write this essay?
2. What social issues does she examine and what, if any, conclusions does she come to?
3. What reasons could Susan Straight have had for writing this essay?

RESPONDING TO READING

Discuss these questions.

1. How do you think Henry and Freddy view their father?

2. What do you think José will decide to do?

3. What are some differences in parent-child relationships across cultures you are familiar with? Think, for example, about parents' attitudes towards children leaving home.

4. What strains does separation of families put on immigrants?

5. How might the author's relationship with her daughter and her parenting style be affected by the fact she is a single parent?

ABOUT THE READING

David Michael Kaplan (1946–) is an American writer and professor of writing. The story, "Love, Your Only Mother," first appeared in *Comfort*, then in *Sudden Fiction International* where Kaplan is quoted as saying, "Reading a good short story is like coming into the theater to see the magic show. We have come to be astonished and delighted and mystified."

BEFORE YOU READ

Thinking about the Topic

Discuss these questions.

1. Under what circumstances do children grow up with only one parent?
2. How might growing up in a single-parent home affect a child? Does it make a difference if the single parent is a mother or a father?

READ

Love, Your Only Mother

By David Michael Kaplan

1   I received another postcard from you today, Mother, and I see by the blurred postmark that you're in Manning, North Dakota now and that you've dated the card 1961. In your last card you were in Nebraska, and it was 1962; you've lost some time, I see. I was a little girl, nine years old, in 1961. You'd left my father and me only two years before. Four months after leaving, you sent me—always me, never him—your first postcard, of a turnpike[1] in the Midwest, postmarked Enid, Oklahoma. You called me "My little angel"[2] and said that the sunflowers by the side of the road were tall and very pretty. You signed it, as you always have, "Your only mother." My father thought, of course, that you were in Enid, and he called the police there. But we quickly learned that postmarks meant nothing: you were never where you had been, had already passed through in the wanderings only you understand.

(continued)

---

[1]**turnpike** *major highway which people pay to use, also called a toll road*
[2]**angel** *expression of endearment or love*

2   A postcard from my mother, I tell my husband, and he grunts.

3   Well, at least you know she's still alive, he says.

4   Yes.

5   This postcard shows a wheat field bending in the wind. The colors are badly printed: the wheat's too red, the sky too blue—except for where it touches the wheat, there becoming aquamarine, as if sky and field could somehow combine to form water. There's a farmhouse in the distance. People must live there, and for a moment I imagine you do, and I could walk through the red wheat field, knock on the door, and find you. It's a game I've always played, imagining you were hiding somewhere in the postcards you've sent. Your scrawled message, as always, is **brief**: "The beetles are so much larger this year. I know you must be enjoying them. Love, your only mother."

6   What craziness is it this time? my husband asks. I don't reply.

7   Instead, I think about your message, measure it against others. In the last postcard seven months ago, you said you'd left something for me in a safety deposit box[3] in Ferndale. The postmark was Nebraska, and there's no Ferndale in Nebraska. In the card before that, you said you were making me a birthday cake that you'd send. Even though I've vowed I'd never do it again, I try to understand what you are telling me.

8   "Your only mother." I've **mulled** that signature **over** and over, wondering what you meant. Are you worried I'd forget you, my only mother? In favor of some other? My father, you know, never divorced you. It wouldn't be fair to her, he told me, since she might come back.

9   Yes, I said.

10   Or maybe you mean singularity: out of all the mothers I might have had, I have you. You exist for me alone. Distances, you **imply**, mean nothing. You might come back.

11   And it's true: somehow, you've always found me. When I was a child, the postcards came to the house, of course; but later, when I went to college, and then to the first of several apartments, and finally to this house of my own, with husband and daughter of my own, they still kept coming. How you did this I don't know, but you did. You pursued me, and no matter how far away, you always found me. In your way, I guess, you've been faithful.

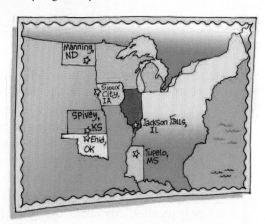

12   I put this postcard in a box with all the others you've sent over the years— postcards from Sioux City, Jackson Falls, Horseshoe Bend, Truckee, Elm City, Spivey. Then I pull out the same atlas I've had since a child and look up Manning, North Dakota, and yes, there you are, between Dickinson and Killdeer, a blip on the red highway line.

---

[3]**safety deposit box** *small box in a bank vault for keeping valuables*

brief
a. long
b. short

mulled over
a. thought about
b. forgotten

imply
a. suggest
b. worry

panorama
a. view, scene
b. building

13   She's in Manning, North Dakota, I tell my husband, just as I used to tell my friends, as if that were explanation enough for your absence. I'd point out where you were in the atlas, and they'd nod.

14   But in all those postcards, Mother, I imagined you: you were down among the trees in the mountain **panorama**, or just out of frame on that street in downtown Tupelo, or already through the door to The World's Greatest Reptile Farm. And I was there, too, hoping to find you and say to you, Come back, come back, there's only one street, one door, we didn't mean it, we didn't know, whatever was wrong will be different.

15   Several times I decided you were dead, even wished you were dead, but then another postcard would come, with another message to ponder. And I've always read them, even when my husband said not to, even if they've driven me to tears or rage or a blankness when I've no longer cared if you were dead or anyone were dead, including myself. I've been faithful, too, you see. I've always looked up where you were in the atlas, and put your postcards in the box. Sixty-three postcards, four hundred-odd lines of scrawl: our life together.

16   Why are you standing there like that? my daughter asks me.

17   I must have been away somewhere, I say. But I'm back.

18   Yes.

19   You see, Mother, I always come back. That's the distance that separates us.

20   But on summer evenings, when the windows are open to the dusk, I sometimes smell cities . . . wheat fields . . . oceans—strange smells from far away—all the places you've been to that I never will. I smell them as if they weren't pictures on a postcard, but real, as close as my outstretched hand. And sometimes in the middle of the night, I'll sit bolt upright, my husband instantly awake and frightened, asking, What is it? What is it? And I'll say, She's here, she's here, and I am terrified that you are. And he'll say, No, no, she's not, she'll never come back, and he'll hold me until my terror passes. She's not here, he says gently, stroking my hair, she's not—except you are, my strange and only mother: like a buoy[4] in a fog, your voice, dear Mother, seems to come from everywhere.

---

[4]**buoy** *object that floats on the water and marks where it is safe for boats to go; many buoys emit warning sounds*

COMPREHENSION CHECK

Answer these questions.

1. Who is the narrator of the story? Who is the narrator addressing?
2. How old was the daughter when the mother left? Approximately how old is she now?
3. How does the mother communicate with her daughter? And vice versa?
4. Where does the mother send postcards from? How far away are these places from each other? Are they big cities or small towns?
5. What does the daughter tell other people about her mother?

(continued)

6. What does the daughter find curious about the messages and the signature on the cards? Why does she keep the postcards?
7. What does the husband think about this situation?
8. How has this mother affected her daughter's life? What does the simile "like a buoy in the fog" (¶20) add to our understanding of the daughter and her relationship with her mother?
9. Reread the story and write questions that the story doesn't seem to answer.

VOCABULARY

Vocabulary Building

Read the underlined word or expression in its context and match it with the correct meaning. Use a dictionary if necessary.

---- 1. . . . the <u>wanderings</u> only you understand. (¶1)

---- 2. . . . I tell my husband, and he <u>grunts</u>. (¶2)

---- 3. What <u>craziness</u> is it this time? (¶6)

---- 4. . . . I've <u>vowed</u> I'd never do it again . . . (¶7)

---- 5. . . . I've mulled that signature over and over, <u>wondering</u> what you meant. (¶8)

---- 6. You <u>pursued</u> me, and . . . you always found me. (¶11)

---- 7. . . . with another message to <u>ponder</u>. (¶15)

---- 8. I've always read them (the postcards) . . . even if they've driven me to tears or <u>rage</u> . . . (¶15)

---- 9. . . . , and I am <u>terrified</u> that you are (here) . . . (¶20)

---- 10. . . . you are, my strange and only mother: like a buoy in a <u>fog</u> . . . (¶20)

a. asking oneself

b. cloudy air making it impossible to see much

c. extremely afraid

d. followed

e. made a serious promise

f. nonsense

g. think carefully and seriously about

h. trips to different places where you don't stay long

i. uncontrollable anger

j. makes short, low sound

Vocabulary Review

Complete the following statements about the reading selection with the correct word from the list below. Use each word only once.

brief	terrified	wandered
grunts	vowed	wonders

1. The mother in this story left home years ago. The different postmarks on the mother's postcards suggest that she has _____ from place to place over the years.

2. The messages on the postcards are always _____, never more than a few lines.

3. The daughter _____ what "your only mother" means. Once she _____ never to think about what the messages mean again, but she cannot get them out of her mind.

4. The daughter has mixed feelings about her mother. She saves the cards to show that she has remained faithful to her, but she is also _____ by a dream that her mother has come back.

5. When she tells her husband that she got another postcard from her mother, he _____ to show that he is listening, but he knows the postcard won't tell them very much.

TEXT ANALYSIS *Details in Stories*

Writers of short stories must say and suggest a lot in a few words. Therefore, they select details carefully to communicate something important about a character or the situation. The meaning readers get from stories can depend on what details they notice.

Reread parts of the story as needed to do the following tasks.

1. In paragraph 1, note that the mother always sent the postcards to her daughter and not to her husband. What reasons could she have had? Does this detail help us understand the mother or the situation in any way?
2. What details in the story can a reader use to calculate approximately how long the mother has been gone?
3. What details help a reader understand the husband's attitude in this situation?
4. Notice the many times *distance, leaving, being away,* or *coming back* are mentioned in the story. Do all the examples refer to physical distance? How might the repeated references to distance contribute to the meaning of the story?

RESPONDING TO READING Discuss these questions.

1. What similarities and differences are there in the way the father and daughter have reacted to the mother's desertion of the family? Do you think the reactions would have been the same if the father had left home? Explain.

2. How does this story relate to the styles of parenting you read about on page 32?

3. Share with your classmates the unanswered questions you wrote in the Comprehension Check #9 on page 56. Try to answer them. Support your answers with evidence from the story. If you find no evidence, talk about what might be true.

4. Did Kaplan's story "astonish, delight, or mystify" you? Explain.

Extending Your Vocabulary

Word Families

Study the chart below to learn other forms of some of the words in this unit. If a box is blank, either there is no word to fill it, or the word is missing because it is not one you need to know now.

	NOUNS	VERBS	ADJECTIVES	ADVERBS
1.	consolation	console	(in)consolable	inconsolably
2.	flattery	flatter	flattered flattering	—
3.	fury	infuriate	furious	furiously
4.	frustration	frustrate	frustrated frustrating	—
5.	guilt	—	guilty	—
6.	illiteracy	—	illiterate	—
7.	pride	—	proud	proudly
8.	resentment	resent	resentful	—
9.	shame	shame (a person)	ashamed shameful	shamefully
10.	terror	terrify	terrified terrifying	—

For each item, look at the row in the chart above with the same number. Choose the word that correctly completes the sentence; be sure it is in the correct form.

1. When José's sons left California, it was no _____ to him to hear that parents have to let their children go.

2. Saying nice things about a person is not always a good idea if you are not sincere. There is a saying, "_____ will get you nowhere."

3. Mr. Fenner _____ Hank by humiliating his father. Hank was so _____ that he threw a can of furniture polish at Fenner.

4. Do you think that Mr. López was as _____ as Hank was that he couldn't read or write?

5. Hank felt _____ that he had yelled at his father.

6. There are languages that have no writing system; in those societies everyone is _____, and it is not a reason for shame.

7. Chang walked _____ across the stage to receive his diploma.

8. I have always _____ the fact that my parents didn't support my career choice.

9. It's a _____ that you couldn't go on the trip with us.

10. Living through an earthquake is the most _____ experience Tsuneko can remember.

Polysemous Words

Read each sentence. Match the underlined word with the correct meaning. In some cases, you will use the same answer twice. An asterisk indicates a meaning that was used in this unit.

1. ____ Hank López could not <u>bear</u>* the fact that his father was illiterate.

   ____ If all women <u>bear</u> only two children, we will have zero population growth.

   ____ It will be at least five years before those trees <u>bear</u> fruit.

   ____ Some parents can't <u>bear</u> it when their children leave home.

   ____ Can that platform <u>bear</u> the weight of the band and all their equipment?

   a. give birth to
   b. produce
   c. support, carry, hold
   d. tolerate

2. ____ She tried to <u>look up</u>* the towns in the atlas.

   ____ Things will <u>look up</u> if Ali gets a scholarship.

   ____ I'll <u>look</u> your parents <u>up</u> when I go to Osaka.

   a. become better
   b. try to find (information)
   c. try to visit someone

3. ____ Mrs. Michelotti <u>made up for</u>* the shortcomings of the local school.

   ____ Will you please <u>make up your mind</u>* about what you're going to do?

   ____ The couple didn't speak to each other for days, but they finally <u>made up</u>.

   ____ I didn't want to tell the truth, so I <u>made up</u> a story.

   a. reconciled, repaired a relationship
   b. decide
   c. invent
   d. compensated for

(continued)

4. ___ The Michelotti's <u>managed</u>* to send all their children to college and graduate school.

    ___ Mr. Karkambasis <u>managed</u> his own restaurant for 25 years.

    ___ I <u>managed</u> to graduate from college in three years.

a. directed, controlled a business and employees

b. succeeded in doing something

5. ___ The mother had written four hundred-<u>odd</u>* lines of scrawl.

    ___ Do you believe that <u>odd</u> numbers, such as 1, 3, 5 are unlucky?

    ___ Luisa is an <u>odd</u> person; you never know what she is going to say.

a. approximately

b. different, strange, unusual

c. numbers that cannot be divided by two

6. ___ Her daughter asked her why she was <u>standing</u>* there like that.

    ___ The judge let the decision <u>stand</u>.

    ___ You can <u>stand</u> the umbrella in the corner over there.

    ___ Hank couldn't <u>stand</u> the fact that his father was illiterate.

    ___ <u>Where do you stand</u> on the issue of disciplining children?

a. tolerate, bear

b. be on your feet in an upright position

c. what is your opinion

d. place in an upright position

e. stay the same, not change

7. ___ José came to the United States because he couldn't <u>support</u>* his family in Guatemala.

    ___ Should parents always <u>support</u> their children in the things they want to do?

    ___ These columns <u>support</u> the roof.

    ___ Which candidate will you <u>support</u>?

    ___ The results of the experiment <u>support</u> our hypothesis.

a. favor, agree with (in politics)

b. help and encourage

c. help prove the truth of

d. hold the weight of

e. provide enough money to live

8. ___ The daughter <u>wondered</u>* what her mother meant.

    ___ There were seven <u>wonders</u> of the ancient world.

    ___ <u>No wonder</u> you're exhausted! You're getting three hours of sleep a night.

a. asked oneself

b. it's no surprise

c. marvels, great things

WRITING **Choose one of the suggestions for writing below. Talk about what you plan to say in your writing with a classmate who chose the same topic. Then follow the instructions for writing.**

Personal Writing

1. Which of the parents portrayed in these selections do you admire most? Why? Which of the parents, if any, do you not admire? How would you feel if they were your parents?
2. Write about one of your own parents or grandparents or about being a parent. Start with a general statement and support it with specific examples from your own experience.

Academic Writing

> When you write a reaction, you make general statements such as "I like [title of selection] a lot." or "I found [title of selection] very disturbing." Remember that you must then write about specific things that you liked or that you found disturbing. In other words, in writing a reaction you must support your general statements with details as in any other piece of writing.

3. Write at least one paragraph describing your reaction to one of the selections in this unit. Why did you react as you did? Make specific reference to the reading. If you quote words exactly, use quotation marks.

Creative Writing

4. Write a letter from one character to another. For example from:
   a. one of the Michelotti children to their mother or Carlo Michelotti to his wife.
   b. Mrs. López to a relative in Mexico or an adult Hank López to his father.
   c. Henry or Freddy to their father or José to his wife or daughter in Guatemala.
   d. one of the characters in *Love, Your Only Mother* to the absent mother.

   Focus the letter on a specific issue and use relevant information or inferences from the reading.

Try to use some of the following vocabulary in writing about the topic you choose: *annoyed, ashamed, bolster (my) confidence, console, convince, furious, inspire, let go, make up your mind, potential, resent, vow, wonder, yell.*

Parenting styles: *authoritarian, authoritative, permissive, disengaged/detached/ uninvolved.*

Discuss

1. What causes stress for you and for other people you know?
2. How does stress affect people physically and emotionally?
3. What can people do to handle stress well?

> [Stress comes from] any circumstances that threaten or are perceived to threaten our well-being and that thereby tax our coping abilities. The threat may be to our immediate physical safety, our long-range security, our self-esteem, our reputation, our peace of mind, or many other things that we value.
>
> Wayne Weiten, social psychologist

> Reality is the leading cause of stress amongst those in touch with it.
>
> Lily Tomlin, actress and comedian

"Plain Talk about Handling Stress" is from an information sheet published by the National Institute of Mental Health (NIMH), a division of the Department of Health and Human Services.

BEFORE YOU READ

Thinking about the Topic

Read about types of stress and discuss the questions.

ACUTE STRESS AND CHRONIC STRESS

According to Wayne Weiten,[1] "acute stressors are threatening events that have a relatively short duration and a clear endpoint." An example would be the threat of damage to your home by a natural disaster.

Chronic stressors, on the other hand, are "threatening events that have a relatively long duration and no readily apparent time limit." An example would be long-term financial problems.

[1] *Weiten, Wayne (2007).* Psychology: Themes and Variations, *7th edition. Belmont, CA: Thomson-Wadsworth.*

1. What forms of acute stress have you experienced? What forms of chronic stress have you experienced? Comparing answers with your classmates, which seems more common? Which type of stress do you think is more harmful?
2. What are some of the things people can do to handle or cope with chronic stress? What can people do to handle acute stress, such as experiencing a car accident, an earthquake, or a death in the family?

Previewing

Preview the selection appropriately. Then answer these questions.

1. What does "plain talk" mean?
2. Who do you suppose is the audience for this information sheet?
3. What do you predict Dr. Kopolow will tell his readers about?
4. What is the main purpose of this type of reading material? Where would you be likely to find government information sheets of this type?

Before you read, turn to Comprehension Check, First Reading on page 66. Your purpose for the first reading is to answer those questions.

Plain Talk about Handling Stress
By Louis E. Kopolow, M.D.

1   You need stress in your life! Does that surprise you? Perhaps so, but it is quite true. Without stress, life would be dull and unexciting. Stress adds flavor, challenge, and opportunity to life. Too much stress, however, can seriously affect your physical and mental well-being. A major challenge in this stress-filled world of today is to learn how to cope with stress so that it does not become too much.

2   What kinds of things can cause too much stress in our lives? We often think of major crises such as natural disasters, war, and death as main sources of stress. These are, of course, stressful events. However, according to psychologist Wayne Weiten, on a day-to-day basis, it is the small things that cause stress: waiting in line, having car trouble, getting stuck in a traffic jam, having too many things to do in a limited time.

3   Interestingly, stress is unique and personal to each of us. So personal, in fact, that what may be relaxing to one person may be stressful to another. For example, if you are an executive who likes to keep busy all the time, "taking it easy" at the beach on a beautiful day may feel extremely frustrating, non-productive, and upsetting. You may be emotionally distressed from "doing nothing."

4   Hans Selye, M.D., a recognized expert in the field, has defined stress as a "non-specific response of the body to a demand." For the busy executive, the demand to relax might cause stress. For most of us, it is a demand to act. If we feel overwhelmed by the pressure to do too many things, we may not be able to function at all. In this case, the stress that can be good for us becomes distress, or bad stress. When stress becomes **prolonged** or particularly frustrating, it can become harmful, causing physical illness.

REACTING TO STRESS

5   The body responds to stressful events by going through three stages: (1) alarm, (2) resistance, and (3) exhaustion. Let's take the example of a typical commuter in rush-hour traffic. If a car suddenly pulls out in front of him, his initial alarm reaction may include fear of an accident, anger at the driver who committed the action, and general frustration. His body may respond in the alarm stage by releasing hormones[1] into the bloodstream which cause his face to flush, perspiration to form, his stomach to have a sinking feeling, and his arms and legs to tighten. The next stage is resistance, in which the body repairs damage caused by the stress. If the stress of driving continues with repeated close calls or traffic jams, however, his body will not have time to make repairs. He may become so conditioned[2] to expect potential problems when he drives that he tightens up at the beginning of each commuting day. The third stage, exhaustion, occurs if the stress continues over a long period of time, and the body **depletes** its resources for fighting stress. A result may be illnesses such as insomnia,[3] migraine headaches, backaches, ulcers,[4] high blood pressure, and even heart disease.

6   While you can't live completely free of stress and distress, you can prevent some distress as well as **minimize its impact**. By recognizing the early signs of distress

---

[1]**hormones** *chemicals formed in one part of the body that travel through the blood and affect the functions of cells in other parts of the body*
[2]**conditioned** *trained to associate a stimulus and a response, for example, Pavlov's dogs were trained to associate a bell with getting food; then they would salivate every time they heard a bell*
[3]**insomnia** *not being able to sleep*
[4]**ulcers** *sore areas, especially in the stomach*

---

prolonged
a. lasting a long time
b. very productive

depletes
a. describes
b. uses up

minimize its impact
a. increase the damage
b. reduce the effect

and then doing something about them, you can improve the quality of your life and perhaps even live longer.

HELPING YOURSELF

7   When stress does occur, it is important to recognize and deal with it. Here are some suggestions for ways to handle stress. As you begin to understand more about how stress affects you as an individual, you will come up with your own ideas of helping to ease the tensions.

8   *Try physical activity.* When you are nervous, angry, or upset, release the pressure through exercise or physical activity. Running, walking, playing tennis, or working in your garden are just some of the activities you might try. Physical exercise will **relieve that "up tight" feeling**, relax you, and turn the frowns into smiles. Remember, your body and your mind work together.

9   *Share your stress.* It helps to talk to someone about your concerns and worries. Perhaps a friend, family member, teacher, or counselor can help you see your problem in a different light. If you feel your problem is serious, you might seek professional help from a psychologist, psychiatrist, social worker, or mental health counselor. Knowing when to ask for help may avoid more serious problems later.

10   *Know your limits.* If a problem is beyond your control and cannot be changed at the moment, don't fight the situation. Learn to accept what is—for now—until such time when you can change it.

11   *Take care of yourself.* You are special. Get enough rest and eat well. If you are irritable and tense from lack of sleep or if you are not eating correctly, you will have less ability to deal with stressful situations. If stress repeatedly keeps you from sleeping, you should ask your doctor for help.

12   *Make time for fun.* Schedule time for both work and recreation. Play can be just as important to your well-being as work; you need a break from your daily routine to just relax and have fun.

13   *Be a participant.* One way to keep from getting bored, sad, and lonely is to go where it's all happening. Sitting alone can make you feel frustrated. Instead of feeling sorry for yourself, get involved and become a participant. Offer your services in neighborhood or volunteer organizations. Help yourself by helping other people. Get involved in the world and the people around you, and you'll find they will be attracted to you. You will be on your way to making new friends and enjoying new activities.

14   *Check off your tasks.* Trying to take care of everything at once can seem overwhelming, and, as a result, you may not accomplish anything. Instead, make a list of what tasks you have to do, then do one at a time, checking them off as they're completed. Give priority to the most important ones and do those first.

15   *Must you always be right?* Do other people upset you—particularly when they don't do things your way? Try **cooperation instead of confrontation**; it's better than fighting and always being "right." A little give and take on both sides will reduce the strain and make you both feel more comfortable.

16   *It's OK to cry.* A good cry can be a healthy way to bring relief to your anxiety, and it might even prevent a headache or other physical consequence. Take some deep breaths; they also release tension.

17   *Create a quiet scene.* You can't always run away, but you can "dream the impossible dream." A quiet country scene painted mentally, or on canvas, can take you out of the turmoil of a stressful situation. Change the scene by reading a good book or playing beautiful music to create a sense of peace and **tranquility**.

(continued)

relieve that "up tight" feeling
a. make you feel more relaxed
b. make you feel more nervous

cooperation instead of confrontation
a. working together and not fighting
b. facing problems alone

tranquility
a. peace
b. anger

18   ***Avoid self-medication.*** Although you can use prescription or over-the-counter medications[5] to relieve stress temporarily, they do not remove the conditions that caused the stress in the first place. Medications, in fact, may be habit-forming and also may reduce your efficiency, thus creating more stress than they take away. They should be taken only on the advice of your doctor.

THE ART OF RELAXATION

19   The best **strategy** for avoiding stress is to learn how to relax. Unfortunately, many people try to relax at the same pace that they lead the rest of their lives. For a while, tune out your worries about time, productivity, and "doing right." You will find satisfaction in just *being,* without **striving.** Find activities that give you pleasure and that are good for your mental and physical well-being. Forget about always winning. Focus on relaxation, enjoyment, and health. Whatever method works for you, be good to yourself. If you don't let stress get out of hand, you can actually make it work for you instead of against you.

strategy
a. story
b. plan

striving
a. making an effort
b. walking quickly

---

[5]**over-the-counter (OTC) medications** *medications you can buy without a doctor's prescription*

COMPREHENSION CHECK

First Reading

Answer these questions.

1. In what ways is stress good for you? When does good stress become bad stress, or distress? (Note that the word *stress* is usually used to refer to both good and bad stress.)
2. Which is the best statement of the main idea of the reading?
   a. The best way to avoid acute stress is to relax.
   b. Stress is both good and bad for you.
   c. If we recognize chronic stress and deal with it successfully, we will live better.
3. Find a sentence in the selection that expresses the main idea.

Second Reading

Reread parts of the selection as needed to answer these questions. As you read, highlight or jot down helpful words or phrases.

1. What three stages does the body go through in reacting to stress? Explain each one in your own words.
2. On a separate piece of paper, make three columns. List each of Dr. Kopolow's suggestions for handling stress in column one. In column two, paraphrase each one. In a third column, list the causes that you can infer from each suggestion. Follow the examples.

Suggestion	Paraphrase	Inferred Cause
Try physical activity.	Exercise.	You are not exercising enough.
Share your stress.	Talk to people about your problems.	You tend to keep your problems inside you.

Vocabulary Building

Read the underlined word or expression in its context and match it with the correct meaning. Use a dictionary if necessary.

PART 1

____ 1. We often think of major <u>crises</u> such as natural disasters, war, and death as main sources of stress. (¶2) (*crisis*, singular)

____ 2. . . . we feel <u>overwhelmed</u> by the pressure to do too many things . . . (¶4)

____ 3. . . . his initial <u>alarm reaction</u> may include fear of an accident . . . (¶5)

____ 4. . . . anger at the driver who <u>committed</u> the action . . . (¶5)

____ 5. . . . <u>releasing</u> hormones into the bloodstream . . . (¶5)

____ 6. . . . which cause his face to <u>flush</u> . . . (¶5)

____ 7. . . . <u>perspiration</u> to form . . . (¶5)

a. did something wrong or illegal

b. feeling of fear or anxiety because something dangerous might happen

c. letting out

d. liquid that appears on skin when you are hot or nervous, sweat

e. turn red

f. unable to think clearly or act because of too many obligations

g. very bad or dangerous situations

PART 2

____ 8. The next stage is <u>resistance</u>, in which the body repairs damage caused by the stress. (¶5)

____ 9. . . . you will come up with your own ideas of helping to ease the <u>tensions</u>. (¶7)

____ 10. If you are <u>irritable</u> and tense from lack of sleep . . . (¶11)

____ 11. One way to keep from getting <u>bored</u>, sad, and lonely is to go where it's all happening. (¶13)

____ 12. A little give and take on both sides will reduce the <u>strain</u> and make you both feel more comfortable. (¶15)

____ 13. A quiet country scene painted mentally, or on canvas, can take you out of the <u>turmoil</u> of a stressful situation. (¶17)

____ 14. Unfortunately, many people try to relax at the same <u>pace</u> that they lead the rest of their lives. (¶19)

h. chaos and trouble

i. easily annoyed or angered

j. feelings of anxiety and worry

k. fighting against something

l. uninterested

m. speed

n. uncomfortable feeling; pressure

Multiword Expressions

Recognizing multiword expressions as meaningful units is an important reading skill to develop. For each definition below, scan the indicated paragraph to find the equivalent multiword expression and write it on the line.

1. handle stress (¶1) _____

2. relaxing (¶3) _____

3. condition of heavy traffic on the road (¶5) _____

4. events in which something bad almost happens (¶5) _____

5. handle (¶7) _____

6. produce, invent (¶7) _____

7. feeling or taking pity on (¶13) _____

8. moving toward (¶13) _____

9. flexibility, willingness to compromise (¶15) _____

10. forget about, ignore (¶19) _____

11. get out of control (¶19) _____

Vocabulary Review

Complete the following statements about the reading selection with the correct words or expression from the list below. Use each word or expression only once.

bored	get out of hand	prolonged	take it easy
close call	overwhelmed	relieve	tune out

1. There are two types of stress. Acute stress is generally temporary. It can be caused by a _____, for example, almost getting hit by a car.

2. Chronic stress, on the other hand, is _____. It is caused by everyday difficulties in our lives, both large and small.

3. Many of us feel _____ and stressed by everyday problems at work or in our families.

4. Kopolow makes numerous suggestions to help us change the way we live in order to _____ chronic stress and that "uptight" feeling we so often have.

5. It isn't good to work 24/7; everyone needs to _____, get enough exercise, and sometimes _____ problems.

6. If we don't allow stress to _____ and become distress, it can actually be good for us. If we didn't have any tension and excitement, most of us would be _____.

Participial Adjectives

> The italicized words in the sentences below are all adjectives* that come from verbs, that is participial adjectives.
>
> Examples:
>
> v
>
> The three-mile run exhausted all the runners.
>
> The run was *exhausting*, and the runners were *exhausted*.
>
> v
>
> The responsibility of raising children alone overwhelms some single parents.
>
> The responsibility of raising children alone is *overwhelming*; some single parents are *overwhelmed*.

*The -ing *form is the present participle of a verb, and the* -ed *form is the past participle.*

A. Study the sentences in the box. Then answer these questions.

1. Which form (*-ing* or *-ed*) is used to describe the cause of the feeling?
2. Which form is used to describe the way people (or animals) feel?

B. Complete the following sentences with the correct participial adjective from the verb in parentheses.

1. I had nothing to do last summer. Summer vacation was extremely

   _____. I was _____ for two months.

   (bore)

2. A reasonable amount of stress makes our lives _____.

   (excite)

3. Some people become very _____ if they have nothing to

   do. (frustrate)

4. I always feel _____ after a good walk. Exercise, in general,

   is _____. (relax)

5. It's very _____ to have your mother criticize the way you

   dress. I was really _____ that my mother didn't like the

   dress I bought. (irritate)

RESPONDING TO READING

Discuss these questions.

1. Read the following statements. Circle *S* if you can support the statement or *R* if you prefer to refute it. What evidence from the reading or your personal experience can you give to support or refute each statement?

   a. Most people have similar reactions to stressful events.　　　　S　　R

   b. Stress has physical effects over a long period of time.　　　　S　　R

   c. Your objective in handling stress should be to eliminate it.　　S　　R

   d. Self-medication is a bad idea.　　　　　　　　　　　　　　S　　R

   e. Everyone finds it easy to relax.　　　　　　　　　　　　　S　　R

2. Will you change your ways of dealing with chronic stress after reading this article? Explain.

3. What are some unhealthy or dangerous ways of reacting to stress? Why do people choose these negative ways and why do they fail?

ABOUT THE READING

"Energy Walks" is about the results of research conducted by Robert E. Thayer, Professor of Psychology at California State University, Long Beach. He is the author of *Calm Energy: How People Regulate Mood with Food and Exercise* and *The Biopsychology of Mood and Arousal.* The following article appeared in *Psychology Today.*

BEFORE YOU READ

Thinking about the Topic

Discuss these questions.

1. What do you do in order to feel energetic and alert, for example, when you have exams?
2. Which do you think gives you more energy, eating something sweet or doing some physical exercise?
3. How do you think an article on walking might relate to the topic of stress?

Previewing

Preview the selection appropriately. Then answer these questions.

1. How does this article answer question 2 in Thinking about the Topic? Where did you find that information?

2. The word *boost* in the subhead means a(an) ___.

    a. decrease   b. increase

Before you read, turn to Comprehension Check, First Reading on page 73. Your purpose for the first reading is to answer those questions.

READ

Energy Walks *By Robert E. Thayer*

Don't touch that candy bar. A short walk gives you a longer energy boost and improves your mood.

1   Recently, I met one of my students at a candy machine on our college campus. He told me he was about to attend a long and boring lecture and needed his favorite sweet to stay alert. I suggested that he join me for a brisk walk instead. When we returned, he thanked me for the **tip**. As he left for the lecture hall, he said he felt great.

tip
a. suggestion
b. payment

2   Another one of my students suffered badly from test anxiety. She knew of my work on the psychology of mood and asked me for help because she had an important exam coming up. I suggested she take a 10-minute walk, moderately fast-paced but not exhausting, before the test. She took the advice and later reported that she "aced"[1] the exam.

(continued)

---

[1]**aced** *got a grade of* A

3   I have been doing research for many years on the mood changes that occur with short, rapid walks. My latest findings clearly indicate that brisk walks increase people's feelings of energy, sometimes for several hours. They are a more effective (and less fattening) pick-me-up than a candy bar and can reduce tension and make personal problems appear less serious. These changes can be **subtle**, but repeated over time they become very apparent. Short walks may even make it easier to quit smoking.

4   I learned of these effects from several experiments with young or middle-aged people who were in fairly good shape. In an early experiment, I had a group of college students sit for a few minutes and **rate** their feelings of energy and tension using a short checklist. They then joined me for a moderately fast 10-minute walk around the campus. We returned and sat down, and within five minutes people completed the checklist again.

5   People felt more energetic and less tired following the walk. I later repeated this procedure with people who walked on a treadmill[2] in a bare-walled room, to ensure that the mood shift was not due simply to a stroll through the attractive campus surroundings. Again, the energizing effect held true. Other aspects of this research made it clear that the mood change did not occur because people expected walking would make them feel better—it was the walk itself that was responsible. Cardiologist James Rippe has also found that walking—specifically a three-mile walk—reduces people's anxiety and tension, as well as their blood pressure.

6   My next step was to discover how long the energized mood lasted. This time, people walked on a number of occasions during a three-week period. Each time, they rated their energy and tension levels, then walked briskly for 10 minutes and repeated the ratings several times during the following two hours.

7   Twenty minutes after the walk, there were significant increases in energy and decreases in fatigue and tension. The effects lasted for at least an hour, **impressive** results when you consider that it took only 10 minutes of rapid walking to produce them. Even after two hours, the increased energy from walking was still present **to a small degree**.

8   As part of this experiment I compared walking to the effects of eating a sugar snack. I had people eat an average-sized candy bar instead of taking the walk. The immediate mood change from the candy bar was similar to the effect of walking: increased energy. But one hour after snacking, some negative changes began to show up: People felt more tired and a lot more tense (the tension was gone after two hours).

9   Other researchers have found that eating sugar can cause fatigue, perhaps because it leads to higher levels of the neurotransmitter serotonin in the brain, which acts as a sedative (see "Food for Thought," *Psychology Today*, April 1988).

subtle
a. small, slight
b. large, noticeable

rate
a. speed up
b. evaluate

impressive
a. impossible
b. notable, good

to a small degree
a. at a low temperature
b. in a small amount

---

[2]**treadmill** *exercise equipment on which a person walks or runs without going anywhere*

I found that the first reaction to sugar is enhanced energy, and fatigue seems to occur half an hour to an hour later. This might explain why people who ate candy bars subsequently felt tense. The sugar, after providing a short burst of energy, **eventually** caused fatigue. People felt tired but were not able to sleep (it was during the day and they were busy), which made them tense. The people who walked enjoyed an energy boost, avoided the effects of a sugar sedative, and didn't experience tension later on.

10   Short, rapid walks can also help make personal problems appear less serious and increase optimism. During the course of three weeks, one group of people repeatedly assessed the severity of a continuing personal problem, such as marital troubles or a **stubborn** weight problem. Another group rated their level of optimism. In addition to completing these ratings at fixed times each day, people in both groups took a brisk 10-minute walk.

11   After the walk, chronic personal problems appeared less serious. The walk also increased general optimism. These improvements were small and were not noticeable every day, but after three weeks the difference became obvious.

12   Walking produces some other interesting psychological effects, according to studies **currently underway** by various graduate students and myself. One especially important benefit may be for cigarette smokers who are trying to cut down or quit. Since people often smoke to increase their energy or reduce tension, we have asked smokers to take 5-minute walks before they light up. So far the results are very impressive. Following a walk, smokers wait two times longer than nonwalking smokers do between cigarettes during free-smoking periods. And those who report the greatest energy increases from the walk wait the longest to smoke the next cigarette.

currently under way
a. in progress now
b. below the road

13   Walking is, of course, very good physical exercise. Beyond that, it feels good to walk and at moderate walking speeds those good feelings occur right away. Try it after you have been sitting for a while. Keep your posture erect but otherwise relaxed, swing your arms freely and breathe naturally. You don't have to be a dedicated athlete to walk, nor do you need to invest a lot of time and money. Ten minutes should do it and the benefits—both mental and physical—should last a lot longer.

COMPREHENSION CHECK

First Reading

Answer these questions.

1. What kind of walking does Thayer recommend and for how long?
2. In what ways is walking better than eating a candy bar for energy?
3. What good effects does walking have in addition to increasing energy?

Second Reading

Reread parts of the selection as needed to answer these questions. As you read, highlight or jot down helpful words or phrases.

1. Whose research is reported? _____

2. Who were the subjects, the people who participated in the study?

   _____

(continued)

3. The facts about several experiments are given in paragraphs 4 to 11. Identify each experiment, and answer the questions below. Then write your answers in the chart that follows.

- What questions was the researcher trying to answer?
- What procedures did the researcher follow to answer the research questions?
- What were the findings?

Experiment	Research Questions	Procedures	Findings
1 (¶4)			
2 (¶5)			
3A (¶6–7)			
3B (¶8)			
4 (¶10–11)			

4. Why might sugar actually make you more tired in the long run?

VOCABULARY

Vocabulary Building

Read the underlined word or expression in its context. Choose the meaning that makes sense in this context. Use a dictionary if necessary.

1. He told me he was about to attend a long and boring lecture . . . (¶1)

   a. criticism from a professor

   b. a long talk

   c. a reading assignment

2. He . . . needed his favorite sweet to stay alert. (¶1)

   a. attentive, able to think clearly

   b. intelligent, well-educated

   c. strong, physically fit

3. I suggested that he join me for a brisk walk instead. (¶1)

   a. long and difficult

   b. quick and energizing

   c. slow and lazy

4. I suggested she take a 10-minute walk, <u>moderately</u> fast-paced . . . (¶2)

    a. extremely, very

    b. somewhat, reasonably

    c. uncontrollably

5. They [brisk walks] are a more effective (and less fattening) <u>pick-me-up</u> than a candy bar . . . (¶3)

    a. open truck for carrying things

    b. something that gives you energy

    c. unplanned activity

6. . . . to <u>ensure</u> that the mood shift was not due simply to a stroll through the attractive campus . . . (¶5)

    a. believe

    b. make certain

    c. promise

7. . . . there were significant. . . decreases in <u>fatigue</u> and tension. (¶7)

    a. anxiety

    b. physical relaxation

    c. tiredness

8. . . . neurotransmitter serotonin in the brain, which acts as a <u>sedative</u> . . . (¶9)

    a. antidepressant

    b. drug that energizes

    c. drug that calms

9. . . . people who ate candy bars <u>subsequently</u> felt tense. (¶9)

    a. afterwards

    b. suddenly

    c. surprisingly

10. . . . one group of people repeatedly <u>assessed</u> the severity of a continuing personal problem . . . (¶10)

    a. assumed

    b. discussed

    c. evaluated

11. <u>Keep your posture erect</u> . . . (¶13)

    a. maintain a positive mental attitude

    b. stand up straight

    c. stay comfortable

Vocabulary Review

Complete the following statements about the reading selection with the correct words or expression from the list below. Use each word or expression only once.

alert	fatigue	tip
brisk	pick-me-up	

1. When you have an exam coming up, you want to be well-rested, calm, and
   _____. Feeling nervous and tired isn't going to help you
   ace the test.

2. A short, _____ walk, whether it is in an attractive setting
   or on a treadmill in a gym, can do a lot to calm your nerves and help you feel
   more energetic.

3. Walking is a better _____ than eating a sugar snack
   because the positive effect of the walk lasts longer. Eating a sugar snack
   provides only a brief boost to your energy level and eventually leads to

   _____.

4. So take a(an) _____ from Robert Thayer and walk.

TEXT ANALYSIS   Text Organization

Skim the reading again and describe the contribution of each paragraph or set of paragraphs to the whole piece of writing.

Paragraphs	Contribution
¶1–2	*Introduces the topic with two examples*
¶3–12	_____
¶13	_____

How is the reading selection organized?

RESPONDING TO READING

Discuss these questions.

1. Why do you think this article appears in a unit on stress?

2. How does walking compare to other forms of physical exercise to relieve stress?

3. Survey a minimum of five people outside your class to find out how they cope with stress. Use the following questions as a guide.

   a. Do you suffer from stress? If so, what causes it?

   b. What do you do to relieve stress?

   c. Do you exercise? What type of exercise do you do? How does it make you feel?

   d. Note the person's gender and guess the person's age. (It is not polite to ask.) Combine your findings with those of your classmates. Summarize your conclusions for the population of people you surveyed.

ABOUT THE READING

"Stressed to Death" and "Heartfelt Fear" appeared in *Science News* December, 2004, and February, 2005, respectively. *Science News* is a magazine for the general public that publishes short reports on important research that is published in scientific journals.

BEFORE YOU READ

Thinking about the Topic

Discuss these questions.

1. What are some of the physical conditions that stress might cause?
2. Which type of stress, acute or chronic, do you think has a more serious effect on the body?

Previewing

Read the title, subhead, and the first paragraph of each article. Then answer these questions and decide which article you want to read.

1. Which article will be about acute stress?
2. Which article will be about chronic stress?

Choose Part 1 or Part 2. Before you read, turn to Comprehension Check, First Reading on page 80. Your purpose for the first reading is to answer those questions.

READ

Part 1: Stressed to Death

By C. Brownlee

Mental tension ages cells.

adage
a. wise saying
b. horror movie

1   A new study puts evidence behind the old **adage** that stressful experiences can give a person gray hairs. Scientific data now indicate that prolonged psychological stress might cause a person's cells to age, and possibly die, significantly faster than normal.

2   Previous research had shown that protein-DNA complexes called telomeres serve as a cell's timekeeper, telling it how long to live. Telomeres protect the ends of chromosomes, much as plastic tips protect shoelaces. Each time a cell divides, enzymes[1] chew off a tiny portion of its telomeres. When the caps are **whittled down to nubs**, cells cease dividing and soon die.

whittled down to nubs
a. reduced in size
b. thrown away

3   Scientists have long known that stress can harm a person's health by, for instance, lowering immunity or raising blood pressure. "We wanted to look at

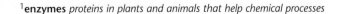

[1]**enzymes** *proteins in plants and animals that help chemical processes*

underpinnings
a. hormones
b. causes

play a role
a. be partly responsible
b. be in the theater

some of the molecular **underpinnings** of why that might be true. No one actually has clear ideas," says Elizabeth Blackburn of the University of California, San Francisco.

4   Blackburn and her colleagues examined whether telomeres might **play a role**. Her team recruited 58 healthy women between the ages of 20 and 50. While all the women were mothers of at least one child, 39 members of the group were primary caregivers for a child who was chronically ill with a disease such as cerebral palsy.

5   Each volunteer answered a questionnaire on how much day-to-day stress she perceived in her life. Not surprisingly, mothers with chronically ill children generally reported more stress than did women with healthy children.

6   Blackburn's team measured telomere lengths in immune cells called mononucleocytes collected from blood samples of each volunteer. The researchers also assessed the activity of an enzyme called telomerase, which maintains telomeres.

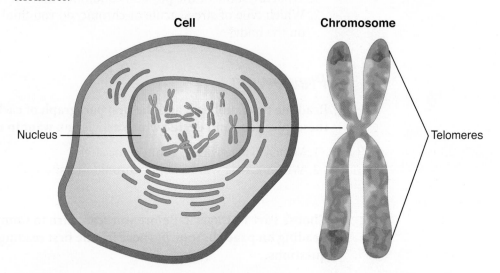

striking
a. unimportant
b. very notable, large

estimate
a. know for sure
b. guess, judge

7   "There was a very **striking** connection" between stress and telomere length, Blackburn reports. Mothers who perceived their stress levels as high had significantly shorter telomeres and less telomerase activity than did women reporting lower stress. From the telomere lengths, the researchers **estimate** that cells from the highly stressed women resembled cells of low-stressed volunteers who were 10 years older.

8   The researchers aren't sure how stress affects telomere length and telomerase activity, but they speculate that chemicals known as free radicals[2] might impede telomerase function. Further tests showed that women who reported higher stress also had more free radical damage to their cells than women under less psychological strain did.

upcoming
a. old
b. future

9   The findings, to be published in an **upcoming** *Proceedings of the National Academy of Sciences,* are "very provocative, in the best sense of the word," says Robert Sapolsky, a biologist at Stanford University. "This is very exciting because it ties in stress to, arguably, the best cellular pacemaker of aging out there."

10   Blackburn's results "make sense," says Fred Goldman, a pediatric oncologist[3] who studies telomere biology at the University of Iowa in Iowa City. "We know that people who are stressed-out look haggard. . . . If we have less stress in our lives, we might live longer."

---

[2]**free radicals** *atoms which attack molecules in the body and disturb their normal function*
[3]**pediatric oncologist** *medical doctor who specializes in treating cancer in children*

Part 2: Heartfelt Fear *By N. Seppa*

Findings link stress and cardiac symptoms.

1 Terrible sadness, a sudden fright, or other emotional stress can bring on heart attack symptoms in people not actually experiencing a heart attack, according to two new reports.

2 The researchers examined people who showed up at hospitals with chest pain and an impaired capacity to pump blood but no heart-tissue damage or **clogged** coronary arteries.[1] Rather, the patients turned out to be experiencing physical effects after stressful events, such as the death of a loved one.

3 Cardiologist[2] Hunter C. Champion of Johns Hopkins Medical Institutions in Baltimore and his colleagues treated 18 women and one man with severe symptoms. After initial tests had ruled out a heart attack, bedside talks revealed that all the patients had recently had a stressful experience. These included the death of a spouse, a car accident, an armed robbery, a family dispute, a court appearance, and a surprise party.

4 The patients had blood concentrations of catecholamine hormones that were more than seven times normal and two to three times as great as those in five patients having heart attacks **triggered** by coronary artery blockages. Catecholamines, which include adrenaline and dopamine, are powerful hormones that regulate heart rate, blood pressure, and other body processes. The researchers report their findings in the Feb. 10 *New England Journal of Medicine*.

5 In the other study, cardiologist Scott W. Sharkey of the Minneapolis Heart Institute and his colleagues identified 22 women who were brought to a hospital shortly after a stressful incident. "These patients came in with what looked like **massive** heart attacks," Sharkey says. But tests of their hearts showed no blockage and no tissue damage.

6 However, magnetic resonance images[3] revealed an unusual **abnormality** in the movement of the wall of the heart's strongest pumping chamber,[4] Sharkey and his colleagues report in the Feb. 1 *Circulation*. This condition prevents the heart from circulating enough blood.

7 All patients in both studies **recovered**, but some of them received assistance from a machine in pumping blood for a few days.

8 Sharkey points out that heart tissue is rich in nerve endings that can **stimulate** the release of catecholamines. The flood of these chemicals brought on by stress might cause spasms in small arteries that nourish the heart, he says.

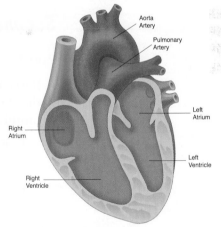

Chambers of the heart and coronary arteries

(continued)

---

[1]**coronary arteries** *blood vessels that carry blood from the heart (see picture above)*
[2]**cardiologist** *a doctor who specializes in treating heart disease*
[3]**magnetic resonance images** *(MRIs) pictures of the inside of the body produced by using strong magnetic fields*
[4]**the heart's strongest pumping chamber** *The heart has two pumping chambers called ventricles (see picture above).*

clogged
a. blocked
b. cut

triggered
a. killed
b. caused

massive
a. good, excellent
b. major, serious

abnormality
a. something not normal
b. something routine or normal

recovered
a. died
b. got better

stimulate
a. cause
b. stop

excess
a. too few
b. too many

mend
a. break
b. fix

9   The new findings also suggest that **excess** catecholamines have a toxic effect on heart tissue, says Yoshihiro J. Akashi of St. Marianna University School of Medicine in Kawasaki, Japan.

10   Sharkey adds, "This process is an example of the strong physical connection between the brain and the heart, in women especially."

11   Emergency room physicians should ask patients about stressful events when apparent heart attack patients have no sign of a coronary artery blockage, Champion says. Then after stabilizing the patient, it's a matter of waiting it out.

12   "Time really does **mend** a broken heart," Champion says.

COMPREHENSION CHECK

First Reading

Answer these questions with a partner who read the same article as you. Then share information about the article and the answers to the questions with students who read the other article.

PART 1

1. Who were the two groups of volunteers studied?
2. Which group suffered more stress? Was it acute or chronic stress?
3. What do scientists conclude about the effect of stress?

PART 2

1. When can patients show up in the emergency room with signs of a heart attack that is not a real heart attack? What type of stress are their symptoms related to?
2. Why is this important for emergency room physicians to know?
3. What happened to the patients mentioned in this article?

Second Reading

PART 1

A. Reread parts of the article you read as needed to answer these questions. Mark the statements *T* (true) or *F* (false). Write the paragraph number(s) where you found evidence for each answer.

1. T F Scientists have known for a long time that stress can affect the immune system and blood pressure. ¶____

2. T F Scientists have long understood how stress affects the immune system and blood pressure. ¶____

3. T F Dr. Blackburn built her research on previous research that showed that telomeres influence how long cells live. ¶____

4. T F Women who reported high levels of stress had shorter telomeres and less telomerase activity than did women reporting lower stress. ¶____

5. T F The researchers did more tests and found that the women who reported more stress showed more free-radical damage to their cells. ¶____

6. T F We can infer that aging may be related to how long our cells continue to divide. ¶____

7. T F This study shows that women with children are more stressed and age more rapidly than women without children. ¶____

B. Use the flowchart as a guide to fill the blanks in the summary of what Dr. Blackburn and her colleagues think is happening to the women in the more stressed group.

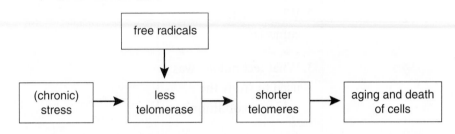

Chronic stress may lead to a reduction in (1)_____, an enzyme which is necessary to maintain cell function. Scientists speculate that (2)_____ impede the function of telomerase. The result is (3)_____. When there is not enough (4)_____ left, the cell cannot (5)_____. When cells stop dividing, they (6)_____ and the person looks older.

PART 2

A. Reread parts of the article you read as needed to answer these questions. Mark the statements *T* (true) or *F* (false). Write the paragraph number(s) where you found evidence for each answer.

1. T F The subjects in these studies were hospital patients who had blocked blood vessels in the heart that caused them to have heart attacks. ¶____

2. T F The patients had chest pains and their hearts didn't pump well. ¶____

3. T F The patients had suffered a recent, stressful experience. ¶____

4. T F The patients had smaller quantities of catecholamine hormones in their blood than five patients having real heart attacks. ¶____

5. T F Sharkey thinks that stress may cause heart nerves to release high levels of catecholamine into the blood, causing the symptoms of a heart attack. ¶____

6. T F All the patients recovered mainly by waiting the symptoms out. ¶____

7. T F The effects of the catecholamine hormones seem to be more common in men than in women. ¶____

B. There are two studies reported in this article. Fill in the information about both studies in the chart below.

	Study 1 (Johns Hopkins, Baltimore)	Study 2 (Minneapolis Heart Institute)
1. Who was the researcher?		
2. Who were the subjects?		
3. What technology was used to study the subjects' condition?		
4. What did the researchers find?		

VOCABULARY

Vocabulary Building

Do the vocabulary matching exercise for the part you read. If you want to learn more vocabulary, do the other part as well. Read the underlined word or expression in its context and match it with the correct meaning. Use a dictionary if necessary.

PART 1

___ 1. . . . cells <u>cease</u> dividing and soon die. (¶2)

___ 2. . . . stress can harm a person's health by . . . lowering <u>immunity</u> . . . (¶3)

___ 3. Her team <u>recruited</u> 58 healthy women . . . (¶4)

___ 4. . . . immune cells . . . collected from blood <u>samples</u> of each volunteer. (¶6)

___ 5. . . . cells from the highly stressed women <u>resembled</u> cells of low-stressed volunteers who were 10 years older. (¶7)

___ 6. . . . they <u>speculate</u> that . . . free radicals might impede . . . (¶8)

___ 7. . . . chemicals known as free radicals might <u>impede</u> telomerase function. (¶8)

___ 8. The findings . . . are "very <u>provocative</u> . . ." (¶9)

___ 9. . . . people who are stressed out look <u>haggard</u> . . . (¶10)

a. ability of body to fight off disease

b. were similar to, looked like

c. small amounts

d. causing thought and discussion

e. got, found

f. slow down, make something difficult

g. stop

h. tired and worried

i. think about possible causes

____ 1. Findings link stress and <u>cardiac symptoms</u> (subhead)

____ 2. . . . an <u>impaired</u> capacity to pump blood . . . (¶2)

____ 3. <u>Rather</u>, the patients turned out to be experiencing physical effects after stressful events . . . (¶2)

____ 4. . . . the death of a <u>spouse</u> . . . (¶3)

____ 5. . . . a family <u>dispute</u> . . . (¶3)

____ 6. This condition prevents the heart from <u>circulating</u> enough blood. (¶6)

____ 7. . . . might cause <u>spasms</u> in small arteries that nourish the heart . . . (¶8)

____ 8. . . . excess catecholamines have a <u>toxic</u> effect on heart tissue . . . (¶9)

____ 9. Then after <u>stabilizing</u> the patient, it's a matter of waiting it out. (¶11)

a. getting back to a constant, normal state

b. instead

c. husband or wife

d. moving within a system

e. poisonous

f. not as good as it should be

g. argument or disagreement

h. signs of heart problems

i. sudden, uncontrolled tightening

Finding Definitions in the Text

In scientific or academic writing, technical terms are often defined in the text. Find the definition of each of the following terms, and write the definition on the line.

PART 1

1. telomeres (¶2) _____

2. mononucleocytes (¶6) _____

3. telomerase (¶6) _____

PART 2

1. catecholamine (¶4) _____

2. adrenaline and dopamine (¶4) _____

Vocabulary Review

Complete the following statements about the reading selection with the correct word from the list below. Use each word only once.

PART 1

haggard	resembled	striking
impede	speculate	underpinnings

1. In the study described in this article the cells of women who suffered from chronic stress _____ the cells of older people.

2. The researchers found a(an) _____ difference between the length of telomeres and telomerase activity in immune cells of the two groups of women in the study.

3. Telomeres were much shorter, and telomerase activity was much lower among the more stressed women, leading the researchers to _____ that free radicals, which damage cells, also _____ telomerase activity.

4. The old adage that stress wears us out may turn out to have scientific _____. There may be scientific explanations for why stressed people look tired and _____.

PART 2

abnormal	impaired	symptoms
circulated	recovered	triggered
clogged		

1. People who have _____ of a heart attack but no physical damage to the heart may be showing the effect of acute stress, _____ by a traumatic or stressful experience.

2. The subjects in these studies had chest pain, but they did not have _____ coronary blood vessels. However, blood samples showed _____ levels of catecholamines, hormones that affect body processes, such as heart rate and blood pressure.

3. Furthermore, MRIs showed that the pumping capacity of their hearts was _____, so less blood _____.

4. These physical effects are temporary, and all the patients in both studies described in this article _____.

TEXT ANALYSIS   *Citing Sources in a Magazine*

> *Science News* is a magazine, not an academic journal. The audience for magazines is ordinary people. The audience for a journal, on the other hand, is limited to scholars in a particular field. In a journal or in academic books, strict rules about citing sources are followed. (See Text Analysis in Unit 1, Chapter 3, page 20.) The rules for citing sources in magazines are less rigid.

To see how the citation of sources in a magazine such as *Science News* is different from more academic writing found in journals, answer these questions about "Stressed to Death" and "Heartfelt Fear."

1. Is there a list of references?
2. Where can you locate the original research?
3. How do the writers of these articles support their statements?
4. Does the reader know where or when the people quoted made their statements?
5. What information do you get about the person quoted?
6. Why do you think the citing of sources is stricter in academic journals than in magazines?

RESPONDING TO READING

Work with a partner who did not read the same article as you. Discuss these questions so each of you can get a better understanding of the article you did not read. Ask appropriate questions to clarify anything you do not understand.

1. How do chronic and acute stress affect the body?

2. What tools or techniques do researchers use to determine physiological changes in the body caused by stress?

3. Which type of stress do you now think is more harmful?

4. Talk about times when stress affected the health of people you know. What circumstances caused the stress? How harmful and long-lasting were the effects?

ABOUT THE READING

"The Dinner Party" is a fictional story that takes place in India during the period when India was a British colony, from 1876 to 1948.

**BEFORE
YOU READ**

Thinking about the Topic

Discuss these questions.

1. Who do you think might have been at a dinner party in India before it was an independent nation?
2. What type of stress do you think might occur at a dinner party?

READ

The Dinner Party *By Mona Gardner*

spacious
a. cold
b. large

1   The country is India. A colonial official and his wife are giving a large dinner party. They are seated with their guests—army officers and government attachés[1] and their wives, and a visiting American naturalist[2]—in their **spacious** dining room, which has a bare marble floor, open rafters, and wide glass doors opening onto a veranda.

2   A spirited discussion springs up between a young girl who insists that women have outgrown the jumping-on-a-chair-at-the-sight-of-a-mouse era and a colonel[3] who says that they haven't.

---

[1]**attachés** *diplomatic officials*
[2]**naturalist** *someone who studies animals and plants, a biologist*
[3]**colonel** *high-ranking military officer*

scream
a. shout when frightened
b. sing and dance

3   "A woman's unfailing reaction in any crisis," the colonel says, "is to **scream**. And while a man may feel like it, he has that ounce more of nerve control than a woman has. And that last ounce is what counts."

4   The American does not join in the argument but watches the other guests. As he looks, he sees a strange expression come over the face of the hostess. She is staring straight ahead, her muscles contracting slightly. With a slight gesture she summons the native boy standing behind her chair and whispers to him. The boy's eyes widen: he quickly leaves the room.

5   Of the guests, none except the American notices this or sees the boy place a bowl of milk on the veranda just outside the open doors.

6   The American comes to with a start. In India, milk in a bowl means only one thing—bait for a snake. He realizes there must be a cobra in the room. He looks up at the rafters—the likeliest place—but they are bare. Three corners of the room are empty, and in the fourth the servants are waiting to serve the next course. There is only one place left—under the table.

7   His first impulse is to jump back and warn the others, but he knows the commotion would frighten the cobra into striking. He speaks quickly, the tone of his voice so arresting that it sobers everyone.

8   "I want to know just what control everyone at this table has. I will count to three hundred—that's five minutes—and not one of you is to move a muscle. Those who move will forfeit fifty rupees.[4] Ready!"

like stone images
a. moving
b. not moving

9   The twenty people sit **like stone images** while he counts. He is saying " . . . two hundred and eighty. . . . " when, out of the corner of his eye, he sees the cobra emerge and make for the bowl of milk. Screams ring out as he jumps to slam the veranda doors safely shut.

exclaims
a. asks
b. cries out

10   "You were right, Colonel!" the host **exclaims**. "A man has just shown us an example of perfect control."

11   "Just a minute," the American says, turning to his hostess. "Mrs. Wynnes, how did you know that cobra was in the room?"

crawling
a. moving slowly
b. jumping

12   A faint smile lights up the woman's face as she replies: "Because it was **crawling** across my foot."

---

[4]**rupee** *monetary unit of India*

COMPREHENSION CHECK

Answer these questions.

1. What question were the dinner guests discussing? What opinions were expressed?
2. How does the American naturalist know there is a danger?
3. What is clever about what he does?
4. Why didn't the cobra attack Mrs. Wynnes?
5. How was the question of the dinner conversation resolved?

Vocabulary Building: Using Paraphrases

Work with a partner. Study the sentence on the left. Underline the difficult words in the sentence and find their meanings in the paraphrase on the right. Use a dictionary if necessary.

Sentence from the Text	Paraphrase
1. A spirited discussion springs up between a young girl who insists that women have outgrown the jumping-on-a-chair-at-the-sight-of-a-mouse era and a colonel who says that they haven't. (¶2)	There's a lively discussion between a young girl and a colonel. She insists women have changed and the period of time when they jumped on a chair at the sight of a mouse has passed.
2. With a slight gesture she summons the native boy standing behind her chair and whispers to him. (¶4)	With a slight gesture, she calls the native boy standing behind her chair to come and she speaks very softly to him.
3. The American comes to with a start. In India, milk in a bowl means only one thing—bait for a snake. (¶6)	The American is suddenly on the alert. He knows that in India, milk in a bowl is used to attract a snake.
4. His first impulse is to jump back and warn the others, but he knows the commotion would frighten the cobra into striking. (¶7)	His immediate reaction is to jump back and warn the others, but he realizes the chaos and noisy reaction of the guests will frighten the cobra into attacking or biting someone.
5. He speaks quickly, the tone of his voice so arresting that it sobers everyone. (¶7)	He speaks quickly in a tone of voice that stops everyone and makes them listen seriously.
6. Those who move will forfeit fifty rupees. (¶8)	Guests who move will lose fifty rupees. (He is challenging the guests to a bet.)
7. . . . out of the corner of his eye, he sees the cobra emerge and make for the bowl of milk. (¶9)	Out of the corner of his eye, he sees the cobra come out and move towards the bowl of milk.

Vocabulary Review

Complete the following statements about the reading selection with the correct words from the list below. Use each word only once.

bait   emerge   outgrown
commotion   impulse

1. Having a cobra as an unexpected dinner guest would certainly cause acute

   stress for many people, even people who think they have

   _____ most of their fears.

2. Instead of warning the guests about the danger and causing a great

_____, the American naturalist distracted the guests by

challenging them to keep still for five minutes.

3. This gave the cobra time to _____ from under the table

and find the _____ Mrs. Wynnes had directed a servant

to place outside on the veranda.

4. This situation could have turned out badly if either Mrs. Wynnes or the

American naturalist had acted on _____. Instead they

stayed calm, used their heads, and Mrs. Wynnes proved that women can have

as much or more control than men.

TEXT ANALYSIS *Elements of Fiction*

> Short stories and novels have three principal elements: the **setting**, the
> **characters**, and the **plot**.
>
> **Setting:** the place, time, and conditions under which a story takes place
>
> **Characters:** the people in a story
>
> **Plot:** the events that happen in a story
>
> Story plots need **conflict** of some sort. The characters must struggle with some
> problem. The **climax** of the plot is the point at which the action reaches its
> highest emotional intensity. Most stories have a part after the climax, the
> **resolution** or **denouement,** which shows how things turn out in the end.

Answer these questions.

1. What is the setting of this story?
2. Who are the characters? What are their important personality traits?
3. What are the events in the plot? What is the conflict? Where does the plot
   reach its climax? Is there a part you would call the resolution?
4. Which of the elements—setting, characters, or plot—do you think is most
   important in this story, or are they almost equally important? Explain with
   reference to the story.

RESPONDING TO READING Discuss these questions.

1. How did you feel as you read this story? Were you surprised by the ending?
   Explain.

2. How would the story have been different if there had been no discussion about
   men's and women's behavior?

3. What is the point of this story? Is it only meant to be entertaining? Explain.

4. Do you think men and women differ in the way they handle stress? If so, what
   do you think the differences are, and who do you think handles stress better?

Extending Your Vocabulary

Word Families

Study the chart below to learn other forms of some of the words in this unit. If a box is blank, either there is no word to fill it, or the word is missing because it is not one you need to know now.

	NOUNS	VERBS	ADJECTIVES	ADVERBS
1.	abnormality	—	abnormal	abnormally
2.	boredom	bore	boring bored	—
3.	energy	energize	energetic	energetically
4.	estimation estimate	estimate	estimated	—
5.	exhaustion	exhaust	exhausting exhausted	—
6.	immunity immunization	immunize	immune	—
7.	relaxation	relax	relaxing relaxed	—
8.	relief	relieve	relieved	—
9.	sedative sedation	sedate	sedated	—
10.	tranquility tranquilizer	tranquilize	tranquil	tranquilly

For each item, look at the row in the chart above with the same number. Choose the word that correctly completes the sentence; be sure it is in the correct form.

1. It is _____ for people to have no stress in their lives. But

    excess stress can release _____ high amounts of

    hormones into the blood and trigger some serious symptoms.

2. A totally stress-free life, if it were possible, would probably

    _____ us.

3. If you get enough sleep, you will feel more _____ and be able to accomplish more.

4. The _____ cost of the trip was higher than expected.

5. Physical exercise does not have to be _____, but it should be strenuous enough to raise your heart rate.

6. We have reduced the incidence of infectious disease through _____, but not all parents want to _____ their children.

7. What do you do for _____? I find reading a good book at the beach very _____.

8. I didn't think I did very well on my biology test, but I aced it. What a _____! I feel so _____.

9. There are many different drugs doctors can use to _____ people.

10. Some people hate to travel by airplane and take a _____ before the trip. For others, who prefer to avoid medication, it is enough to imagine a _____ scene.

Polysemous Words

Read each sentence. Match the underlined word with the correct meaning. In some cases, you will use the same answer twice. An asterisk indicates a meaning that was used in this unit.

1. ____ . . . his initial alarm reaction may include . . . anger at the driver who committed* the action (of pulling out in front of him).

____ Abdul commits himself 100% to anything he agrees to do.

____ A person who commits a murder might be mentally ill.

____ Alice had a nervous breakdown and was committed to a mental institution.

____ The board of directors has committed $500,000 to the project.

a. use all of the time and energy you can in order to do something

b. do something wrong or illegal

c. put in a hospital or prison

d. promise to use something for a specific purpose

(continued)

2. ____ After two hours the increased energy from walking was still present to a small <u>degree</u>.*

    ____ Water boils at 212 <u>degrees</u>.

    ____ When will you graduate and get your bachelor's <u>degree</u>?

    ____ An angle of 45 <u>degrees</u> is an acute angle.

a. a unit for measuring temperature

b. a unit for measuring the size of an angle

c. a document proving that someone has successfully completed a course of study at a college or university

d. amount or level

3. ____ She had a <u>faint</u>* smile on her face.

    ____ Some people think they will <u>faint</u> at the sight of a snake or a mouse.

    ____ There was a <u>faint</u> odor of fire.

a. slight, difficult to perceive

b. become unconscious

4. ____ Thayer had subjects <u>rate</u>* their feelings of energy and tension.

    ____ They walked at a moderately fast <u>rate</u>.

    ____ What is the interest <u>rate</u> now?

    ____ There is a special <u>rate</u> for children.

    ____ The movie was <u>rated</u> PG-13.

a. speed

b. evaluate, assess

c. charge or payment according to a standard scale

5. ____ Stress <u>releases</u>* hormones into the blood.

    ____ Rafael was <u>released</u> from the hospital.

    ____ The movie will be <u>released</u> next month.

    ____ It's easy to forget to <u>release</u> the emergency brake before you move the car.

a. made public

b. let something flow out

c. permitted to leave

d. take off

6. ____ The difference between the two groups was <u>striking</u>.*

    ____ The naturalist and Mrs. Wynnes were afraid the cobra would <u>strike</u>* one of the guests.

    ____ Some people don't think public employees should have the right to <u>strike</u>.

a. attack, hit, bite

b. notable, impressive

c. stop working as a form of protest against pay or work conditions

7. ___ Dr. Thayer gave the student a tip*;
he told him to take a walk instead
of eating a candy bar.

___ It is customary to leave a 15%
tip when you pay your bill in
a restaurant.

___ The word was on the tip of
my tongue.

___ If you aren't careful, that
bookcase is going to tip over.

a. fall over

b. suggestion, piece of advice

c. extra money for a service

d. end of something, usually
something pointed

WRITING

**Choose one of the suggestions for writing below. Talk about what you plan to
write with a classmate who chose the same topic. Then follow the instructions
for writing.**

Personal Writing

1. Change is one source of stress. Write about a change you have had to make in
your life such as changing schools, moving to a new culture, or starting a new
job. What stress did it cause in your life? Use the question words: *who, what,
where, when, why, how,* and *how long* to be sure that you provide the necessary
background information and explain the situation clearly.

2. Write at least one paragraph giving advice to the person suffering from stress
described below in *a* or *b*. Provide reasons for the advice. Support it with
factual information.
   a. Kim is a single mother with two small children, a six-year-old boy and an
   eight-year-old girl. She is a police officer. Since she is the only parent, she
   says she has almost no time for herself.
   b. Andrew is working full time as a store clerk and studying for his bachelor's
   degree at night. He has a wife and small baby. His wife is always
   complaining that they never have time for fun.

Academic Writing

3. Write a summary of one of the research reports in Chapter 11. Use the notes
you made in Comprehension Check—Second Reading on page 82. If you
choose "Stressed to Death" you will need to take additional notes.

Try to use some of the following vocabulary in writing about the topic you choose:
*acute, alert, chronic, close call, cope (with), crisis, ease tensions, exhaustion, fatigue,
feel sorry for, frustration, get out of hand, haggard, impede, impulse, irritated/
irritating/irritable, minimize the impact, overwhelmed/overwhelming, pick-me-up,
relaxed/relaxing, release pressure, relieve stress/that up tight feeling, rush hour traffic,
scream, symptoms, take it easy, traffic jam, tranquility, trigger, tune out, turmoil.*

UNIT 4

Cultures in Contact

Discuss

1. What does culture include?
2. What types of reactions might people have when they visit or live in a different culture?
3. What problems and what benefits are possible when people from different cultures come into contact?

> *When you understand another culture or language, it does not mean that you have to lose your own culture.*
>
> Edward T. Hall, anthropologist

ABOUT THE READING

This reading selection is from a classic anthropology textbook by Clyde Kluckhohn, *Mirror for Man: The Relation of Anthropology to Modern Life*, first published in 1959. It comes from a chapter entitled "Queer Customs." Cultural or social anthropologists, like Clyde Kluckhohn, study people, their societies, their behavior, and their beliefs.

BEFORE YOU READ

Thinking about the Topic

Discuss these questions.

1. All of the following are food to people in some parts of the world. Which ones would be the easiest for you to learn to eat? Which would be the most difficult? Compare answers with your classmates.

ants	eels	octopus
blood sausage	giant waterbugs	rose petals
cactus fruit	grasshoppers	seaweed
camel hump meat	horsemeat	snake
dog	kangaroo tails	

Previewing

Preview the selection appropriately. Then check the things you think the author will do.

____ define culture

____ explain how cultures have changed over the years

____ give examples of how cultures differ

____ evaluate cultures

Before you read, turn to Comprehension Check, First Reading on page 97. Your purpose for the first reading is to answer those questions.

READ

Culture *By Clyde Kluckhohn*

1   Why do the Chinese dislike milk and milk products? Why would the Japanese die willingly in a Banzai charge[1] [in World War II] that seemed senseless to Americans? Why do some nations trace descent through the father, others through the mother, still others through both parents? Not because different peoples have different **instincts**, not because the weather is different in China and Japan and the

(continued)

instincts
a. natural tendencies
b. friends

[1]**Banzai charge** *suicide attacks to avoid surrender and dishonor*

United States. Sometimes shrewd common sense has an answer that is close to that of an anthropologist: "because they were brought up that way." By *culture*, anthropology means the total life way of a people, the social legacy the individual acquires from his group. Or *culture* can be regarded as that part of the environment that is the creation of man.[2]

2   This technical term has a wider meaning than the *culture* of history and literature. A humble cooking pot is as much a cultural product as is a Beethoven sonata. In ordinary speech a man of culture is a man who can speak languages other than his own, who is familiar with history, literature, philosophy, or the fine arts. . . . To the anthropologist, however, to be human is to be cultured. There is culture in general, and then there are the specific cultures, such as Russian, American, British, Hottentot, Inca. . . . Each specific culture constitutes a kind of **blueprint** for all of life's activities.

3   . . . A good deal of human behavior can be understood and, indeed, predicted, if we know a people's design for living. Many acts are neither accidental nor due to personal peculiarities nor caused by supernatural forces nor simply mysterious. Even those of us who pride ourselves on our individualism follow most of the time a pattern not of our own making. We brush our teeth on arising. We put on pants—not a loincloth[3] or grass skirt. We eat three meals a day—not four or five or two. We sleep in a bed—not in a hammock[4] or on a sheep **pelt**. I do not have to know the individual and his life history to be able to predict these and countless other regularities. . . .

4   To the American woman a system of plural wives seems "instinctively" abhorrent. She cannot understand how any woman can fail to be jealous and uncomfortable if she must share her husband with other women. She feels it is "unnatural" to accept such a situation. On the other hand, a Koryak woman of Siberia, for example, would find it hard to understand how a woman could be so selfish and so undesirous of feminine companionship in the home as to wish to restrict her husband to one mate.

5   Some years ago I met in New York City a young man who did not speak a word of English and was obviously **bewildered** by American ways. By "blood" he was American, for his parents had gone from Indiana to China as missionaries.[5] Orphaned in infancy, he was reared in a remote village. All who met him found him more Chinese than American. The facts of his blue eyes and light hair were **less impressive** than a Chinese style of gait, Chinese arm and hand movements, Chinese facial expression, and Chinese **modes** of thought. The biological heritage was American, but the cultural training had been Chinese. He returned to China.

6   Another example of another kind: I once knew a trader's wife in Arizona who took a somewhat devilish interest in producing a cultural reaction. Guests who came her way were often served delicious sandwiches filled with a meat that seemed to be neither chicken nor tuna fish yet was **reminiscent of** both. To queries she gave no reply until each had eaten his fill. She then explained that what they had eaten was not chicken, not tuna fish, but the rich white flesh of freshly killed rattlesnakes. The response was instantaneous—vomiting, often violent vomiting. A biological process is caught in a cultural web.

blueprint
a. plan, design
b. blue paper

pelt
a. bed with blankets
b. animal skin with
    hair on it

bewildered
a. helped
b. confused

less impressive
a. less noticeable
b. less frequent

modes
a. ways, styles
b. moods

reminiscent of
a. much worse tasting
    than
b. reminding you of,
    similar to

---

[2]**man** *humans in general (male and female); contemporary English uses* humans *or* humankind
[3]**loincloth** *a piece of cloth worn around the loins or hips, especially in warmer climates, as the only item of clothing*
[4]**hammock** *(see picture at right)*
[5]**missionaries** *members of a religion sent to foreign countries to persuade nonmembers to join their religion*

7 A highly intelligent teacher with long and successful experience in the public schools of Chicago was finishing her first year in a [North American] Indian[6] school. When asked how her Navaho pupils compared in intelligence with Chicago youngsters, she replied, "Well, I just don't know. Sometimes the Indians seem just as bright. At other times they just act like dumb animals. The other night we had a dance in the high school. I saw a boy who is one of the best students in my English class standing off by himself. So I took him over to a pretty girl and told them to dance. But they just stood there with their heads down. They wouldn't even say anything." I inquired if she knew whether or not they were members of the same clan.[7] "What difference would that make?"

in a huff
a. angrily
b. with a smile

8 "How would you feel about getting into bed with your brother?" The teacher walked off **in a huff**, but, actually, the two cases were quite comparable in principle. To the Indian, the type of bodily contact involved in our social dancing has a directly sexual connotation. The incest taboos between members of the same clan are as severe as between true brothers and sisters. The shame of the Indians at the suggestion that a clan brother and sister should dance and the indignation of the white teacher at the idea that she should share a bed with an adult brother represent equally nonrational responses, culturally standardized unreason.

potentialities
a. possibilities
b. impossibilities

9 All this does not mean that there is no such thing as raw human nature. The very fact that certain of the same institutions are found in all known societies indicates that, at bottom, all human beings are very much alike. . . . The members of all human groups have about the same biological equipment. All men undergo the same poignant life experiences, such as birth, helplessness, illness, old age, and death. The biological **potentialities** of the species are the blocks with which cultures are built. Some patterns of every culture crystallize around focuses provided by the inevitables[8] of biology: the difference between the sexes, the presence of persons of different ages, the varying physical strength and skill of individuals.

---

[6]**Indian** *refers to indigenous people of North America; contemporary English uses* Native American
[7]**clan** *a large group of families who have the same ancestor*
[8]**inevitables** inevitable *(adjective) means* unavoidable. *In the last sentence Kluckhohn means: Human biology, the same for all cultures, accounts for the similarities among cultures.*

COMPREHENSION CHECK

First Reading

Answer these questions.

1. What is culture and how do we learn it? Highlight or jot down phrases in paragraphs 1 and 2 that help define culture as an anthropologist defines it.
2. What prevents cultures from being even more different from each other than they are?

Second Reading

Reread parts of the selection as needed to answer these questions. Mark the statements *T* (true) or *F* (false). Write the paragraph number(s) where you found evidence for each answer.

1. T F We learn our culture by the way we are brought up. ¶____

2. T F When anthropologists refer to culture, they mean primarily history, literature, philosophy, the fine arts. ¶____

3. T F Each human is different, so behavior cannot be predicted. ¶____

4. T F In some cultures women view polygamy (having multiple wives) as desirable. ¶____

5. T F People will always fit into the culture of their biological parents. ¶____

6. T F Conscious knowledge of what you eat can trigger a negative reaction even if it tastes good. ¶____

7. T F Incest taboos are the same in all cultures. ¶____

8. T F All humans are biologically similar, so all cultures deal with many of the same life events. ¶____

VOCABULARY

Vocabulary Building

Read the underlined word or expression in its context and match it with the correct meaning. Use a dictionary if necessary.

PART 1

____ 1. Why do some nations <u>trace descent</u> through the father, others through the mother, still others through both parents? (¶1)

____ 2. By *culture*, anthropology means . . . the social <u>legacy</u> the individual acquires from his group. (¶1)

____ 3. Each specific culture <u>constitutes</u> a kind of blueprint for all of life's activities. (¶2)

____ 4. To the American woman a system of plural wives seems "instinctively" <u>abhorrent</u>. (¶4)

____ 5. . . . a Chinese style of <u>gait</u> . . . (¶5)

a. completely unacceptable because it seems morally wrong

b. walking

c. describe family history (ancestry)

d. forms, is considered to be

e. what comes to a person through parents, ancestors, or society

PART 2

_____ 6. The biological <u>heritage</u> was American . . . (¶5)

_____ 7. . . . I once knew a trader's wife in Arizona who took a somewhat <u>devilish</u> interest in producing a cultural reaction. (¶6)

_____ 8. To <u>queries</u> she gave no reply . . . (¶6)

_____ 9. To the Indian, the type of bodily contact involved in our social dancing has a directly sexual <u>connotation</u>. (¶8)

_____ 10. The <u>incest taboos</u> between members of the same clan are as severe as between true brothers and sisters. (¶8)

_____ 11. All men <u>undergo</u> the same poignant life experiences . . . (¶9)

_____ 12. Some patterns of every culture <u>crystallize</u> around focuses provided by the inevitables of biology . . . (¶9)

f. form, take shape

g. cultural rules against sexual relations between members of the same family

h. traditions and values inherited from parents, ancestors, or culture

i. live through or have

j. playfully bad or evil, mischievous

k. meaning, suggestion

l. questions

Using Paraphrases

Work with a partner. Study the sentence on the left. Underline the difficult words in the sentence and find their meanings in the paraphrase on the right. Use a dictionary if necessary.

Sentence from the Text	Paraphrase
1. . . . a Koryak woman of Siberia, for example, would find it hard to understand how a woman could be so selfish and so undesirous of feminine companionship in the home as to wish to restrict her husband to one mate. (¶4)	A Koryak woman of Siberia, for example, would find it hard to understand how a woman could care so much only about herself as to limit her husband to one sexual partner and how she could not want the company of other women in the home.
2. Orphaned in infancy, he was reared in a remote village. (¶5)	Because his parents died when he was a young baby, he was raised, or brought up in a faraway village not near any city.
3. The shame of the Indians at the suggestion that a clan brother and sister should dance and the indignation of the white teacher at the idea that she should share a bed with an adult brother represent equally nonrational responses, culturally standardized unreason. (¶8)	The shame of the Indians . . . and the anger of the white teacher . . . represent equally unreasonable responses, a culturally regularized rule that is not logical or reasonable.

Vocabulary Review

Complete the following statements about the reading selection with the correct word from the list below. Use each word only once.

| abhorrent | infancy | modes | standardized |
| bewildered | legacy | restrict | undergo |

1. From reading Kluckhohn, we learn that much of human behavior is determined by our social _____, the culture we have inherited from our ancestors. We start acquiring our culture in _____ and learn whatever culture we are brought up in.

2. As a result, our behavior is more _____ and predictable than many individuals realize or want to admit.

3. When faced with values, customs, and _____ of thinking different from our own, we may feel _____ or puzzled.

4. We usually _____ ourselves to eating what our culture dictates. Eating something we are not accustomed to may seem _____ to us and may provoke vomiting when we find out what we have eaten.

5. Due to the biological similarity of all humans, we _____ many of the same types of experiences; as a result, human cultures are not entirely different.

TEXT ANALYSIS   ## Text Organization: Paragraph Purpose

Each of Kluckhohn's paragraphs or groups of paragraphs serves a clear purpose, making this selection a good example of well-organized writing. Skim the reading and describe the contribution of each paragraph or set of paragraphs to the whole piece of writing.

Paragraphs	Contribution
¶1–2	_____
¶3	_____
¶4–8	_____
¶9	_____

Word Order

English sentences typically have the following word order:

subject + verb + object + adverbials and some prepositional phrases.

Adverbials and some prepositional phrases, however, can sometimes be located in different places in the sentence.

Rewrite each of Kluckhohn's sentences in a more common word order by moving the underlined phrases. The first one is done as an example.

1. Even those of us who pride ourselves on our individualism follow <u>most of the time</u> a pattern not of our own making. (¶3)

   Even those of us who pride ourselves on our individualism follow a

   pattern (that is) not of our own making most of the time.

2. <u>To the American woman</u> a system of plural wives seems "instinctively" abhorrent. (¶4)

   _____

3. <u>Some years ago</u> I met <u>in New York City</u> a young man who did not speak a word of English . . . (¶5)

   _____

4. <u>To queries</u> she gave no reply . . . (¶6)

   _____

RESPONDING TO READING

Discuss these questions.

1. Refer back to the Thinking about the Topic exercise (on page 95) in which you thought about different foods. How would you explain your food preferences now?

2. What are some incidents in which you felt bewildered, out-of-place, or annoyed in a foreign culture? Were any of these incidents caused because of taboos in one of the cultures?

3. What are some problems that might occur when there is a cultural difference between teachers and students?

4. What are some areas in which cultures differ that are not mentioned in this selection? Consider areas such as excuses, apologies, punctuality, and nonverbal communication. In general, which types of cultural differences are easiest to adapt to? Which are most difficult?

"Touching" is from the book, *Gestures: The Do's and Taboos of Body Language Around the World*. The author, who has traveled and lived abroad for many years as vice-president of a major company, has written several books of use to international business people and travelers.

**BEFORE
YOU READ**

Thinking about the Topic

Discuss these questions.

1. What do you think cultural anthropologists do in order to learn about different cultures?
2. Sit in a park, a mall or shopping center, or a café for 30 minutes. Observe pairs or small groups of people (excluding couples in love) who pass by or who are sitting near you. Do this *covertly*; no one should know what you are doing. Take notes on the questions below. For questions that ask *how often*, indicate frequency on the scale that follows. Share your findings with your classmates.

never	infrequently	fairly frequently	very frequently

- What are the people's gender and approximate age?
- How close are they as they walk, stand, or sit?
- How often do they touch each other? Where?
- How often do they look each other in the eye?
- How loudly do they speak?
- How often do they gesture with their hands? Do they use any other part of the body to gesture?

Previewing

Preview the selection appropriately. Then answer these questions.

1. Where was the author at the time of the first incident? Where is he from?
2. What kinds of cultural differences does he discuss?

Before you read, turn to Comprehension Check, First Reading on page 106. Your purpose for the first reading is to answer those questions.

Note: This selection is quite long. If desired, it can be read in two parts: paragraphs 1–12 and paragraphs 13–17.

Touching *By Roger E. Axtell*

1   On my first trip to the Middle East, my Arab business contact and I toured the city, walking along the street visiting customers. He wore his long robe, the air was hot and dusty, a priest chanted the call to prayers from a nearby minaret,[1] and I felt as far away from my American home as one could possibly be. At that moment, my business friend reached over, took my hand in his, and we continued walking along, his hand holding mine.

2   It didn't take me long to realize that something **untoward** was happening here, that some form of communication was being issued . . . but I didn't have the faintest idea what that message was. Also, I suddenly felt even farther from home.

3   Probably because I was so **stunned**, the one thing I didn't do was pull my hand away. I later learned that if I had **jerked** my hand out of his, I could have committed a Sahara-sized[2] *faux pas.*[3] In his country, this act of taking my hand in his was a sign of great friendship and respect.

4   That was my first lesson about space relationships between different people. I quickly learned that it was a world of extremes—important extremes—with some cultures seeking bodily contact and others studiously avoiding it. Ken Cooper, in his book *Nonverbal Communication For Business Success* (AMACOM, NY 1979), writes that he once covertly observed conversations in outdoor cafes in several different countries and counted the number of casual touches (of self or of the other party) per hour. The results: San Juan, Puerto Rico, 180 per hour; Paris, 110 per hour; Florida, 2 per hour; London, 0 per hour.

5   I also learned that the Middle East was not the only region where it is quite acceptable for two men to walk cradling an elbow, arm-in-arm, or even holding hands. Indochina,[4] Greece, and Italy are also regarded as "touch-oriented" countries. Such physical displays in those countries usually signal friendship. Touching between men—often seen as an indication of homosexuality in North America—is quite the opposite. In some of the most "touch-oriented" areas homosexuality is coldly **rejected**.

6   Here, on a scale of "touch" or "don't touch," is a geographic measuring stick:

Don't Touch	*Touch*	*Middle Ground*
Japan	Middle East countries	France
United States & Canada	Latin countries	China
England	Italy	Ireland
Scandinavia	Greece	India
Other Northern	Spain & Portugal	
European countries	Some Asian countries	
Australia	Russia	
Estonia		

7   Can the casual act of touching be all that important? The answer is "yes"—important enough to make bold headlines in at least one country's national newspapers:

---

[1]**minaret** *small thin tower on a mosque (Muslim place of worship)*
[2]**Sahara-sized** *referring to the Sahara Desert in Africa, meaning very large*
[3]**faux pas** *social mistake (French, literally:* false step*)*
[4]**Indochina** *older name for the region east of India and south of China*

untoward
a. unusual, different
b. understandable

stunned
a. surprised
b. bored

jerked
a. waved rapidly
b. pulled suddenly

rejected
a. accepted
b. not accepted

When Queen Elizabeth paid one of her periodic visits to Canada, a Canadian provincial transport minister escorted her through a crowd by gently touching her elbow; he may have even touched the small of her back. Newspaper headlines in England screamed protests: "Hands off our Queen," said one; "Row Over Man Who Touched Queen," read another.

uproar
a. party
b. complaint, protest

The reason behind that **uproar** was that it is an unwritten rule among the British that no one touches the Queen. Even when shaking hands, the rule is that she must make the first move.

8   In the United States, office workers and school teachers are warned and trained to avoid any casual touching of their employees or students. A university professor of communications explains that "an innocuous touch on someone's hand or arm can be misconstrued as a sexual move, especially if we let it linger." Unwanted touching in U.S. business offices can lead to lawsuits for sexual harassment while teachers may be accused of molestation if they frequently hug, pat, or touch their students.

9   Yet there are strange contradictions, especially in the United States. Here are two examples:

I once asked an audience of U.S. businessmen what they would do if they boarded a crowded airplane, sat next to a large man and found themselves pressing elbows, maybe even shoulders and upper arms as well, throughout the whole trip. "Nothing," was the consensus. "It happens all the time," they agreed. I countered, "Well, what would you do then if that same man then touched your knee with his hand?" The reaction was unanimous: "Move the knee." "And," one added, "if, God forbid, he *grabbed* my knee, I would punch him in the nose."

The second contradiction regarding rules for touching occurs on elevators and subways. On a crowded elevator or an underground train at commuting time, people will stand shoulder-to-shoulder, arm-to-arm, and accept such rubbing of shoulders without complaint. But, the rule is "Touch *only* from shoulder to elbow. No other parts of the body."

10   Cultures are colliding every day over this dilemma of "to touch or not to touch." In New York City, Korean immigrants in recent years have started new lives by opening retail shops of all kinds. But, when American customers make a purchase and receive their change, the Korean merchants place the money on the counter to avoid any physical contact. "They won't touch my hand," one customer noticed. "They won't even place coins in my hand. It's **somewhat** cold and insulting. And furthermore, they won't look me in the eyes."

somewhat
a. a little
b. not at all

11   One Korean merchant explained in a national television interview that in his homeland they are taught to avoid physical contact of any kind. The same with direct eye contact. "We are taught that either gesture could have sexual connotations," he added, "so we carefully avoid them."

12   And here's a surefire way for a North American to make a Japanese acquaintance feel uncomfortable. Just go up and place your arm around him, as you would a college buddy or big brother. Even though the Japanese permit themselves to be **jammed** into subways and trains, they are not regarded as a touching society. To explain this, anthropologist Edward T. Hall says the Japanese handle any unease about being packed into public places by **averting eyes**, avoiding eye contact, drawing within themselves and thus "touching without feeling."

jammed
a. crowded
b. sweetened

averting eyes
a. looking at
b. looking away

invades
a. runs away from
b. enters

13   Closely related to the societal customs of touching is that of spatial relationships. Anthropologists tell us that each of us walks around inside "bubbles of personal space."[5] The size of the bubble represents our personal territory, territorial imperative,[6] or "personal buffer zones."[7] We neither like nor tolerate it when someone **invades** our bubble. We become distinctly uncomfortable.

14   But as we travel to different places around the world, we learn that some cultural bubbles are larger or smaller than others. Here is a ruler for measuring the bubbles between nationalities:

- The American "bubble" extends about 12 to 15 inches, and so we may stand a combined 24 to 30 inches apart. Scientists point out this just happens to be an arm's length away (which carries a certain symbolism, doesn't it?). Anthropologist George Renwick says, "When two Americans stand facing one another in any normal social or business situation, one could stretch out his arm and put his thumb in the other person's ear."
- Orientals,[8] and especially the Japanese, stand even farther apart, Renwick adds. When it comes to ordinary business or social situations, they have the largest bubbles of all. However, as we have learned, in their own public settings, where crowding is impossible to avoid, they accept body contact or just seem to ignore it by "retreating within themselves."
- Latins and Middle Easterners, on the other hand, stand much closer than Americans. They may stand, literally, toe-to-toe. They may even place a hand on the other's forearm[9] or elbow, or finger the lapel[10] of the other person.

Americans claim it takes years of experience, plus steely resolve, to stand that close and smell that many breaths. Some observers in Latin America even have a name for this charade.[11] They call it "the conversational tango." That's the "dance" done by an American or European freshly arrived in Latin America who is **confronted by** this sudden and startling custom of closeness. The first reaction of the visitor is to step backward. But the Latin will follow. So, the visitor steps back again. The Latin follows. And so it goes, in a poorly choreographed tango. . . . As one observer put it, "The dance stops only when the American is backed into a corner."

confronted by
a. faced with
b. comforted by

(continued)

---

[5]**bubbles of personal space** *amount of space (defined by culture) that keeps people from getting uncomfortably close to each other*
[6]**territorial imperative** *the need to have a certain amount of space we must consider our own*
[7]**personal buffer zones** *neutral spaces between two places, things, or people to keep them safely apart*
[8]**Orientals** *refers to people from Asia; contemporary English uses the word* Asian
[9]**forearm** *(see picture at right)*
[10]**lapel** *(see picture at right)*
[11]**charade** *game*

lapel
forearm

codes
a. numbers
b. rules

finger-crunching handshakes
a. firm, strong handshakes
b. weak, gentle handshakes

aloofness
a. unfriendliness
b. friendliness

15   But even as these words are written, touch **codes** are changing all over the world. In the United States, politicians have learned the value of touch. They frequently give two-handed handshakes, casually touch the elbow of another, or lightly touch the back of the person standing next to them. "Pressing flesh" has become a byword on political campaigns. Also, Japanese managers posted in U.S. factories are steeling themselves and learning to accept **finger-crunching handshakes**, back patting, and maybe even a friendly arm around the shoulder for the softball team photo.

16   The "hugging professor," Leo Buscaglia, tours cities and campuses presenting captivating lectures on the joy of hugging. His popular books and video and audio tapes make his audiences realize that separateness and **aloofness** can be a lonely, cold existence.

17   Finally, in Helen Colton's wonderful book, *The Gift of Touch,* she describes how Swedish actress Liv Ullman was once touring famine-stricken lands on behalf of UNICEF.[12] In Bangladesh, after a warm visit with a woman there, Ullman gave the woman a hug. But she felt the woman suddenly draw away. Through her interpreter, Ullman asked why. The woman answered, "In my country, we kiss feet when we say goodbye." Ullman, the quintessential lady, unhesitatingly bent down and kissed the woman's feet. Then they hugged, each woman having exchanged the parting ritual of her own world.

---

[12]**UNICEF** *United Nations International Children's Fund*

COMPREHENSION CHECK

First Reading

Answer these questions.

1. What did the author's Arab business contact do? How did the author react and why? What does this custom mean in Arab culture?
2. What is a "bubble of personal space"?

Second Reading

Reread parts of the selection as needed to answer these questions. As you read, highlight or jot down helpful words or phrases.

1. Where did Ken Cooper observe people? Do his observations match Axtell's categories? Explain.
2. How did the British press react to a Canadian government official guiding the Queen through a crowd? Why?
3. How do people in the United States and Japan, two nontouching countries, handle crowded places?
4. What was the problem between Korean storekeepers in New York City and their American customers? What are the rules in Korea that conflict with American rules?
5. What is the "conversational tango"?
6. How are the rules about touching and personal space changing?
7. How did Liv Ullman handle the difference between parting rules in Sweden and Bangladesh? What did her decision illustrate about intercultural relations?

 **VOCABULARY**

Vocabulary Building: Using Paraphrases

Work with a partner. Study the sentence on the left. Underline the difficult words in the sentence and find their meanings in the paraphrase on the right. Use a dictionary if necessary.

Sentence from the Text	Paraphrase
1. Newspaper headlines in England screamed protests: "Hands off our Queen," said one; "Row Over Man Who Touched Queen," read another. (¶7)	Newspaper headlines in England screamed strong complaints: "Hands off our Queen," said one; "Angry Argument Over Man Who Touched Queen," read another.
2. . . . an innocuous touch on someone's hand or arm can be misconstrued as a sexual move, especially if we let it linger." (¶8)	A harmless or innocent touch on someone's arm can be misunderstood as a sexual move, especially if we let our hand stay there.
3. Unwanted touching in U.S. business offices can lead to lawsuits for sexual harassment while teachers may be accused of molestation if they frequently hug, pat, or touch their students. (¶8)	Unwanted touching in U.S. business offices can lead to lawsuits for unwanted sexual advances while teachers may be said to be guilty of sexually abusing students if they frequently hug, pat, or touch them.
4. The reaction was unanimous: "Move the knee." (¶9)	Everyone agreed that they would move their knee.
5. Cultures are colliding every day over this dilemma of "to touch or not to touch." (¶10)	Cultures are in conflict every day over this problem of whether to touch or not.
6. . . . they accept body contact or just seem to ignore it by "retreating within themselves." (¶14)	They accept body contact or simply don't pay attention to it by pulling into themselves.
7. . . . it takes years of experience, plus steely resolve, to stand that close . . . (¶14)	It takes years of experience, and strong determination, to stand that close . . .
8. . . . she describes how Swedish actress Liv Ullman was once touring famine-stricken lands on behalf of UNICEF. (¶17)	She describes how Swedish actress Liv Ullman was once traveling as a representative of UNICEF to countries where there was extreme hunger.
9. Ullman, the quintessential lady, unhesitatingly bent down and kissed the woman's feet. (¶17)	Ullman, the perfect example of a lady, without stopping to think, bent down and kissed the woman's feet.
10. Then they hugged, each woman having exchanged the parting ritual of her own world. (¶17)	Then they hugged, each woman having exchanged the traditional way to say good-bye in her world.

Vocabulary Review

Complete the following statements about the reading selection with the correct word from the list below. Use each word only once.

aloof	collide	invade	reject
codes	dilemma	jerk	rituals

1. One way cultures differ is in touch _____ and rules for personal space.

2. North Americans or Northern Europeans will feel uncomfortable if Arabs or Latin Americans _____ their personal bubble; Arabs or Latin Americans may think North Americans or Northern Europeans seem _____ and unfriendly.

3. Generally we are not aware of the cultural rules we live by until they _____ with those of another culture. Then we are faced with a(an) _____: Which set of rules should we follow?

4. Roger Axtell did not _____ his hand away from his Arab host and was later glad that he didn't. Liv Ullman and the Bangladeshi woman used both the Bangladeshi and Swedish _____ for saying good-bye.

5. As the examples of Axtell and Ullman show, we can follow foreign modes of behavior and do not necessarily have to _____ our own when interacting cross culturally.

TEXT ANALYSIS   *Supporting General Statements*

> General statements require examples to make ideas clear; Axtell provides them in great number. Some of his examples are anecdotes, that is, specific incidents that really occurred.

In paragraphs 1–2 and 17, Axtell uses anecdotes to introduce and conclude this selection. In between, he supports his general statements with examples. Find the general statements that these examples support.

1. Cooper's report on touching in various cultures (¶4)

2. the incident involving the Queen of England and the examples of touching in United States offices and schools (¶7–8)

3. the examples of touching on planes and subways (¶9)

4. the Korean and Japanese examples (¶10–12)

5. the conversational tango (¶14)

6. examples of United States politicians, Japanese managers, and Leo Buscaglia (¶15–16)

RESPONDING TO READING

Discuss these questions.

1. If your country of origin is included in paragraph 6, is it listed as a "Don't Touch," a "Middle Ground," or a "Touch" country? Do you agree with this label? If your country is not listed, where would you list it?

2. How do you feel when confronted with touching or space behavior that conflicts with yours?

3. What does *direct eye contact* mean in your culture? How do you feel if someone violates the rule of your culture with regard to eye contact?

ABOUT THE READING

"Change of Heart" appeared in the March, 2005 *Reader's Digest*. It is a true story.

BEFORE YOU READ

Thinking about the Topic

Discuss these questions.

1. What things can affect how well neighbors *get along,* in other words, whether or not they have friendly relationships?
2. In cases where neighbors are from different ethnic groups, what role might *prejudice,* an unreasonable dislike of people from different ethnic groups, play in relations between neighbors?

Previewing

Preview the selection appropriately. Then answer these questions.

1. What was Mary Fischer's attitude in the beginning with regard to getting along with people from other ethnic groups?
2. What was her attitude in the end?
3. What do you think the expression "change of heart" means?

Before you read, turn to Comprehension Check, First Reading on page 112. Your purpose for the first reading is to answer those questions.

READ

riots
a. parties
b. violent protests

plaintively
a. sadly
b. cheerfully

Change of Heart *By Mary A. Fischer*

My neighbors and I just couldn't get along.

1   In 1992, like many people in Los Angeles, I watched TV news reports of Rodney King[1] speaking to the press after four officers accused of beating him in 1991 were acquitted, leading to **riots** in the city. As King spoke to reporters, he **plaintively** asked, "Can we all get along?"

2   "No! We can't," I shouted back at the TV, though no one else was in the room to hear me. Mine was not an idle, uninformed response. I knew what I was talking about. In late 1989, I had bought a house in an affordable eastside neighborhood of Los Angeles called Highland Park, which was being transformed by waves of new immigrants, and I was convinced racial harmony was impossible. Statistics said that each year, tens of thousands of new immigrants, mostly from Latin America and Asia, were pouring into Southern California, yet for most whites, these trends remained in the abstract realm of statistics.

---

[1]**Rodney King** *an African American, stopped for speeding and beaten by police; the incident was videotaped by a private citizen.*

fortressed
a. visited
b. protected

restore
a. bring back
b. buy again

surmising
a. surprising
b. guessing

grief
a. extreme sadness
b. deep water

make ends meet
a. have enough money
   to cover expenses
b. be able to meet
   someone

3   When I moved to Highland Park, however, the statistics became my daily reality and brought my prejudices to the surface. Many of my neighbors were from Mexico, El Salvador, the Philippines and Vietnam, and for the first time, I was in the minority and I didn't like it.

4   Convinced that we had nothing in common, I **fortressed** myself in my lovely pink Spanish house on the hill. I rarely spoke to my neighbors, waving occasionally when we took out our trash cans or passed by in our cars. I fit their stereotype—the unfriendly white "gringa"[2] who owned the nicest house on the block—just as they fit my preconceived notions of immigrants who stubbornly refused to assimilate.

5   I was annoyed when Hispanic salespeople in Radio Shack didn't understand when I asked for lithium batteries or extension cords. It irritated me that the local supermarkets didn't carry things like blue cheese or soy milk, and that some billboard ads for movies and cars were written in Spanish.

6   For years, I complained to various officials when my neighbors behaved in ways I didn't agree with. One woman from El Salvador kept a rooster in her backyard that woke me up at 5:00 every morning. When I reported her to the Animal Regulation Department, she responded to the complaint by cutting off the bird's head. I felt guilty about being the impetus for the rooster's brutal demise,[3] but rationalized it as being necessary to **restore** peace and quiet to the neighborhood.

7   When my neighbors from Mexico played their music too loud, I called the police, who put a stop to it. **Surmising** that I had reported them, my neighbors stopped speaking to me. It was a punishment I could live with, since I reasoned that I was bringing the neighborhood into compliance with my values.

8   Then two years ago, something happened that changed me and how I live in my neighborhood. In a matter of two days, I lost the things that mattered most to me. My six-figure job as a senior writer for a national magazine came to an end, and a relationship with a man I loved ended badly. Suddenly, all my anchors were gone and, sunk deep in **grief**, I wondered how—or if—I would be able to pull myself out.

9   The losses I experienced humbled me and made me vulnerable, but as a consequence I began to connect more fully with my neighbors and the world around me. I discovered how extraordinary they were. They were nothing like my biases had made them out to be. They were hard-working, honorable people who, like me, were just looking to live well and experience some measure of happiness.

10   I learned that the woman from El Salvador had fled her country with two young daughters after death squads murdered her husband. She cleaned houses to **make ends meet** and send her daughters to college.

11   I learned that when my neighbors from Mexico came to Los Angeles 15 years ago, they did not speak English and the father cleaned offices for $8 an hour. Later, he drove delivery trucks. Today he owns three apartment buildings and has made more money than I probably will in my lifetime.

12   Now, many of my neighbors are my friends. At Christmas, I give them red wine and cakes and they give me potted flowers and platters of burritos. When my car wouldn't start a few months ago, and it looked like it would have to be towed, another neighbor from Guatemala, a sweet man named Angel who's a gardener, quickly brought out his jumper cables[4] and got the car started.

(continued)

---

[2]**gringa** *informal term in Spanish to refer to an American (feminine form)*
[3]**impetus for the rooster's brutal demise** *the cause of the rooster's death*
[4]**jumper cables** *electrical cables joining two cars to re-start a dead battery*

13   Today, I would answer Rodney King's question differently. I'd say that it is possible for us to get along if people from different cultures don't make the mistake I did. When I first moved to my neighborhood, I neglected to view my neighbors as individuals and I saw them as different and apart from me. I see now how their lives and mine include experiences universal to us all: loss, disappointment, hope and love.

14   Last month, I heard a rooster crow early in the morning. It seems my neighbor from El Salvador got another one, but I no longer mind. I like watching the rooster as it wanders the neighborhood. Somehow, he makes me feel like I'm home.

COMPREHENSION CHECK

First Reading

Answer these questions.

1. What kind of neighborhood did the author move into?
2. How did the author's attitude toward her neighbors change? What caused the change?
3. What mistake did she realize she had made?

Second Reading

Reread parts of the selection as needed to answer these questions.

1. Why was she unfriendly toward her neighbors?
2. How did she appear to them?
3. What were some things about the neighborhood that she didn't like?
4. What actions did she take to try to change her neighbors' behavior?
5. After her change of heart, what did she learn about her neighbors? How did these facts change her attitude?
6. What kind of relationship did she finally develop with her neighbors?

> This essay has some of the same elements as a fictional short story, which were pointed out in Unit 1, Chapter 4 (see page 27). Short stories have a plot, which involves a problem or conflict. The conflict causes tension, which reaches a high point (climax or turning-point) and is followed by a resolution, or denouement.

7. In this story:
   a. What is the problem or conflict? What tension is created?
   b. What is the climax or turning point?
   c. What is the resolution or denouement?

Vocabulary Building

Read the underlined word or expression in its context and match it with the correct meaning. Use a dictionary if necessary.

PART 1

_____ 1. . . . four officers accused of beating him . . . were <u>acquitted</u>

_____ 2. . . . I was convinced <u>racial harmony</u> was impossible. (¶2)

_____ 3. . . . for most whites, these <u>trends</u> remained in the abstract realm of statistics. (¶2)

_____ 4. I fit their <u>stereotype</u>—the unfriendly white "gringa" who owned the nicest house on the block . . . (¶4)

_____ 5. . . . just as they fit my <u>preconceived notions</u> of immigrants . . . (¶4)

_____ 6. . . . immigrants who stubbornly refused to <u>assimilate</u>. (¶4)

a. idea formed before you have enough knowledge

b. found not guilty

c. situation where people of different races live and work together without problems

d. directions things are going in, general tendencies

e. become similar to those around you

f. idea of what a particular group of people is like that many people have, which may be wrong or unfair

PART 2

_____ 7. I felt guilty . . . but <u>rationalized</u> it as being necessary . . . (¶6)

_____ 8. . . . I was bringing the neighborhood into <u>compliance</u> with my values. (¶7)

_____ 9. Suddenly, all my <u>anchors</u> were gone . . . (¶8)

_____ 10. . . . and made me <u>vulnerable</u> . . . (¶9)

_____ 11. They were nothing like my <u>biases</u> had made them out to be. (¶9)

_____ 12. They were nothing like my biases <u>had made them out</u> to be. (¶9)

_____ 13. . . . I <u>neglected to</u> view my neighbors as individuals . . . (¶13)

g. easily hurt

h. unfair one-sided opinions, prejudices

i. invented reasons to explain behavior, especially when the reasons are not good or sensible

j. did not

k. things that provide a feeling of safety

l. agreement

m. had made me imagine them

Vocabulary Review

Complete the following statements about the reading selection with the correct word from the list below. Use each word only once.

grief	neglected	prejudices	vulnerable
harmony	preconceived	restore	

1. Even though Mary Fischer had many _____ against immigrants and didn't think that she could ever live in _____ with them, she bought a house in an interethnic neighborhood in Los Angeles because it was affordable.

2. She complained to the authorities about her neighbors' loud music and a crowing rooster in an effort to _____ peace to the neighborhood, at least according to her definition of peace.

3. Then she lost her job, and her relationship with the man she loved ended. She fell into a period of _____ and felt alone and _____.

4. At this low point in her life, she realized she had _____ to see her neighbors as individuals and began to see them in a different light.

5. As she learned about their hardships and their successes, she realized that her _____ notions about them were wrong, and she began to admire and appreciate them.

TEXT ANALYSIS   Essays

There is a definition of *essay* in the Text Analysis section of Chapter 7 on page 52. Read the definition and then answer these questions.

1. How well does this essay fit the definition on page 52?
2. What social issue does Fischer examine?
3. What conclusions does she come to?
4. What reasons could she have had for writing this essay?

RESPONDING TO READING

Discuss these questions.

1. How would you feel if a neighbor called the police or the Animal Regulation Department to register a complaint about you or your family? Did the author do the right thing? If not, what could she have done instead?

2. Why do people have stereotypes about others? Are stereotypes ever accurate? What is their danger?

3. What prevents different groups from living in harmony? What can be done to build better relationships?

4. Why is it important to have good relationships with your neighbors? What role do you think neighbors should play in each other's lives?

CHAPTER 16

ABOUT THE READING

Although very little is known about B. Traven, the author of "Assembly Line," it is believed he was born in Chicago in 1890 and died in 1969. He lived most of his life in Mexico. His many books and stories have been published in thirty languages, but he has been largely neglected as a writer in the United States, perhaps because at the time he was writing, his views were considered too radical. He wrote mainly about oppressed Indians in Mexico, a theme of universal relevance.

BEFORE YOU READ

Thinking about the Topic

Discuss these questions.

1. What is an assembly line? What kinds of products are usually produced on assembly lines? What things would never be produced on an assembly line?
2. In which countries are assembly lines common and well-accepted?

This selection is quite long. If desired, it can be read in two parts: paragraphs 1–44 and paragraphs 45–98. You will find two questions to answer at the end of Part 1. After you have answered those questions, continue reading Part 2.

READ

Assembly Line *By B. Traven*

PART 1

1   Mr. E. L. Winthrop of New York was on vacation in the Republic of Mexico. It wasn't long before he realized that this strange and really wild country had not yet been fully and satisfactorily explored by Rotarians and Lions,[1] who are forever conscious of their glorious mission on earth. Therefore, he considered it his duty as a good American citizen to do his part in correcting this **oversight**.

2   In search for opportunities to indulge in his new avocation[2], he left the beaten track and **ventured into** regions not especially mentioned, and hence not recommended, by travel agents to foreign tourists. So it happened that one day he found himself in a little, quaint Indian village somewhere in the State of Oaxaca.

3   Walking along the dusty main street of this pueblecito,[3] which knew nothing of pavements, drainage, plumbing, or of any means of artificial light save candles or pine splinters, he met with an Indian squatting on the earthen-floor front porch of a palm hut, a so-called jacalito.

4   The Indian was busy making little baskets from bast and from all kinds of fibers gathered by him in the immense tropical bush which surrounded the village

(continued)

oversight
a. good vision
b. failure to notice something

ventured into
a. went to
b. ignored

---

[1]**Rotarians and Lions** *members of Rotary Clubs and Lions Clubs, which are international service organizations for men; the author thinks of them as promoters of capitalism*
[2]**avocation** *Winthrop's avocation (personal interest) is to promote capitalism in this part of Mexico.*
[3]**pueblecito** *little town (pueblo means town; -ito is a Spanish suffix meaning small)*

dyes
a. colors
b. nutrients

dawdle
a. keep busy
b. waste time

weaving
a. painting
b. crossing fibers

gone astray
a. wandered off
b. died

wares
a. clothing he is
   wearing
b. products for sale

sinful
a. unfair
b. fair

on all sides. The material used had not only been well prepared for its purpose but was also richly colored with **dyes** that the basket-maker himself extracted from various native plants, barks, roots and from certain insects by a process known only to him and the members of his family.

5   His principal business, however, was not producing baskets. He was a peasant who lived on what the small property he possessed—less than fifteen acres of not too fertile soil—would yield, after much sweat and labor and after constantly worrying over the most wanted and best suited distribution of rain, sunshine, and wind and the changing balance of birds and insects beneficial or harmful to his crops. Baskets he made when there was nothing else for him to do in the fields, because he was unable to **dawdle**. After all, the sale of his baskets, though to a rather limited degree only, added to the small income he received from his little farm.

6   In spite of being by profession just a plain peasant, it was clearly seen from the small baskets he made that at heart he was an artist, a true and accomplished artist. Each basket looked as if covered all over with the most beautiful, sometimes fantastic ornaments, flowers, butterflies, birds, squirrels, antelope, tigers, and a score of other animals of the wilds. Yet, the most amazing thing was that these decorations, all of them symphonies of color, were not painted on the baskets but were instead actually part of the baskets themselves. Bast and fibers dyed in dozens of different colors were so cleverly—one must actually say intrinsically—interwoven that those attractive designs appeared on the inner part of the basket as well as on the outside. Not by painting but by **weaving** were those highly artistic effects achieved. This performance he accomplished without ever looking at any sketch or pattern. While working on a basket these designs came to light as if by magic, and as long as a basket was not entirely finished one could not perceive what in this case or that the decoration would be like.

7   People in the market town who bought these baskets would use them for sewing baskets or to decorate tables with or window sills, or to hold little things to keep them from lying around. Women put their jewelry in them or flowers or little dolls. There were in fact a hundred and two ways they might serve certain purposes in a household or in a lady's own room.

8   Whenever the Indian had finished about twenty of the baskets he took them to town on market day. Sometimes he would already be on his way shortly after midnight because he owned only a burro to ride on, and if the burro had **gone astray** the day before, as happened frequently, he would have to walk the whole way to town and back again.

9   At the market he had to pay twenty centavos[4] in taxes to sell his **wares**. Each basket cost him between twenty and thirty hours of constant work, not counting the time spent gathering bast and fibers, preparing them, making dyes and coloring the bast. All this meant extra time and work. The price he asked for each basket was fifty centavos, the equivalent of about four cents. It seldom happened, however, that a buyer paid outright the full fifty centavos asked—or four reales as the Indian called that money. The prospective buyer started bargaining, telling the Indian that he ought to be ashamed to ask such a **sinful** price. "Why, the whole dirty thing is nothing but ordinary petate straw which you find in heaps wherever

---

[4]**centavo** *cent, 1/100th of a Mexican peso; a peso is the monetary unit of Mexico*

you may look for it; the jungle is packed full of it," the buyer would argue. "Such a little basket, what's it good for anyhow? If I paid you, you thief, ten centavitos for it you should be grateful and kiss my hand. Well, it's your lucky day, I'll be generous this time, I'll pay you twenty, yet not one green centavo more. Take it or run along."

10   So he sold finally for twenty-five centavos, but then the buyer would say, "Now, what do you think of that? I've got only twenty centavos change on me. What can we do about that? If you can change me a twenty-peso bill, all right, you shall have your twenty-five fierros."[5] Of course, the Indian could not change a twenty-peso bill and so the basket went for twenty centavos.

11   He had little if any knowledge of the outside world or he would have known that what happened to him was happening every hour of every day to every artist all over the world. That knowledge would perhaps have made him very proud, because he would have realized that he belonged to the little army which is the salt of the earth and which keeps culture, urbanity and beauty for their own sake from **passing away**.

12   Often it was not possible for him to sell all the baskets he had brought to market, for people here as elsewhere in the world preferred things made by the millions and each so much like the other that you were unable, even with the help of a magnifying glass, to tell which was which and where was the difference between two of the same kind.

13   Yet he, this craftsman, had in his life made several hundreds of those exquisite baskets, but so far no two of them had he ever turned out **alike** in design. Each was an individual piece of art and as different from the other as was a Murillo from a Velásquez.[6]

14   Naturally he did not want to take those baskets which he could not sell at the market place home with him again if he could help it. In such a case he went **peddling** his products from door to door where he was treated partly as a beggar and partly as a vagrant apparently looking for an opportunity to steal, and he frequently had to swallow all sorts of insults and nasty remarks.

15   Then, after a long run, perhaps a woman would finally stop him, take one of the baskets and offer him ten centavos, which price through talks and talks would perhaps go up to fifteen or even to twenty. Nevertheless, in many instances he would actually get no more than just ten centavos, and the buyer, usually a woman, would grasp that little marvel and right before his eyes throw it carelessly upon the nearest table as if to say, "Well, I take that piece of nonsense only for charity's sake. I know my money is wasted. But then, after all, I'm a Christian and I can't see a poor Indian die of hunger since he has come such a long way from his village." This would remind her of something better and she would hold him and say, "Where are you at home anyway, Indito?[7] What's your pueblo? So, from Huehuetonoc? Now, listen here, Indito, can't you bring me next Saturday two or three turkeys from Huehuetonoc? But they must be heavy and fat and very, very cheap or I won't even touch them. If I wish to pay the regular price I don't need you to bring them. Understand? Hop along, now, Indito."

16   The Indian squatted on the earthen floor in the portico of his hut, attended to his work and showed no special interest in the curiosity of Mr. Winthrop watching him. He acted almost as if he **ignored** the presence of the American altogether.

17   "How much that little basket, friend?" Mr. Winthrop asked when he felt that he at least had to say something as not to appear idiotic.

(continued)

passing away
a. coming along
b. disappearing, dying

alike
a. beautiful
b. similar

peddling
a. selling
b. kicking

ignored
a. didn't pay attention to
b. was interested in

---

[5]**fierro** *25 fierros = 5 centavos*
[6]**Murillo, Velázquez** *famous Spanish painters of the 1600s, each had a very distinctive style*
[7]**Indito** *lowly Indian (the Spanish suffix -ito can suggest that a person is of lower rank)*

apiece
a. for each one
b. for all of them

in stock
a. bought
b. ready to sell

18 "Fifty centavitos, patroncito,[8] my good little lordy, four reales," the Indian answered politely.

19 "All right, sold," Mr. Winthrop blurted out in a tone and with a wide gesture as if he had bought a whole railroad. And examining his buy he added, "I know already who I'll give that pretty little thing to. She'll kiss me for it, sure. Wonder what she'll use it for?"

20 He had expected to hear a price of three or even four pesos. The moment he realized that he had judged the value six times too high, he saw right away what great business possibilities this miserable Indian village might offer to a dynamic promoter like himself. Without further delay he started exploring those possibilities. "Suppose, my good friend, I buy ten of these little baskets of yours which, as I might as well admit right here and now, have practically no real use whatsoever. Well, as I was saying, if I buy ten, how much would you then charge me **apiece**?"

21 The Indian hesitated for a few seconds as if making calculations. Finally he said, "If you buy ten I can let you have them for forty-five centavos each, señorito gentleman."

22 "All right, amigo. And now, let's suppose I buy from you straight away one hundred of these absolutely useless baskets, how much will cost me each?"

23 The Indian, never fully looking up to the American standing before him and hardly taking his eyes off his work, said politely and without the slightest trace of enthusiasm in his voice, "In such a case I might not be quite unwilling to sell each for forty centavitos."

24 Mr. Winthrop bought sixteen baskets, which was all the Indian had **in stock**.

25 After three weeks' stay in the Republic, Mr. Winthrop was convinced that he knew this country perfectly, that he had seen everything and knew all about the inhabitants, their character and their way of life, and that there was nothing left for him to explore. So he returned to good old Nooyorg and felt happy to be once more in a civilized country, as he expressed it to himself.

26 One day going out for lunch he passed a confectioner's and, looking at the display in the window, he suddenly remembered the little baskets he had bought in that faraway Indian village.

27 He hurried home and took all the baskets he still had left to one of the best-known candy-makers in the city.

28 "I can offer you here," Mr. Winthrop said to the confectioner, "one of the most artistic and at the same time the most original of boxes, if you wish to call them that. These little baskets would be just right for the most expensive chocolates meant for elegant and high-priced gifts. Just have a good look at them, sir, and let me listen."

29 The confectioner examined the baskets and found them extraordinarily well suited for a certain line in his business. Never before had there been anything like them for originality, prettiness and good taste. He, however, avoided most carefully showing any sign of enthusiasm, for which there would be time enough once he knew the price and whether he could get a whole load exclusively.

30 He shrugged his shoulders and said, "Well, I don't know. If you asked me I'd say it isn't quite what I'm after. However, we might give it a try. It depends, of course, on the price. In our business the package mustn't cost more than what's in it."

31 "Do I hear an offer?" Mr. Winthrop asked.

32 "Why don't you tell me in round figures how much you want for them? I'm not good in guessing."

---

[8]**patroncito** *my good boss (the Spanish suffix -ito can also suggest respect)*

33   "Well, I'll tell you, Mr. Kemple: since I'm the smart guy who discovered these baskets and since I'm the only Jack who knows where to lay his hands on more, I'm selling to the highest bidder, on an exclusive basis, of course. I'm positive you can see it my way, Mr. Kemple."

34   "Quite so, and may the best man win," the confectioner said. "I'll talk the matter over with my partners. See me tomorrow same time, please, and I'll let you know how far we might be willing to go."

35   Next day when both gentlemen met again Mr. Kemple said: "Now, to be frank with you, I know art on seeing it, no getting around that. And these baskets are little works of art, they surely are. However, we are no art dealers, you realize that of course. We've no other use for these pretty little things except as fancy packing for our French pralines made by us. We can't pay for them what we might pay considering them pieces of art. After all to us they're only wrappings. Fine wrappings, perhaps, but nevertheless wrappings. You'll see it our way I hope, Mr.—oh yes, Mr. Winthrop. So, here is our offer, take it or leave it: a dollar and a quarter apiece and not one cent more."

36   Mr. Winthrop made a gesture as if he had been struck over the head.

37   The confectioner, misunderstanding this involuntary gesture of Mr. Winthrop, added quickly, "All right, all right, no reason to get excited, no reason at all. Perhaps we can do **a trifle** better. Let's say one-fifty."

a trifle

a. no

b. a little

38   "Make it one-seventy-five," Mr. Winthrop snapped, swallowing his breath while wiping his forehead.

39   "Sold. One-seventy-five apiece free at port of New York. We pay the customs and you pay the shipping. Right?"

40   "Sold," Mr. Winthrop said also and the deal was closed.

41   "There is, of course, one condition," the confectioner explained just when Mr. Winthrop was to leave. "One or two hundred won't do for us. It wouldn't pay the trouble and the advertising. I won't consider less than ten thousand, or one thousand dozens if that sounds better in your ears. And they must come in no less than twelve different patterns well assorted. How about that?"

42   "I can make it sixty different patterns or designs."

43   "So much the better. And you're sure you can deliver ten thousand let's say early October?"

44   "Absolutely," Mr. Winthrop avowed and signed the contract.

Before you read Part 2, answer these questions:

1. Was Mr. Winthrop smart in dealing with Mr. Kemple? Explain.
2. Do you think he will be smart in negotiating with the Indian? Explain.

PART 2

45   Practically all the way back to Mexico, Mr. Winthrop had a notebook in his left hand and a pencil in his right and he was writing figures, long rows of them, to find out exactly how much richer he would be when this business had been put through.

46   "Now, let's sum up the whole goddamn thing," he muttered to himself. "Damn it, where is that cursed pencil again? I had it right between my fingers. Ah, there it is. Ten thousand he ordered. Well, well, there we got a clean-cut profit of fifteen thousand four hundred and forty genuine dollars. Sweet smackers.[9] Fifteen grand[10]

---

[9]**smackers** *dollars (old-fashioned slang)*
[10]**grand** *$1,000 (slang)*

right into papa's pocket. Come to think of it, that Republic isn't so backward after all."

47   "Buenas tardes, mi amigo,[11] how are you?" he greeted the Indian whom he found squatting in the porch of his *jacalito* as if he had never moved from his place since Mr. Winthrop had left for New York.

48   The Indian rose, took off his hat, bowed politely and said in his soft voice, "Be welcome, patroncito. Thank you, I feel fine, thank you. Muy buenas tardes. This house and all I have is at your kind disposal." He bowed once more, moved his right hand in a gesture of greeting and sat down again. But he excused himself for doing so by saying, "Perdóneme,[12] patroncito, I have to take advantage of the daylight, soon it will be night."

49   "I've got big business for you, my friend," Mr. Winthrop began.

50   "Good to hear that, señor."[13]

51   Mr. Winthrop said to himself, "Now, he'll jump up and go wild when he learns what I've got for him." And aloud he said: "Do you think you can make one thousand of these little baskets?"

52   "Why not, patroncito? If I can make sixteen, I can make one thousand also."

53   "That's right, my good man. Can you also make five thousand?"

54   "Of course, señor. I can make five thousand if I can make one thousand."

55   "Good. Now, if I should ask you to make me ten thousand, what would you say? And what would be the price of each? You can make ten thousand, can't you?"

56   "Of course, I can, señor. I can make as many as you wish. You see, I am an expert in this sort of work. No one else in the whole state can make them the way I do."

57   "That's what I thought and that's exactly why I came to you."

58   "Thank you for the honor, patroncito."

59   "Suppose I order you to make me ten thousand of these baskets, how much time do you think you would need to deliver them?"

60   The Indian, without interrupting his work, cocked his head to one side and then to the other as if he were counting the days or weeks it would cost him to make all these baskets.

61   After a few minutes he said in a slow voice, "It will take a good long time to make so many baskets, patroncito. You see, the bast and the fibers must be very dry before they can be used properly. Then all during the time they are slowly drying, they must be worked and handled in a very special way so that while drying they won't lose their softness and their flexibility and their natural brilliance. Even when dry they must look fresh. They must never lose their natural properties or they will look just as lifeless and dull as straw. Then while they are drying up I got to get the plants and roots and barks and insects from which I brew the dyes. That takes much time also, believe me. The plants must be gathered when the moon is just right or they won't give the right color. The insects I pick from the plants must also be gathered at the right time and under the right conditions or else they produce no rich colors and are just like dust. But, of course, jefecito,[14] I can make as many of these canastitas[15] as you wish, even as many as three dozens if you want them. Only give me time."

62   "Three dozens? Three dozens?" Mr. Winthrop yelled, and threw up both arms in desperation. "Three dozens!" he repeated as if he had to say it many times in his

---

[11]**Buenas tardes, mi amigo** *Good afternoon, my friend*
[12]**Perdóneme** *Pardon me, excuse me*
[13]**señor** *sir, mister*
[14]**jefecito** *boss, chief*
[15]**canastitas** *little baskets*

own voice so as to understand the real meaning of it, because for a while he thought that he was dreaming. He had expected the Indian to go crazy on hearing that he was to sell ten thousand of his baskets without having to peddle them from door to door and be treated like a dog with a skin disease.

63   So the American took up the question of price again, by which he hoped to activate the Indian's ambition. "You told me that if I take one hundred baskets you will let me have them for forty centavos apiece. Is that right, my friend?"

64   "Quite right, jefecito."

65   "Now," Mr. Winthrop took a deep breath, "now, then, if I ask you to make me one thousand, that is, ten times one hundred baskets, how much will they cost me, each basket?"

66   That figure was too high for the Indian to grasp. He became slightly confused and for the first time since Mr. Winthrop had arrived he interrupted his work and tried to think it out. Several times he shook his head and looked vaguely around as if for help. Finally, he said, "Excuse me, jefecito, little chief, that is by far too much for me to count. Tomorrow, if you will do me the honor, come and see me again and I think I shall have my answer ready for you, patroncito."

67   When on the next morning Mr. Winthrop came to the hut he found the Indian as usual squatting on the floor under the overhanging palm roof working at his baskets.

68   "Have you got the price for ten thousand?" he asked the Indian the very moment he saw him, without taking the trouble to say "Good Morning!"

69   "Sí, patroncito, I have the price ready. You may believe me when I say it has cost me much labor and worry to find out the exact price, because, you see, I do not wish to cheat you out of your honest money."

70   "Skip that, amigo. Come out with the salad. What's the price?" Mr. Winthrop asked nervously.

71   "The price is well calculated now without any mistake on my side. If I got to make one thousand canastitas each will be three pesos. If I must make five thousand, each will cost nine pesos. And if I have to make ten thousand, in such a case I can't make them for less than fifteen pesos each." Immediately he returned to his work as if he were afraid of losing too much with such idle talk.

72   Mr. Winthrop thought that perhaps it was his faulty knowledge of this foreign language that had played a trick on him.

73   "Did I hear you say fifteen pesos each if I eventually would buy ten thousand?"

74   "That's exactly and without any mistake what I've said, patroncito," the Indian answered in his soft courteous voice.

75   "But now, see here, my good man, you can't do this to me. I'm your friend and I want to help you get on your feet."

76   "Yes, patroncito, I know this and I don't doubt any of your words."

77   "Now, let's be patient and talk this over quietly as man to man. Didn't you tell me that if I would buy one hundred you would sell each for forty centavos?"

78   "Sí, jefecito, that's what I said. If you buy one hundred you can have them for forty centavos apiece, provided that I have one hundred, which I don't."

79   "Yes, yes, I see that." Mr. Winthrop felt as if he would go insane any minute now. "Yes, so you said. Only what I can't comprehend is why you cannot sell at the same price if you make me ten thousand. I certainly don't wish to chisel[16] on the price. I am not that kind. Only, well, let's see now, if you can sell for forty centavos at all, be it for twenty or fifty or a hundred, I can't quite get the idea why the price has to jump that high if I buy more than a hundred."

(continued)

---

[16]**chisel** *cheat (slang)*

80 "Bueno, patroncito, what is there so difficult to understand? It's all very simple. One thousand canastitas cost me a hundred times more work than a dozen. Ten thousand cost me so much time and labor that I could never finish them, not even in a hundred years. For a thousand canastitas I need more bast than for a hundred, and I need more little red beetles and more plants and roots and bark for the dyes. It isn't that you just can walk into the bush and pick all the things you need at your heart's desire. One root with the true violet blue may cost me four or five days until I can find one in the jungle. And have you thought how much time it costs and how much hard work to prepare the bast and fibers? What is more, if I must make so many baskets, who then will look after my corn and my beans and my goats and chase for me occasionally a rabbit for meat on Sunday? If I have no corn, then I have no tortillas to eat, and if I grow no beans, where do I get my frijoles from?"

81 "But since you'll get so much money from me for your baskets you can buy all the corn and beans in the world and more than you need."

82 "That's what you think, señorito, little lordy. But you see, it is only the corn I grow myself that I am sure of. Of the corn which others may or may not grow, I cannot be sure to feast upon."

83 "Haven't you got some relatives here in this village who might help you to make baskets for me?" Mr. Winthrop asked hopefully.

84 "Practically the whole village is related to me somehow or other. Fact is, I got lots of close relatives in this here place."

85 "Why then can't they cultivate your fields and look after your goats while you make baskets for me? Not only this, they might gather for you the fibers and the colors in the bush and **lend you a hand** here and there in preparing the material you need for the baskets."

86 "They might, patroncito, yes, they might. Possible. But then you see who would take care of their fields and cattle if they work for me? And if they help me with the baskets it turns out the same. No one would any longer work his fields properly. In such a case corn and beans would get up so high in price that none of us could buy any and we all would starve to death. Besides, as the price of everything would rise and rise higher still how could I make baskets at forty centavos apiece? A pinch of salt or one green chili would set me back more than I'd collect for one single basket. Now you'll understand, highly estimated caballero[17] and jefecito, why I can't make the baskets any cheaper than fifteen pesos each if I got to make that many."

87 Mr. Winthrop was hard-boiled, no wonder considering the city he came from. He refused to give up the more than fifteen thousand dollars which at that moment seemed to slip through his fingers like nothing. Being really desperate now, he talked and bargained with the Indian for almost two full hours, trying to make him understand how rich he, the Indian, would become if he would take this greatest opportunity of his life.

88 The Indian never ceased working on his baskets while he explained his points of view.

89 "You know, my good man," Mr. Winthrop said, "such a wonderful chance might never again knock on your door, do you realize that? Let me explain to you in ice-cold figures what fortune you might miss if you leave me flat on this deal."

90 He tore out leaf after leaf from his notebook, covered each with figures and still more figures, and while doing so told the peasant he would be the richest man in the whole district.

lend you a hand
a. help you
b. buy your baskets

---

[17]**estimated caballero** *mistranslation of the Spanish* estimado cabalerro, *meaning* esteemed *gentleman*

91   The Indian without answering watched with a genuine expression of awe as Mr. Winthrop wrote down these long figures, executing complicated multiplications and divisions and subtractions so rapidly that it seemed to him the greatest miracle he had ever seen.

92   The American, noting this growing interest in the Indian, misjudged the real significance of it. "There you are, my friend," he said. "That's exactly how rich you're going to be. You'll have a bankroll of exactly four thousand pesos. And to show you that I'm a real friend of yours, I'll throw in a bonus. I'll make it a round five thousand pesos, and all in silver."

93   The Indian, however, had not for one moment thought of four thousand pesos. Such an amount of money had no meaning to him. He had been interested solely in Mr. Winthrop's ability to write figures so rapidly.

94   "So, what do you say now? Is it a deal or is it? Say yes and you'll get your advance this very minute."

95   "As I have explained before, patroncito, the price is fifteen pesos each."

96   "But, my good man," Mr. Winthrop shouted at the poor Indian in **utter despair**, "where have you been all this time? On the moon or where? You are still at the same price as before."

97   "Yes, I know that, jefecito, my little chief," the Indian answered, entirely unconcerned. "It must be the same price because I cannot make any other one. Besides, señor, there's still another thing which perhaps you don't know. You see, my good lordy and caballero, I've to make these canastitas my own way and with my song in them and with bits of my soul woven into them. If I were to make them in great numbers there would no longer be my soul in each, or my songs. Each would look like the other with no difference whatever and such a thing would slowly eat up my heart. Each has to be another song which I hear in the morning when the sun rises and when the birds begin to chirp and the butterflies come and sit down on my baskets so that I may see a new beauty, because, you see, the butterflies like my baskets and the pretty colors on them, that's why they come and sit down, and I can make my canastitas after them. And now, señor jefecito, if you will kindly excuse me, I have wasted much time already, although it was a pleasure and a great honor to hear the talk of such a distinguished caballero like you. But I'm afraid I've to attend to my work now, for day after tomorrow is market day in town and I got to take my baskets there. Thank you, señor, for your visit. Adiós."[18]

98   And in this way it happened that American garbage cans escaped the fate of being turned into receptacles for empty, torn, and crumpled little multicolored canastitas into which an Indian of Mexico had woven dreams of his soul, throbs of his heart: his unsung poems.

---

[18]**adiós** *good-bye*

utter despair
a. complete hopelessness
b. tremendous happiness

COMPREHENSION CHECK

Answer these questions.

PART 1

1. Mr. Winthrop was on vacation in Mexico. What other purpose or mission did he discover while he was there?
2. How does the Indian make a living?

(continued)

3. What was exceptional about the baskets that the Indian made? How did people use them? Are these uses worthy of the baskets? Explain.
4. How did Mexican townspeople treat the Indian? How were prices for the baskets established when the Indian sold them in town? What does this suggest about the attitude of some Mexican townspeople toward rural Indians?
5. How does Mr. Winthrop view the Indian?
6. Who would benefit most from the business deal Mr. Winthrop wants to make with the Indian?
7. What business principle does Mr. Winthrop use in negotiating prices with the Indian?
8. What business strategies do Mr. Winthrop and Mr. Kemple, the confectioner, use on each other in making their deal?

PART 2

9. When Mr. Winthrop returns to Mexico, what does he propose to the Indian? How will Mr. Winthrop benefit from the deal?
10. How does the Indian respond to Mr. Winthrop's proposal? Can he make the number of baskets Mr. Winthrop wants? Why can't they come to an agreement?
11. Mr. Winthrop cannot understand the Indian's point of view on two levels, economic and artistic. What exactly does he not understand?
12. What does the Indian not understand? How do the different views of Mr. Winthrop and the Indian relate to the title?

VOCABULARY

Vocabulary Building

Read the underlined word or expression in its context and match it with the correct meaning. Use a dictionary if necessary.

PART 1

_____ 1. . . . he was an artist, a true and <u>accomplished</u> artist. (¶6)

_____ 2. The prospective buyer started <u>bargaining</u>, telling the Indian that he ought to be ashamed to ask such a sinful price. (¶9)

_____ 3. . . . he belonged to the little army which is <u>the salt of the earth</u> . . . (¶11)

_____ 4. . . . which keeps culture, urbanity and beauty <u>for their own sake</u> from passing away. (¶11)

_____ 5. . . . he had seen everything and knew all about the <u>inhabitants</u>, their character and their way of life . . . (¶25)

_____ 6. . . . once he [Mr. Kemple] knew the price and whether he could get a whole load <u>exclusively</u>. (¶29)

a. for their own value

b. people who are ordinary but good and honest

c. people who live in a particular place

d. very skillful

e. for him alone, not shared

f. discussing the price, trying to get a lower price

____ 7. . . . I'm selling to the
    <u>highest bidder</u> . . . (¶33)

____ 8. This house and all I have is
    <u>at your</u> kind <u>disposal</u>. (¶48)

____ 9. That figure was too high for
    the Indian to <u>grasp</u>. (¶66)

____ 10. Mr. Winthrop felt as if he would
    <u>go insane</u> any minute now. (¶79)

____ 11. . . . corn and beans would get
    up so high in price that none
    of us could buy any and we all
    would <u>starve to death</u>. (¶86)

____ 12. . . . I'll throw in a <u>bonus</u>. (¶92)

g. understand

h. die from lack of food, die of
   hunger

i. go crazy

j. something extra

k. person who offers the most
   money

l. available for you to use

Synonyms

Read the underlined word or expression in its context. Mark the *two* choices that are similar in meaning to the underlined word. Use a dictionary if necessary.

1. . . . Rotarians and Lions, who are forever conscious of their glorious <u>mission</u>
   on earth. (¶1)

   a. duty   b. purpose   c. religion

2. . . . colored with dyes that the basket-maker himself <u>extracted</u> from various
   native plants . . . (¶4)

   a. bought   b. took out   c. removed

3. He was a <u>peasant</u> who lived on what the small property he possessed . . . would
   yield . . . (¶5)

   a. poor farmer   b. nice man   c. rural person

4. . . . less than fifteen acres of not too <u>fertile</u> soil . . . (¶5)

   a. fruitful   b. imaginative   c. productive

5. Yet he . . . had . . . made several hundreds of those <u>exquisite</u> baskets . . . (¶13)

   a. expensive   b. beautiful   c. lovely

6. . . . he was treated partly as . . . a <u>vagrant</u> looking for an opportunity to steal . . .
   (¶14)

   a. beggar   b. tourist   c. vagabond

7. . . . he frequently had to swallow all sorts of insults and <u>nasty</u> remarks. (¶14)

   a. mean   b. polite   c. unkind

8. . . . the buyer, usually a woman, would <u>grasp</u> that little marvel . . . throw it
   carelessly . . . upon the nearest table . . .(¶15)

   a. grab   b. take   c. appreciate

(continued)

9. . . . that little <u>marvel</u> . . . (¶15)

    a. amazing thing   b. piece of garbage   c. wonderful creation

10. And they must come in no less than twelve different patterns well <u>assorted</u>.
(¶41)

    a. designed   b. mixed   c. varied

Vocabulary Review

Complete the following statements about the reading selection with the correct word from the list below. Use each word only once.

accomplished	despair	mission	peddles
assorted	exquisite	nasty	sake
bargain	grasp	peasant	

1. The Indian _____, in addition to being a farmer, is also
   a(an) _____ artist who weaves beautiful designs into
   baskets made from plant fibers.

2. In spite of their beauty, selling his _____ baskets is not
   easy. He takes them to market or _____ them from door-
   to-door in town.

3. He rarely gets his asking price because customers _____
   with him to get the lowest price possible. They treat him rudely and often
   make _____ and insulting remarks.

4. Mr. Winthrop, who believes it is his _____ to bring
   capitalism to remote areas of the developing world, strikes a deal with a
   candy maker in New York to deliver 10,000 baskets with varied or
   _____ designs to package expensive candies.

5. Mr. Winthrop returns to Mexico to negotiate with the Indian. Their
   communication is not at all successful, and Mr. Winthrop gives up in utter
   _____.

6. He cannot understand the Indian's way of life or appreciate art for art's
   _____. He simply cannot _____ the
   idea that it is impossible to make 10,000 of those marvelous baskets by hand.

Elements of Fiction: Characters

In some stories, characters come alive as individuals. In others, such as this one, they seem to be important for what they represent. How do Mr. Winthrop and the Indian differ?

Read the areas of difference in the column on the left. Add others that you may think of. Fill in the chart with information about their differences, and then answer the questions that follow.

Areas of Difference	Mr. Winthrop	Indian
a. occupation		
b. personality		
c. communication style		
d. aim in life		
e.		
f.		

1. What do Mr. Winthrop and the Indian represent?
2. What do you infer about Traven's views of North American and Mexican-Indian cultures through these characters? Which is he more sympathetic towards? Which is he more critical of? Which details show his attitude?

RESPONDING TO READING

Discuss these questions.

1. This story involves three cultures: Mexican Indian, Mexican non-Indian, and North American. How do these three cultures differ in (a) how people relate to each other and (b) what they value or consider important? What can you detect about the author's attitude towards these three groups?

(continued)

2. The story is told from the point of view of the omniscient, or all-knowing author. How would the story be different if told from the Indian's point of view? From Mr. Winthrop's point of view?

3. Have you ever tried to negotiate or discuss something with a person who thinks differently from you? Were you able to communicate? How did you feel during the interaction?

UNIT WRAP-UP

Extending Your Vocabulary

Word Families

Study the chart below to learn other forms of some of the words in this unit. If a box is blank, either there is no word to fill it, or the word is missing because it is not one you need to know now.

	NOUNS	VERBS	ADJECTIVES	ADVERBS
1.	assimilation	assimilate	assimilated	—
2.	assortment	—	assorted	—
3.	bewilderment	bewilder	bewildered bewildering	—
4.	collision	collide	—	—
5.	compliance	comply	compliant	compliantly
6.	confrontation	confront	confrontational	—
7.	harmony	harmonize	harmonious	harmoniously
8.	hesitation	hesitate	hesitant	hesitantly
9.	indignation	—	indignant	indignantly
10.	invasion	invade	invasive	invasively

For each item, look at the row in the chart above with the same number. Choose the word that correctly completes each sentence; be sure it is in the correct form.

1. Many people believe immigrants should _____ to their

   new culture. However, _____ is difficult, especially for

   older immigrants.

2. Mr. Kemple wanted the baskets in a(an) _____ of designs.

3. The American raised by Chinese people in China was totally

   _____ by the United States. He found American culture

   _____.

4. A bus and a truck _____ on the freeway. Fifteen vehicles piled up as a result of the _____.

5. The saying, "When in Rome, do as the Romans do," suggests that when you are in a foreign culture you should _____ with the local way of doing things.

6. Some people are _____ and don't mind disagreements; others try to avoid _____.

7. It would be ideal if everyone could live _____.

8. Don't _____ to ask a teacher questions if you don't understand something.

9. I was _____ when a coworker questioned my honesty.

10. In some cultures a personal question like that would be considered a/an _____ of privacy.

Collocations

One way to improve your vocabulary is to learn collocations for new words. Using correct collocations makes you sound more like a native speaker.

mode(s) of (n.)	**mode(s) of** thought/thinking, behavior, expression, transportation
remote (adj.)	**remote** village, area, part of, region, chance, possibility, control
restore (v.)	**restore** peace, civil rights, confidence, democracy, order
utter (adj.)	**utter** despair, confusion, darkness, devastation, disregard for, misery, waste (of time)
the surface (n.)	bring, come, rise **to the surface**
	scratch, skim **the surface**
	below, beneath, on **the surface**

Complete the sentences below with appropriate collocations. Consult the chart above for help. There may be more than one correct collocation.

1. Modes of _____ vary from culture to culture.

2. We are too dependent on cars. We need to find alternative modes of _____.

(continued)

3. There's a remote _____ that I'll get the job I really want.

4. Ludmila is from a remote _____ in Russia.

5. The new government has promised to restore _____.

6. There was utter _____ after the earthquake.

7. I woke up in utter _____ and didn't know where I was.

8. Once the labor union and managers started to negotiate, all sorts of problems _____ to the surface.

9. In a new country, at first you will only see what's _____ the surface, but there is a lot _____ the surface that you won't see until you have been there for a long time.

WRITING

Choose one of the suggestions for writing below. Talk about what you plan to write with a classmate who chose the same topic. Then follow the instructions for writing.

Personal Writing

1. Write about an intercultural experience you or a person you know has had. Consider writing about one of the following:
   a. an intercultural misunderstanding
   b. a change a person made because of contact with another culture
   c. a change a person couldn't make when living in another culture

   Use the question words *who, what, where, when, why, how,* and *how long?* to be sure that you provide the necessary background information and explain the situation clearly.

Academic Writing

2. Research notes: write up your notes from the Thinking about the Topic (#2) observation activity you did before you read "Touching." Use what you have learned in this unit to analyze your findings and draw conclusions.

3. Contrasting two characters: contrast the Indian and Mr. Winthrop using the information you put in the chart in Text Analysis, page 127. Start with a sentence like the following:

   > Both the Indian and Mr. Winthrop see the world only through the lens of their own culture.

Try to use some of the following vocabulary in writing about the topic you choose: *aloof, assimilate, bewildered, bias, codes, collide, confronted by, dilemma, get along, go insane, harmony, heritage, ignore, nasty, preconceived notions, prejudice, rationalize, reject, restrict, ritual, stereotype.*

Discuss

1. In what situations is it not easy for people to decide what to do?
2. What is *ethics*? What do these sentences suggest *ethical* means?

   • It is not ethical to use human beings in research without their consent.

   • It is not ethical for teachers to share personal information about a student with other students.

   • It is not ethical for a doctor to accept money from another physician for referring a patient to him or her.

   • It is not ethical for a writer to use another writer's words without giving proper credit.

> *Be the master of your will and the slave of your conscience.*
>
> Hasidic proverb

> *No man should judge unless he asks himself in absolute honesty whether in a similar situation he might not have done the same.*
>
> Victor Frankl (1905–1997), holocaust survivor, author of *Man's Search for Meaning*

ABOUT THE READING

"Treasures from Troy" was written by William Frey, a university professor of ethics who writes similar materials for online ethics courses for business and engineering students.

BEFORE YOU READ

Thinking about the Topic

Read about ethics and discuss the questions.

WHAT IS ETHICS?

When most people think of ethics, or morals, they think of rules for distinguishing between right and wrong, such as the Golden Rule ("Do unto others as you would have them do unto you"), a code of professional conduct like the Hippocratic Oath ("First of all, do no harm"), a religious creed like the Ten Commandments ("Thou shalt not kill . . ."), or wise aphorisms like the sayings of Confucius. This is the most common way of defining ethics: ethics are norms for conduct that distinguish between acceptable and unacceptable behavior. . . . Another way of defining ethics focuses on the disciplines that study standards of conduct, such as philosophy, theology, law, psychology, or sociology. For example, a "medical ethicist" is someone who studies ethical standards in medicine. Finally, ethics can be defined as a method, procedure, or perspective for deciding how to act and for analyzing complex problems and issues.

from: What Is Ethics in Research & Why Is it Important? *by David B. Resnik, J.D., Ph.D.*
http://www.niehs.nih.gov/research/resources/bioethics/whatis.cfm

1. What are the three ways to define *ethics* according to Resnik? Which, if any, of these ways are you familiar with?
2. What are some ethical decisions students have to make?

Previewing

Read the title, headings, and the first two paragraphs of this selection. Then answer these questions.

1. Which of the three meanings of *ethics* does Gregory Pierce give?
2. Which of the three meanings of *ethics* will this reading selection illustrate?

Before you read, turn to Comprehension Check, First Reading on page 135. Your purpose for the first reading is to answer those questions.

Treasures from Troy:[1] An Introduction to Ethics *By William Frey, Ph.D.*

WHAT IS ETHICS?

nature
a. living things
b. characteristics

1   Gregory Pierce, in *A Dictionary of Common Philosophical Terms,* defines ethics as "the branch of philosophy[2] that investigates and creates theories about the **nature** of right and wrong, duty, obligation, freedom, virtue, and other issues where sentient beings can be harmed or helped." (Sentient beings are conscious and feel pleasure and pain.) But a word of caution! Attempts to define ethics are difficult and controversial. As professional engineer, William Lawson, puts it, "defining ethics is sort of like nailing Jell-O to a tree."[3]

AN ETHICS CASE

airtight
a. long
b. perfect

2   Defining ethics may be difficult, but we don't need an **airtight** definition to do ethics. Almost every day, we are all faced with choices that involve deciding if some action is right or wrong. Doing ethics is unavoidable. So let's begin with an example.

frantically
a. nervously
b. a week ahead

3   *You are studying **frantically** for your exam in a computer engineering course. It will be very difficult. But your roommate, who is also taking the exam tomorrow, seems unconcerned. Apparently, a group of students in the class found out how to hack into the professor's computer and download the exam. They installed a program called a Trojan horse into the professor's computer which gave them unauthorized access. Then they searched the professor's files, found the exam, downloaded it, and distributed copies to their friends. Your roommate has the exam in his hand and asks you if you would like to look at it. What should you do?*

4   Ethics helps us to make decisions in situations like this. For example, you accept your roommate's offer or refuse it. Of course there are other possibilities. You could refuse the exam and keep quiet about it. Or you could refuse the exam and go to the professor and tell him about it. When you tell the professor, you could give him the name of your roommate. Or you could just simply say that you have heard a rumor that some students have obtained copies of the exam. Let's analyze this situation from the viewpoint of ethics. For starters: What would it mean to take the exam from your roommate?

impacts
a. effects
b. electric current

5   Business leaders, engineers, and other professionals use ethics tests to aid the decision-making process. Three common tests ask you to 1) divide expected results into positive and negative **impacts,** 2) reverse roles with those who will be affected by your action, and 3) analyze the action in the spotlight of public opinion. Let's use the three tests to shed some light on the difficult decision in the Treasures from Troy scenario.

(continued)

---

[1]**Treasures from Troy** *The author uses this title because the computer program that allows one to gain unauthorized access to another computer is called a Trojan Horse. The citizens of the ancient city of Troy were called Trojans. Their city was invaded and destroyed by Greeks who got inside the walls of Troy by hiding soldiers inside a big wooden horse which the curious Trojans pulled inside the walls.*

[2]**philosophy** *the study of what it means to exist, what good and evil are, what knowledge is, or how people should live*

[3]**like nailing Jell-O to a tree** *using a hammer and nails to hold gelatin to a tree; a humorous simile meaning it's difficult*

6 **The Consequences Test**

Start by asking yourself, "What will happen if I accept the exam?" This employs a consequences test. You might get caught by the professor along with the other students and fail the class and be **expelled** from the university. But you might not get caught. So if you consider accepting the exam in light of the likely consequences *for you* then you might get away with it or you might not. **Reflecting on** the likely results of accepting the exam helps get things started. But it misses important ethical considerations. To bring these out into the open, consider the next test, reversibility.

7 **The Reversibility Test**

Second, ask yourself "Would accepting the exam be a good choice if you traded places with your teacher?" How about if you traded places with students taking the exam who didn't get to see it beforehand? This "reversibility test" helps you understand your decision by getting you to see it through the eyes of other people. Your teacher would not appreciate your viewing the exam ahead of time because it would deceive her. (She believes that the class is seeing the exam for the first time.) Furthermore, your classmates who didn't view the exam ahead of time would object to having to compete with those who did. They would find this unfair. So seeing this action through the eyes of your teacher and some of your classmates helps you to see that it raises serious ethical problems.

8 **The Publicity Test**

Finally, ask yourself "How would it look on the front page of a newspaper?" You take the exam from your roommate and together you look up the answers. After getting a good night's sleep, you do well on the exam and go out to celebrate. Two days later, you pick up a copy of the school newspaper. There on the first page is the headline, "Cheating Scandal Uncovered." **Horrified**, you read the complete story. The ringleaders were caught and confessed to entering the professor's computer and stealing the exam. Even worse, they cut a deal with university authorities and named the students in the class to whom they had given the exam. There on the list are your name and that of your roommate! Now everybody will know you as a cheater. Your choice doesn't look so good when you imagine it on the front page of the school newspaper.

9 **The Tests Summarized**

This quick exercise helps you to understand ethics by actually doing it. Accepting the exam is risky for you. And this alternative looks poor when seen from the standpoints of the other students and the teacher. Finally, it looks bad on the front page of the school newspaper. So these tests help you to cover all the ethics bases when you **deliberate on** what you should do.

Ethics Test	Basis for Deciding
Consequence Test: What are the consequences of the action under consideration? Which of these are benefits? Which of these are harms?	Choose the action that produces the greatest good for the greatest number of people.
Reversibility Test: Would I think this was a good choice if I traded places? How does my action look when viewed through the eyes of others?	Choose the action which treats others with respect. This means avoiding actions which deceive, manipulate, or force someone to do something.
Publicity Test: How would this choice look on the front page of a newspaper?	Choose actions that express key moral virtues like justice, respect, responsibility, and honesty which a virtuous person would choose if he or she were in the situation.

10 **NOW IT'S YOUR TURN**

Go back to the Trojan horse scenario. You have analyzed one alternative, that of accepting the exam and have decided it looks pretty **grim**. But you haven't yet figured out what to do. So apply the tests to the following alternatives:

1. Refuse the exam and keep quiet about it.
2. Refuse the exam and tell the professor about it. Remember, you can implicate others or not.

grim
a. good
b. bad

Sources for quotes in ¶1: Pierce, Gregory (2000) *A Dictionary of Common Philosophical Terms.* New York, NY: McGraw-Hill Higher Education.
Lawson, William (2006). "Ethics for the Real World," pp. 103–107 in *Engineering Ethics: Concepts, Viewpoints, Cases and Codes.*

COMPREHENSION CHECK

First Reading

Answer these questions.

1. What is the situation in the ethical case presented for analysis?
2. In general terms, what do you think about when you apply the Consequences Test?
3. What do you think about when you apply the Reversibility Test?
4. What do you think about when you apply the Publicity Test?

Second Reading

Reread parts of the selection as needed. Mark the statements *T* (true) or *F* (false). Write the paragraph number(s) where you found evidence for each answer.

1. T F The Consequences Test focuses first on what might happen to the person who makes the decision. ¶___

2. T F The Reversibility Test brings into the picture how the decision might affect other people. ¶___

3. T F The Publicity Test makes people think about whether they want the world to know what they have done. ¶___

4. T F Applying the Consequences Test should lead people to choose the decision that has the best consequences for them personally. ¶___

5. T F The Reversibility Test should lead people to choose actions which treat people as they would like to be treated. ¶___

6. T F The Publicity Test should lead people to choose actions that are good for public relations. ¶___

VOCABULARY

Vocabulary Building

Read the underlined word or expression in its context and match it with the correct meaning. Use a dictionary if necessary.

___ 1. . . . ethics . . . creates theories about the nature of right and wrong . . . virtue, and other issues . . . (¶1)

___ 2. Attempts to define ethics are difficult and controversial. (¶1)

___ 3. . . . you have heard a rumor that some students have obtained copies of the exam. (¶4)

___ 4. Your teacher would not appreciate your viewing the exam ahead of time . . . (¶7)

___ 5. . . . because it would deceive her. (¶7)

___ 6. "Cheating Scandal Uncovered." (¶8)

___ 7. The ringleaders were caught and confessed . . . (¶8)

___ 8. And this alternative looks poor . . . (chart)

___ 9. This means avoiding actions which . . . manipulate . . . someone . . . (chart)

___ 10. You could implicate others or not. (¶10)

a. mislead, misinform

b. choice, option

c. make someone do what you want by influencing them

d. causing disagreement

e. moral goodness

f. name, identify people involved in something wrong

g. admitted guilt for doing something wrong or illegal

h. like or be pleased about

i. information passed from one person to another that may not be true

j. something that has happened that people think is immoral or shocking

Multiword Expressions

For each definition, scan the paragraph and find an equivalent multiword expression and write it on the line.

1. learned (¶3) _____

2. enter a computer illegally (¶3) _____

3. make something easier to understand (¶5) _____

4. be found doing something wrong (¶6) _____

5. escape without consequences (¶6) _____

6. make things clear (¶6) _____

7. exchanged places (¶7) _____

8. made an agreement (¶8) _____

9. do a complete, thorough job (¶9) _____

10. decided (¶10) _____

Vocabulary Review

Complete the following statements about the reading selection with the correct word or expression from the list below. Use each word or expression only once.

alternatives	get away with	implicate
controversial	hack into	reflect on
expelled	horrified	trade places

1. The three ethics tests presented in this reading can help people consider their _____ when they face a difficult decision.

2. The specific case presented for analysis in this reading is that of students who _____ a professor's computer and steal a copy of an exam.

3. Applying the Consequences Test guides people to _____ how their actions might affect their lives. In the case of the stolen exam, accepting the exam might help students pass the exam if they could _____ it; on the other hand, it might get them _____ from the university.

4. Applying the Reversibility Test requires people to _____ with the people who will be affected by the decision.

5. The Publicity Test asks people to consider if they would be _____ to read about what they have done in the newspaper.

(continued)

6. In the case of the stolen exam, it is probably easier for most people to say what they will not do (accept the exam), than to decide what to do—keep quiet or _____ other people.

7. Practice in applying the three tests can help people make good decisions when an issue is _____.

TEXT ANALYSIS   *Providing Transitions*

> One way writers help readers understand their ideas is to make clear connections, or transitions, from one part of a discussion to another. They use words, phrases, sentences and complete paragraphs to make smooth transitions.

Skim the reading as needed to answer the following questions.

1. Paragraph 2 is a transition paragraph.
   a. What is the content of paragraph 1?
   b. What is the content of paragraph 3?
   c. What words in paragraph 2 connect back to paragraph 1?
   d. What words in paragraph 2 point to paragraph 3?
2. Paragraph 4 starts with a sentence transition. Does it connect back or point forward? What words make the connection?
3. Paragraph 5 is a transition paragraph. Does it connect back or point forward? How does it do this?

RESPONDING TO READING   **Discuss these questions.**

1. Why do students cheat?

2. How do children learn ethics?

3. If you can learn ethics as a child, why might it be important to take a college course in ethics?

4. What are some ethical decisions that occur in people's daily lives?

5. What are some ethical decisions faced by people who work in the following fields: advertising, business, food production, law and the criminal justice system, medical research, scientific research, and sports?

CHAPTER 18

ABOUT THE READING

"Why You Shouldn't Do It" appeared on the website of musicunited.org. It states the position of many recording artists and the Recording Industry Association of America (RIAA) concerning how music should be shared over the Internet. According to the website, the RIAA members "create, manufacture and/or distribute approximately 90% of all legitimate sound recordings produced and sold in the United States."

BEFORE YOU READ

Thinking about the Topic

Read about copyright and discuss the questions.

WHAT IS COPYRIGHT?

Copyright refers to laws which protect intellectual property: works that people create with their minds. International laws exist to ensure that a person's right to his creative work is respected around the world, but these laws are not enforced equally in all countries. Copyright laws in the United States protect works in literature, drama, music, art, graphics, and architecture. Such intellectual property is protected from the time it is created until 70 years after the author's death.

1. What kinds of works are protected by the U.S. Copyright Act?
2. Why do you think there is a law giving people the right to determine how their creative work is used and distributed?

Previewing

Preview the selection appropriately. Then answer these questions.

1. What do you think *it* refers to in the title?
2. What do you think was the author's purpose in writing this article?

Before you read, turn to Comprehension Check, First Reading on page 142. Your purpose for the first reading is to answer those questions.

Why You Shouldn't Do It

Real Fans Get the Real Thing

1   You may not think you're doing anything illegal when you burn[1] multiple copies of your favorite CD to give to all your friends or offer copies of your favorite tracks[2] to millions of people on the Internet through "peer to peer" networks like Kazaa or Morpheus. The fact is, however, that when you do this sort of thing, you're taking something that doesn't belong to you. The right to reproduce the music you're copying belongs to the artists, songwriters, record companies and others who hold the copyright. All of which means that when you copy and distribute copyrighted music without permission, you are stealing.

2   This wholesale music theft is dramatically damaging to the entire music community. And contrary to what some people would tell you, it's having a very real and harmful effect on countless musicians, independent record stores, singer/songwriters and virtually everyone who dreams about making a living providing the public with their music.

3   There are many reasons why you shouldn't steal music. Here are four basic ones.

1. Stealing music is against the law.

granted
a. taken from
b. given

For centuries, civilized societies have **granted** artists, authors, and other creative people the right to own and control the original work they produce, be they paintings, poems, songs, or any other form of literary or artistic expression. These rights are protected by what is known as copyright.

4   In the United States, copyright protection is guaranteed under the Constitution as well as the Copyright Act. Recorded music is specifically protected by these laws,

---

[1]**burn** *copy electronically, usually to a CD*
[2]**tracks** *sections of electronic recording*

which means it is against the law to make unauthorized reproductions, distributions, or digital transmissions[3] of copyrighted sound recordings.

> "Congress shall have the power to . . . promote the progress of science and useful arts, by securing for limited times to authors and inventors the exclusive right to their respective writings and discoveries . . ."

U.S. Constitution
Article 1, Section 8

The penalties for breaking these laws are stiff—particularly when digital recordings are involved.

5   ***2. Stealing music betrays the songwriters and recording artists who create it.***
A lot of people who copy and distribute music illegally try to rationalize their behavior by arguing that the people who make recordings are all rich anyway, and that music should be free.

6   To **assert** that music should be free is the same as saying it has no value—that music is worthless. It's not.

> Music doesn't just happen. It's made, note by note, beat by beat, by people who work hard to get it right.

7   For the artist, the hard work requires not only a major emotional and intellectual commitment, but also long hours, intense concentration, and real financial risk. We like to talk about the imagination, soul, and courage involved in creative work. But making music is also about career and financial well-being. It's about putting food on the table and covering the rent. It's about making enough money to pay for all that equipment and rehearsal time, about keeping yourself afloat as you **strive** to succeed in a highly competitive industry.

> What gives the music value is not only that you like it, but also that you buy it. If you steal it, you're not just stealing from a record company. You're stealing from the very artists you love and admire.

8   Most of us would never even consider stealing something of value from a neighbor's house. Our conscience, our sense of right and wrong, keep us from doing it. Sure, we know there are criminal penalties, but the main reason we don't steal is because we know it's wrong.

9   ***3. Stealing music stifles the careers of new artists and up-and-coming bands.***
Another rationalization for stealing music is that illegal copying is a victimless crime that really doesn't hurt anyone.
Tell that to the struggling young musicians in a garage band[4] who can't **get signed** because record sales are down.

10 Or tell it to the young singer-songwriter whose career dead-ends because people would rather download her music for free.

> The cost of recording and promoting a major album can easily top $1 million, and only one out of every ten ever turns a profit.

11 There's no question that Internet exposure can be a great thing for new artists. For many up-and-coming bands, there's no better way of getting noticed and establishing a following than creating a website and putting your stuff out there for the online world to hear. But there's a difference between checking out a band

assert
a. say, claim
b. fear

strive
a. hate
b. try hard

get signed
a. get a contract
b. get arrested

---

[3]**digital transmissions** *information sent electronically*
[4]**garage band** *general term for startup musicians, from the fact that they practice in garages*

that chooses to let people download its music for free and deciding for yourself that somebody's new music should be spread all over the Internet.

12   Making records is an expensive undertaking. So is building a career. If people aren't willing to pay for the music they love, the record companies will find it increasingly difficult to commit the kind of resources it takes to discover and develop new talent.

13   ***4. Stealing music threatens the livelihood of the thousands of working people—from recording engineers to record-store clerks—who are employed in the music industry.***

    Songwriters and artists, whether established or up-and-coming, aren't the only people hurt by illegal copying. In the U.S. alone, the music industry employs some 50,000 people—and very few of them are rich rock stars. Stealing music also threatens the livelihoods of the thousands of technicians, CD-plant[5] workers, warehousemen, and other non-musicians who are employed in the music business helping to create and deliver the music you love.

---

[5]**CD-plant** *factory where compact discs are made*

COMPREHENSION CHECK

First Reading

What are the four major arguments in this reading against copying and distributing music from a CD or the Internet? Express each in your own words on the lines below.

Argument 1:

It is illegal to copy and distribute copyrighted music without permission.

Argument 2:

_____

Argument 3:

_____

Argument 4:

_____

Second Reading

Reread parts of the selection as needed to answer these questions. As you read, highlight or jot down helpful words or phrases.

1. Why did the writers of the U.S. Constitution include copyright protection in it?
2. What are two examples of rationalizations about copying and distributing music from CDs or the Internet?
3. What does this article suggest gives value to things in modern society?
4. Why do some up-and-coming musicians put their music on the Internet for free? What do they risk when they do this?
5. What did you learn about the cost of producing music and who pays for it?
6. If people do not pay for the music they download, what are at least two things that will happen?

Vocabulary Building: Synonyms

Read the underlined word or expression in its context. Mark the *two* choices that are similar in meaning. Use a dictionary if necessary.

1. . . . when you <u>burn</u> multiple copies of your favorite CD . . . (¶1)

   a. copy   b. destroy   c. reproduce

2. . . . when you copy and <u>distribute</u> copyrighted music without permission, you are stealing. (¶1)

   a. die out   b. give out   c. hand out

3. This <u>wholesale</u> music <u>theft</u> . . . (¶2)

   a. large-scale stealing   b. widespread robbery   c. low-priced buying

4. Sure, we know there are criminal <u>penalties</u> . . . (¶4)

   a. bad consequences   b. happy endings   c. punishments

5. The penalties for breaking these laws are <u>stiff</u> . . . (¶4)

   a. light   b. severe   c. strong

6. Stealing music <u>betrays</u> the songwriters and recording artists who create it. (¶5)

   a. is disloyal to   b. is meaningful to   c. is unfair to

7. We like to talk about the imagination, <u>soul</u>, and courage involved in creative work. (¶7)

   a. fear   b. heart   c. spirit

8. But making music is also about career and financial <u>well-being</u>. (¶7)

   a. comfort   b. problems   c. security

9. It's about making enough money to pay for all that equipment and <u>rehearsal time</u> . . . (¶7)

   a. practice time   b. preparation time   c. show time

10. Stealing music <u>stifles</u> the careers of new artists and up-and-coming bands. (¶9)

    a. helps   b. cuts off   c. stops

11. Making records is an expensive <u>undertaking</u>. (¶12)

    a. business   b. enterprise   c. sport

12. . . . the record companies will find it increasingly difficult to commit the kind of <u>resources</u> it takes to discover and develop new talent. (¶12)

    a. finances   b. money   c. natural materials

13. Stealing music <u>threatens</u> the livelihood of the thousands of working people . . . (¶13)

    a. endangers   b. improves slowly   c. will probably harm

14. Stealing music threatens the <u>livelihood</u> of the thousands of working people . . . (¶13)

    a. income   b. talent   c. way a person earns money

Multiword Expressions

Work with a partner. Read the underlined multiword expression in its context. Decide what the expression means and paraphrase it on the line. The first one is done for you. Use a dictionary if necessary.

1. . . . everyone who dreams about <u>making a living</u> providing the public with their music. (¶2) *earning enough money to live decently*

2. Music doesn't just happen. It's made, note by note, beat by beat, by people who work hard to <u>get it right</u>. (¶6) _____

3. It [making music] is . . . about <u>keeping yourself afloat</u> as you strive to succeed in a highly competitive industry. (¶7) _____

4. Stealing music stifles the careers of new artists and <u>up-and-coming</u> bands. (¶9)

   _____

5. Another rationalization for stealing music is that illegal copying is <u>a victimless crime</u> that really doesn't hurt anyone. (¶9) _____

6. Or tell it to the young singer-songwriter whose career <u>dead-ends</u> because people would rather download her music for free. (¶10) _____

7. The cost of recording and promoting a major album can easily top $1 million, and only one out of every ten ever <u>turns a profit</u>. (¶10) _____

8. For many up-and-coming bands, there's no better way of getting noticed and <u>establishing a following</u> than creating a website and putting your stuff out there for the online world to hear. (¶11) _____

9. If people aren't willing to pay for the music they love, the record companies will find it increasingly difficult to <u>commit the</u> kind of <u>resources</u> it takes to discover and develop new talent. (¶12) _____

Vocabulary Review

Complete the following statements about the reading selection with the correct word or expression from the list below. Use each word or expression only once.

betray   distribution   threaten
burn   granted   up-and-coming
copyright

1. This article expresses the point of view of most musicians and the recording industry regarding the illegal copying and _____ of digital music either from a CD or from the Internet.

2. Because the writers of the U.S. Constitution wanted to encourage creativity, they _____ inventors and artists the right to control their inventions and artistic work for a limited period of time.

3. When people _____, or reproduce, illegal copies of digital music, they are stealing the music from the artist or recording company that holds the _____.

4. As this article states, when people do this, they _____ people they admire and they _____ the livelihood of virtually everyone who earns a living in the music industry.

5. If people value something, they should be willing to pay for it. Young musicians may see their careers dead-end if recording companies do not have the money to invest in the careers of _____ artists.

TEXT ANALYSIS

Supporting General Statements

When authors make strong claims, they have to support them. Find the support the writer of this article gives for each of these claims. The support may or may not be directly after the claim.

1. When you reproduce and distribute copyrighted music without permission, you are stealing something that doesn't belong to you.
2. This wholesale music theft is dramatically damaging to the entire music community.
3. Stealing music betrays the songwriters and recording artists who create it.
4. Stealing music stifles the careers of new artists and up-and-coming bands.
5. Stealing music threatens the livelihood of the thousands of working people . . . who are employed in the music industry.

Author's Purpose

Mark the correct answer to the question.

What was the author's purpose for writing this material?
    a. to narrate
    b. to compare and contrast
    c. to persuade
    d. to analyze a process

RESPONDING TO READING

Discuss these questions.

1. Which of the reasons not to reproduce and distribute digital music illegally are most convincing to you? Why?

2. Apply the Consequences, Reversibility, and Publicity tests from Chapter 17 to the following ethical questions:
    a. Should I download songs illegally from a P2P site but not copy them for others?
    b. Should I download songs illegally from a P2P site and copy and distribute them to others?

3. If music were available for free on the Internet, where would the money come from to pay the artists and the various costs of production?

4. People have been able to illegally copy music on tapes for many years. Why have copying and distributing music been a bigger issue in recent years?

ABOUT THE READING

"A Plea for the Chimps" by Jane Goodall appeared in the *New York Times Magazine.* Goodall began observing and writing about chimpanzees in Tanzania, Africa, in the early 1960s. Her work was not immediately accepted by animal behaviorists, who considered it nonscientific because it did not result in numerical data. Ultimately, however, her enormous contribution to our understanding of chimpanzees was acknowledged, and today she is considered the world expert on these animals. In 1977 she founded the Jane Goodall Institute for Wildlife Research, Education and Conservation whose mission is to "empower individuals to take informed and compassionate action to improve the environment for all living things."

BEFORE YOU READ

Thinking about the Topic

Chimpanzees and human beings belong to the biological order *primate* and share 99 percent of their genetic material. *Genes* are segments of deoxyribonucleic acid (DNA) found in the chromosomes of cells that determine what genetic information is passed from parent to child. Because of their genetic similarity to humans, chimps have been used for years in medical research to test *cures,* medicines or treatments, for disease and *vaccines* to prevent disease.

Discuss these questions.

1. What do you know about how similar chimpanzees are to humans in their ability to think, learn, socialize, and feel pain and pleasure?
2. How do you suppose chimpanzees live in a laboratory compared to how they live in the wild?

Previewing

Read the title, the first two paragraphs and the last paragraph of this long article. Then answer these questions.

1. What similarities between chimpanzees and humans does Goodall mention?
2. A *plea* is an urgent, emotional request. What do you think Goodall's plea for the chimps might be?

Before you read, turn to Comprehension Check on page 154. Your purpose in reading this article is to answer those questions.

Note: This selection is quite long. If desired, it can be read in two parts: paragraphs 1–23 and paragraphs 24–46.

A Plea for the Chimps

By Jane Goodall

PART 1

1   The chimpanzee is more like us, genetically, than any other animal. It is because of similarities in physiology, in biochemistry, in the immune system, that medical science makes use of the living bodies of chimpanzees in its search for cures and vaccines for a variety of human diseases.

2   There are also behavioral, psychological and emotional similarities between chimpanzees and humans, resemblances so striking that they raise a serious ethical question: are we justified in using an animal so close to us—an animal, moreover, that is highly endangered in its African forest home—as a human substitute in medical experimentation?

3   In the long run, we can hope that scientists will find ways of exploring human physiology and disease, and of testing cures and vaccines, that do not depend on the use of living animals of any sort. A number of steps in this direction already have been taken, prompted in large part by a growing public awareness of the suffering that is being inflicted on millions of animals. More and more people are beginning to realize that nonhuman animals—even rats and guinea pigs—are not just unfeeling machines but are capable of enjoying their lives, and of feeling fear, pain and despair.

4   But until alternatives have been found, medical science will continue to use animals in the battle against human disease and suffering. And some of those animals will continue to be chimpanzees.

5   Because they share with us 99 percent of their genetic material, chimpanzees can be infected with some human diseases that do not infect other animals. They are currently being used in research on the nature of hepatitis non-A non-B, for example, and they continue to play a major role in the development of vaccines against hepatitis B.

6   Many biomedical laboratories are looking to the chimpanzee to help them in the race to find a vaccine against acquired immune deficiency syndrome. Chimpanzees are not good models for AIDS research; although the AIDS virus stays alive and **replicates** within the chimpanzee's bloodstream, no chimp has yet **come down with** the disease itself. Nevertheless, many of the scientists involved argue that only by using chimpanzees can potential vaccines be safely tested.

7   Given the scientists' professed need for animals in research, let us turn aside from the sensitive ethical issue of whether chimpanzees should be used in medical research, and consider a more important issue: how are we treating the chimpanzees that are actually being used?

8   Just after Christmas I watched, with shock, anger and **anguish**, a videotape—made by an animal rights group during a raid—revealing the conditions in a large biomedical research laboratory, under contract to the National Institutes of Health, in which various primates, including chimpanzees, are maintained. In late March, I was given permission to visit the facility.

9   It was a visit I shall never forget. Room after room was lined with small, bare cages, stacked one above the other, in which monkeys circled round and round and chimpanzees sat huddled, far gone in depression and despair.

10   Young chimpanzees, 3 or 4 years old, were crammed, two together, into tiny cages measuring 22 inches by 22 inches and only 24 inches high. They could

replicates
a. dies
b. copies itself

come down with
a. gotten
b. sent

anguish
a. great hope
b. extreme pain

hardly turn around. Not yet part of any experiment, they had been confined in these cages for more than three months.

11   The chimps had each other for comfort, but they would not remain together for long. Once they are infected, probably with hepatitis, they will be separated and placed in another cage. And there they will remain, living in conditions of severe sensory deprivation, for the next several years. During that time, they will become insane.

12   A juvenile female rocked from side to side, sealed off from the outside world behind the glass doors of her metal isolation chamber. She was in semidarkness. All she could hear was the incessant roar of air rushing through vents into her prison.

13   In order to demonstrate the "good" relationship the lab's caretaker had with this chimpanzee, one of the scientists told him to lift her from the cage. The caretaker opened the door. She sat, unmoving. He reached in. She did not greet him—nor did he greet her. As if drugged, she allowed him to take her out. She sat motionless in his arms. He did not speak to her, she did not look at him. He touched her lips briefly. She did not respond. He returned her to her cage. She sat again on the bars of the floor. The door closed.

14   I shall **be haunted** forever by her eyes, and by the eyes of the other infant chimpanzees I saw that day. Have you ever looked into the eyes of a person who, stressed beyond endurance, has given up, succumbed utterly to the crippling helplessness of despair? I once saw a little African boy, whose whole family had been killed during the fighting in Burundi. He too looked out at the world, unseeing, from dull, blank eyes.

15   Though this particular laboratory may be one of the worst, from what I have learned, most of the other biomedical animal-research facilities are not much better. Yet only when one has some understanding of the true nature of the chimpanzee can the cruelty of these **captive** conditions be fully understood.

16   Chimpanzees are very social by nature. **Bonds** between individuals, particularly between family members and close friends, can be affectionate, supportive, and can endure throughout their lives. The accidental separation of two friendly individuals may cause them intense distress. Indeed, the death of a mother may be

be haunted
a. have bad memories
b. forget quickly

captive
a. free
b. prison-like

bonds
a. connections
b. memories

such a psychological blow to her child that even if the child is 5 years old and no longer dependent on its mother's milk, it may pine away and die.

17   It is impossible to overemphasize the importance of friendly physical contact for the well-being of the chimpanzee. Again and again one can watch a frightened or tense individual relax if she is patted, kissed or **embraced** reassuringly by a companion. Social grooming,[1] which provides hours of close contact, is undoubtedly the single most important social activity.

embraced
a. hit
b. hugged

18   Chimpanzees in their natural habitat are active for much of the day. They travel extensively within their territory, which can be as large as 50 square kilometers for a community of about 50 individuals. If they hear other chimpanzees calling as they move through the forest, or anticipate arriving at a good food source, they typically break into excited charging displays, racing along the ground, hurling sticks and rocks and shaking the vegetation. Youngsters, particularly, are full of energy, and spend long hours playing with one another or by themselves, leaping through the branches and **gamboling** along the ground. Adults sometimes join these games. Bunches of fruit, twigs and rocks may be used as toys.

gamboling
a. playing cards
b. running playfully

19   Chimpanzees enjoy comfort. They construct sleeping platforms each night, using a multitude of leafy twigs to make their beds soft. Often, too, they make little "pillows" on which to rest during a midday siesta.[2]

20   Chimps are highly intelligent. They display **cognitive** abilities that were, until recently, thought to be unique to humans. They are capable of cross-model transfer of information—that is, they can identify by touch an object they previously have only seen, and vice versa. They are capable of reasoned thought, generalization, abstraction and symbolic representation. They have some concept of self. They have excellent memories and can, to some extent, plan for the future. They show a capacity for intentional communication that depends, in part, on their ability to understand the motives of the individuals with whom they are communicating.

cognitive
a. mental
b. simple

---

[1]**social grooming** *one animal taking care of the appearance of another*
[2]**siesta** *rest, nap (from Spanish)*

picked up
a. cleaned
b. learned

sustain
a. maintain
b. destroy

bleak and sterile
a. cold and unpleasant
b. bright and cheerful

condone
a. approve of
b. disapprove of

callous
a. friendly
b. not caring

21 Chimpanzees are capable of empathy and altruistic behavior. They show emotions that are undoubtedly similar, if not identical, to human emotions—joy, pleasure, contentment, anxiety, fear and rage. They even have a sense of humor.

22 The chimpanzee child and the human child are alike in many ways: in their capacity for endless romping and fun; their curiosity; their ability to learn by observation, imitation and practice; and, above all, in their need for reassurance and love. When young chimpanzees are brought up in a human home and treated like human children, they learn to eat at table, to help themselves to snacks from the refrigerator, to sort and put away cutlery, to brush their teeth, to play with dolls, to switch on the television and select a program that interests them and watch it.

23 Young chimpanzees can easily learn over 200 signs of the American language of the deaf and use these signs to communicate meaningfully with humans and with one another. One youngster, in the laboratory of Dr. Roger S. Fouts, a psychologist at Central Washington University, has **picked up** 68 signs from four older signing chimpanzee companions, with no human teaching. The chimp uses the signs in communication with other chimpanzees and with humans.

PART 2

24 The chimpanzee facilities in most biomedical research laboratories allow for the expression of almost none of these activities and behaviors. They provide little—if anything—more than the warmth, food and water, and veterinary care required to **sustain** life. The psychological and emotional needs of these creatures are rarely catered to, and often not even acknowledged.

25 In most labs the chimpanzees are housed individually, one chimp to a cage, unless they are part of a breeding program. The standard size of each cage is about 25 feet square and about 6 feet high. In one facility, a cage described as "large," designed for a chimpanzee of up to 25 kilograms (55 pounds), measures 2 feet 6 inches by 3 feet 8 inches, with a height of 5 feet 4 inches. Federal requirements for cage size are dependent on body size; infant chimpanzees, who are the most active, are often imprisoned in the smallest cages.

26 In most labs, the chimpanzees cannot even lie with their arms and legs outstretched. They are not let out to exercise. There is seldom anything for them to do other than eat, and then only when food is brought. The caretakers are usually too busy to pay much attention to individual chimpanzees. The cages are **bleak and sterile**, with bars above, bars below, bars on every side. There is no comfort in them, no bedding. The chimps, infected with human diseases, will often feel sick and miserable.

27 What of the human beings who administer these facilities—the caretakers, veterinarians and scientists who work at them? If they are decent, compassionate people, how can they **condone**, or even tolerate, the kind of conditions I have described?

28 They are, I believe, victims of a system that was set up long before the cognitive abilities and emotional needs of chimpanzees were understood. Newly employed staff members, equipped with a normal measure of compassion, may well be sickened by what they see. And, in fact, many of them do quit their jobs, unable to endure the suffering they see inflicted on the animals yet feeling powerless to help.

29 But others stay on and gradually come to accept the cruelty, believing (or forcing themselves to believe) that it is an inevitable part of the struggle to reduce human suffering. Some become hard and **callous** in the process, in Shakespeare's words, "all pity choked with custom of fell deeds."[3]

(continued)

---

[3]*"all pity choked with custom of fell deeds"* people don't show pity because the habit of doing something evil desensitizes them; (fell = evil) (From Shakespeare's Julius Caesar, Act 3, Scene 1)

lot
a. condition
b. yard

humane
a. cruel
b. kind

mockery
a. joke
b. perfect example

emulate
a. copy, imitate
b. ignore, not pay
attention to

mandatory
a. free
b. required

infringe on
a. obey, follow
b. disobey, go against

30   A handful of compassionate and dedicated caretakers and veterinarians are fighting to improve the **lot** of the animals in their care. Vets are often in a particularly difficult position, for if they stand firm and try to uphold high standards of **humane** care, they will not always be welcome in the lab.

31   Many of the scientists believe that a bleak, sterile and restricting environment is necessary for their research. The cages must be small, the scientists maintain, because otherwise it is too difficult to treat the chimpanzees—to inject them, to draw their blood or to anesthetize them. Moreover, they are less likely to hurt themselves in small cages.

32   The cages must also be barren, with no bedding or toys, say the scientists. This way, the chimpanzees are less likely to pick up diseases or parasites. Also, if things are lying about, the cages are harder to clean.

33   And the chimpanzees must be kept in isolation, the scientists believe, to avoid the risk of cross-infection, particularly in hepatitis research.

34   Finally, of course, bigger cages, social groups and elaborate furnishings require more space, more caretakers—and more money. Perhaps, then, if we are to believe these researchers, it is not possible to improve conditions for chimpanzees imprisoned in biomedical research laboratories.

35   I believe not only that it is possible, but that improvements are absolutely necessary. If we do not do something to help these creatures, we make a **mockery** of the whole concept of justice.

36   Perhaps the most important way we can improve the quality of life for the laboratory chimps is to increase the number of carefully trained caretakers. These people should be selected for their understanding of animal behavior and their compassion and respect for, and dedication to their charges. Each caretaker, having established a relationship of trust with the chimpanzees in his care, should be allowed to spend time with the animals over and above that required for cleaning the cages and providing the animals with food and water.

37   It has been shown that a chimpanzee who has a good relationship with his caretaker will cooperate calmly during experimental procedures, rather than react with fear or anger. At the Dutch Primate Research Center at Rijswijk, for example, some chimpanzees have been trained to leave their group cage on command and move into small, single cages for treatment. At the Stanford Primate Center in California, a number of chimpanzees were taught to extend their arms for the drawing of blood. In return they were given a food reward.

38   Much can be done to alleviate the pain and stress felt by younger chimpanzees during experimental procedures. A youngster, for example, can be treated when in the presence of a trusted human friend. Experiments have shown that young chimps react with high levels of distress if subjected to mild electric shocks when alone, but show almost no fear or pain when held by a sympathetic caretaker.

39   What about cage size? Here we should **emulate** the animal-protection regulations that already exist in Switzerland. These laws stipulate that a cage must be, at minimum, about 20 meters square and 3 meters high for pairs of chimpanzees.

40   The chimpanzees should never be housed alone unless this is an essential part of the experimental procedure. For chimps in solitary confinement, particularly youngsters, three to four hours of friendly interaction with a caretaker should be **mandatory**. A chimp taking part in hepatitis research, in which the risk of cross-infection is, I am told, great, can be provided with a companion of a compatible species if it doesn't **infringe on** existing regulations—a rhesus monkey, for example, which cannot catch or pass on the disease.

deleterious
a. good
b. bad

stimulating
a. exciting
b. boring

begrudge
a. deny, not provide
b. pay, give

41   For healthy chimpanzees there should be little risk of infection from bedding and toys. Stress and depression, however, can have **deleterious** effects on their health. It is known that clinically depressed humans are more prone to a variety of physiological disorders, and heightened stress can interfere with immune function. Given the chimpanzee's similarities to humans, it is not surprising that the chimp in a typical laboratory, alone in his bleak cage, is an easy prey to infections and parasites.

42   Thus, the chimpanzee also should be provided with a rich and **stimulating** environment. Climbing apparatus should be obligatory. There should be many objects for them to play with or otherwise manipulate. A variety of simple devices designed to alleviate boredom could be produced quite cheaply. Unexpected food items will elicit great pleasure. If a few simple buttons in each cage were connected to a computer terminal, it would be possible for the chimpanzees to feel they at least have some control over their world—if one button produced a grape when pressed, another a drink, or another a video picture. (The Canadian Council on Animal Care recommends the provision of television for primates in solitary confinement, or other means of enriching their environment.)

43   Without doubt, it will be considerably more costly to maintain chimpanzees in the manner I have outlined. Should we **begrudge** them the extra dollars? We take from them their freedom, their health and often their lives. Surely, the least we can do is try to provide them with some of the things that could make their imprisonment more bearable.

44   There are hopeful signs. I was immensely grateful to officials of the National Institutes of Health for allowing me to visit the primate facility, enabling me to see the conditions there and judge them for myself. And I was even more grateful for the fact that they gave me a great deal of time for serious discussions of the problem. Doors were opened and a dialogue begun. All who were present at the meetings agreed that, in light of present knowledge, it is indeed necessary to give chimpanzees a better deal in the labs.

45   Plans are now under way for a major conference to discuss ways and means of bringing about such change. Sponsored by the N.I.H. and organized by Roger Fouts (who toured the lab with me) and myself, this conference—which will be held in mid-December at the Jane Goodall Institute in Tucson, Ariz.—will bring together for the first time administrators, scientists and animal technicians from various primate facilities around the country and from overseas. The conference will, we hope, lead to the formulation of new, humane standards for the maintenance of chimpanzees in the laboratory.

46   I have had the privilege of working among wild, free chimpanzees for more than 26 years. I have gained a deep understanding of chimpanzee nature. Chimpanzees have given me so much in my life. The least I can do is to speak out for the hundreds of chimpanzees who, right now, sit hunched, miserable and without hope, staring out with dead eyes from their metal prisons. They cannot speak for themselves.

(continued)

Since 1987 when this article first appeared in *The New York Times Magazine*, Goodall and many others have worked hard to improve the situation of chimpanzees in research laboratories and to provide them with a decent life in retirement after they are no longer used in research. A 2005 Humane Society article "The Chimpanzee Challenge" reported that "1,300 chimpanzees—the majority of them bred in captivity—currently live in biomedical research labs in the United States . . . " and that they were often still housed in the smallest cages that are legal. However, beginning in the year 2000 the Chimpanzee Health Improvement, Maintenance, and Protection Act (the CHIMP Act), established a system of national sanctuaries where chimps live in a natural setting after they are no longer needed in the laboratories. This landmark legislation made clear that killing chimps that are no longer needed is not ethical. The article also reports that "the number of federally funded research projects involving chimpanzees has dropped by half" and that scientists have discovered ways to use human cells in some kinds of research that, in fact, lead to better scientific results.

COMPREHENSION CHECK

Reread parts of the selection as needed to answer these questions. As you read, highlight or jot down helpful words or phrases.

PART 1

1. Why are chimpanzees used in medical research?
2. What question does Goodall focus on in this article?
3. What are conditions like for chimpanzees in the NIH laboratory that Goodall visited?
4. What are the characteristics of chimpanzees in their natural habitat?

PART 2

5. How do conditions in the lab prevent chimps from behaving as they would in their natural habitat?
6. What dilemma does the cruel treatment of chimpanzees in laboratories present for veterinarians?
7. Why do other people who work in the labs, such as caretakers, allow the cruel treatment?
8. Why do some scientists believe the chimpanzees must be kept in such a bleak, sterile, and restricting environment?
9. What evidence does Goodall give to suggest that the scientists may be wrong?
10. What suggestions does Goodall make for improving conditions in the laboratories?
11. Since this article was first published, what difference, if any, have Goodall's efforts made in the lives of laboratory chimps?

Vocabulary Building

Read the underlined word or expression in its context and match it with the correct meaning. Use a dictionary if necessary.

PART 1

____ 1. . . . are we <u>justified</u> in using an animal so close to us . . . as a human substitute in medical experimentation? (¶2)

____ 2. . . . animals . . . are not just unfeeling machines but are capable of . . . feeling fear, pain and <u>despair</u>. (¶3)

____ 3. chimpanzees can be <u>infected</u> with some human diseases . . . (¶5)

____ 4. . . . they had been <u>confined</u> in these cages for more than three months. (¶10)

____ 5 . . . living in conditions of severe <u>sensory deprivation</u> . . . (¶11)

____ 6. During that time, they will become <u>insane</u>. (¶11)

____ 7. . . . behind the glass doors of her metal <u>isolation chamber</u>. (¶12)

____ 8. Bonds between individuals, particularly between family members and close friends, can be <u>affectionate</u> . . . (¶16)

____ 9. Chimpanzees in their <u>natural habitat</u> are active for much of the day. (¶18)

____ 10. Chimpanzees are capable of <u>empathy</u> and altruistic behavior. (¶21)

a. crazy, mentally ill

b. given a disease

c. hopelessness

d. acting ethically, doing the right thing

e. loving

f. place they normally live

g. with no stimulation of the senses

h. space where the animal is alone; cage

i. ability to understand someone else's feelings

j. imprisoned

_____ 11. Chimpanzees are capable of empathy and <u>altruistic</u> behavior. (¶21)

_____ 12. The chimps, infected with human diseases, will often feel sick and <u>miserable</u>. (¶26)

_____ 13. If they are decent, <u>compassionate</u> people . . . (¶27)

_____ 14. Much can be done to <u>alleviate</u> the pain and stress felt by younger chimpanzees . . . (¶38)

_____ 15. A chimp taking part in hepatitis research . . . can be provided with a companion of a <u>compatible</u> species . . . (¶40)

_____ 16. . . . depressed humans are more <u>prone to</u> a variety of physiological disorders . . . (¶41)

_____ 17. The chimp in a typical laboratory, alone in his bleak cage, is an easy <u>prey to</u> infections and parasites. (¶41)

_____ 18. I have had the <u>privilege</u> of working among wild, free chimpanzees for more than 26 years. (¶46)

k. victim of

l. able to exist together without causing problems

m. relieve, make less severe

n. extremely unhappy and uncomfortable

o. special advantage

p. thinking of the needs of others before your own needs

q. kind, sympathetic

r. likely to suffer from

Vocabulary Review

Complete the following statements about the reading selection with the correct word from the list below. Use each word only once.

alleviating	compassionate	isolation
bleak	confined	miserable
bonds	despair	stimulating

1. Although Jane Goodall hopes that some day no animals will be used in research, her immediate goal in this article is to make the public aware of the _____ and sterile environment in which chimps live in research labs and the inhumane treatment they receive.

2. On a visit to a biomedical research laboratory, under contract to the National Institutes of Health, she found chimpanzees _____ to small cages with almost no room to move and nothing to play with. Their eyes often showed that they had been stressed beyond endurance and were in a state of _____.

3. To understand the cruelty of these laboratory conditions, Goodall argues that we must understand the nature of chimpanzees in their natural habitat where they are social and affectionate animals that establish lifelong _____ with other chimps.

4. Goodall makes several suggestions for _____ the suffering of chimps in labs.

5. Three to four hours of friendly interaction with a(an) _____ caretaker every day should be obligatory.

6. Chimps should not be kept in _____ unless the design of the research requires it.

7. They should have a(an) _____ environment, including climbing apparatus, toys and even interaction with a computer.

8. In addition to ethical reasons for improving the lives of chimpanzees in research laboratories, there are scientific reasons as well. Experiments on depressed, _____ chimps may not produce accurate results. If chimpanzees are well treated, it is easy to train them to cooperate with research procedures, yielding better results.

TEXT ANALYSIS

Text Organization

Goodall's article is well organized. Describe the contribution each paragraph or set of paragraphs makes to the whole piece of writing.

Introduction (¶1–7)

a. states the topic, which is _____

b. raises two ethical questions, which are

_____

_____

c. gets the reader interested by _____

Body (¶8–43)

¶8–14 _____

¶15 _____

¶16–23 _____

¶24–26 _____

¶27 _____

¶28–34 _____

¶35–43 _____

(continued)

Conclusion (¶44–46)

¶44–45 _____

¶46 _____

Discuss these questions.

1. If you worked in a laboratory where animals were suffering, what would you do?

2. What is your opinion of using animals in medical research? List the pros and cons. Why is this a controversial issue?

3. Apply the three tests from Chapter 17 to the issue of using primates in medical research.

   a. The Consequences Test: What are the consequences (harms and benefits) of using primates in medical research in laboratory settings?

   b. The Reversibility Test: What if humans had to trade places with chimpanzees in the laboratories? How would it feel?

   c. The Publicity Test: How does this whole situation look to the public when the conditions Goodall describes are shown on television or written about in newspapers?

4. What other ethical questions can we ask about the way humans treat animals? Consider wild animals, farm animals, pets, and zoo or circus animals.

ABOUT THE READING

"The Wallet" by Andrew McCuaig, was first published in the *Beloit Fictional Journal* (Spring 2003), and then in *Flash Fiction Forward: 80 Very Short Stories*. McCuaig teaches English and Creative Writing at a high school in Madison, Wisconsin. He wrote this story in class while his students were working on their stories.

BEFORE YOU READ

Thinking about the Topic

How do you think a story about a wallet might relate to this unit on ethics?

READ

The Wallet *By Andrew McCuaig*

maid
a. friend
b. servant

1   When Elaine arrived at work the first thing she noticed was that Troy had left his wallet on the small shelf next to a half-finished cup of Coke. Troy left his food regularly, as if she were his **maid**, but he left his wallet less often—about once a month. The first time it happened was just her second night on the job, and she thought maybe he was testing her, or, worse, that he had created some excuse to come back and see her. He had, in fact, returned half an hour later and deliberately rubbed his body up against hers as he retrieved his wallet instead of just standing at the door and asking her to hand it to him. They had made awkward small talk in the cramped booth before he finally raised his wallet in a salute, said good-bye and good luck and rubbed past her again.

2   Now, as she settled onto the stool for her shift, she could smell his lingering presence. She picked up the cup of Coke and placed it in the garbage can at her feet, careful to keep it upright. The cup had sweated out a puddle in the summer heat and she shook her head despairingly. She lined up her piles of quarters and

dimes on the shelf in order to have something to do. Two booths down, José waved at her and gave her two thumbs up, a gesture he thought was cute. He was another lecherous type, always spending his breaks standing at her door looking her up and down and blowing smoke into her booth. She waved at him so he'd turn around.

3   In front of her now the highway was black. Every few minutes headlights would appear in the distance like slow trains but most of the time the drivers would pick the automatic lanes. Then three or four cars might come in a row and she'd be grateful to move into a rhythm—reach, grab, turn, gather, turn, reach, good night. It was **annoying** when people didn't bring their cars close enough, but at least it allowed her to stretch more. By midnight she had made change for twenty-six people. Several weeks ago she had started to keep track out of boredom. Her midnight record was seventy-two, her fewest, twelve.

4   At about three o'clock a car came toward her too fast, weaving like a firefly,[1] before picking her booth. The brakes screeched, the muffler roared: it was a little yellow Chevette, an eighties car pocked with rust. Elaine leaned forward with her hand ready, but the driver, a young woman, made no move to pay her toll. She looked straight ahead, her face hidden by strings of brown hair, both hands locked tight to the wheel. Beside her in the front seat was a small beat-up suitcase overflowing with clothes.

5   Elaine said, "Good morning," and the woman said, "I need money."

6   Elaine hesitated. "You mean you don't have the toll?"

7   "No, I mean I need money." She turned now and Elaine saw her bleary eyes and splotched face. There was an ugly gash below one eye and the skin around it had swollen up and turned purple. There seemed to be an older scar on her nose, and dried blood in the corner of her mouth. Her stare was bitter and bold and it made Elaine look away.

8   She was about to raise the bar and tell her to go on ahead when she saw movement in the backseat. Looking closer, she saw there were two children, one about five, the other barely two, neither in car seats or seatbelts. Their eyes were wide and afraid and Elaine realized it was this that had drawn her attention to them in the dark. The little one held on to a gray stuffed animal, the older one was sucking her thumb.

9   José was watching her; he raised his palms and scowled. She had been trained to signal in a certain way if she was being **held up**, and José seemed to be waiting for this gesture. Instead, she gave him a thumbs up and **surreptitiously** reached for Troy's wallet. She opened the wallet to find ninety-two dollars inside. She pulled these bills out, wadded them in her fist and reached out to the woman, who took the money, **gripped** the wheel harder and sped away. The older girl's face, framed by the back window, receded into the darkness, her eyes like glowing stones.

---

[1] **firefly** *insect that lights up*

annoying
a. amusing, funny
b. irritating, upsetting

held up
a. robbed
b. helped

surreptitiously
a. openly
b. secretly

gripped
a. held tight
b. broke

COMPREHENSION CHECK

Answer these questions.

1. Who is Elaine?
2. Who is Troy?
3. What, apparently, are their usual shifts?
4. How well do they get along?
5. How well does Elaine like her job?

6. What do you think is the story of the woman in the car? Why does she need money?
7. What drew Elaine's attention to the children in the backseat of the car?
8. What does Elaine decide to do for the woman?

VOCABULARY

Vocabulary Building: Using Paraphrases

Work with a partner. Study the sentence on the left. Underline the difficult words in the sentence and find their meanings in the paraphrase on the right. Use a dictionary if necessary.

Sentence from the Text	Paraphrase
1. He had, in fact, returned half an hour later and deliberately rubbed his body up against hers as he retrieved his wallet . . . (¶1)	He had, in fact, returned half an hour later and rubbed his body up against hers on purpose as he got his wallet back . . .
2. They had made awkward small talk in the cramped booth . . . (¶1)	They had talked uncomfortably about unimportant things in the small, crowded booth.
3. Now, as she settled onto the stool for her shift, she could smell his lingering presence. (¶2)	Now, as she got comfortable on the high seat for her eight hours of work, she could smell his continuing presence.
4. (Sam) was another lecherous type . . . (¶2)	Sam was another guy who thought about women as sex objects.
5. The brakes screeched, the muffler roared: it was a little yellow Chevette, an eighties car pocked with rust. (¶4)	The brakes made a high, loud unpleasant sound, the muffler made a deep, very loud sound: it was a little yellow Chevette, an eighties car covered with reddish spots where the paint was gone.
6. [The driver] turned now and Elaine saw her bleary eyes and splotched face. (¶7)	She turned now and Elaine saw her tired, unclear, teary eyes and her face covered with marks.
7. There was an ugly gash below one eye and the skin around it had swollen up and turned purple. (¶7)	There was an ugly cut below one eye and the skin around it had gotten puffy and purple.
8. Her stare was bitter and bold . . . (¶7)	The look on her face didn't change; she looked angry and confident.

Vocabulary Review

Complete the following statements about the reading selection with the correct word or expression from the list below. Use each word or expression only once.

annoying   held up   shift
deliberately   maid   surreptitiously
gripping   screeched   swollen

1. Elaine worked the night _____ at a toll booth. When she came on duty one night she found that a co-worker, Troy, had left his wallet in the booth along with a half drunk Coke.

2. Elaine didn't care much for Troy. For one thing, he had the _____ habit of leaving his food as if she were his _____ and should clean up after him.

3. He also left his wallet occasionally, as an excuse to come back to see her. The first time that happened, he _____ rubbed up against her rather than asking her to hand him the wallet.

4. About 3:00 A.M. the night of this story, a young woman driving an old Chevette _____ to a stop at Elaine's booth.

5. She didn't move to pay the toll, but sat there _____ the steering wheel.

6. The young woman told Elaine she needed money. When she turned toward Elaine, Elaine saw there was a gash on her face and one eye was _____. Elaine also noticed two small, frightened children in the back seat.

7. Signaling a co-worker that she was not being _____, Elaine _____ reached for Troy's wallet, removed the $92 from it and gave the money to the young woman who drove off into the night.

Careful Selection of Details

As you would expect, the writer of this short story chooses every word and detail carefully. Details can reveal the physical characteristics of a person or the person's character, that is, his or her personality.

Fill in the chart below with details about each character. You will only fill in one column for each character. Why did the author choose the details he did?

Name	Physical Description	Personality
Troy		
Elaine		
Woman in the car		

RESPONDING TO READING

Discuss these questions.

1. Why do you think Elaine decided to give Troy's money to the woman? Would Troy or José have done the same thing? Would you have done the same thing? Explain.

2. Apply the three tests from Chapter 17 to the issue in this story.

   a. The Consequences Test: What are the consequences (harms and benefits) of Elaine's giving the $92 to the young woman?

   b. The Reversibility Test: How would Elaine feel if Troy had given her money away in similar circumstances?

   c. The Publicity Test: How would Elaine feel if this story became public knowledge?

3. Do you think Elaine's action was justified? Explain.

4. What questions about this story remain unanswered?

Extending Your Vocabulary

Word Families

Study the chart below to learn other forms of some of the words in this unit. If a box is blank, either there is no word to fill it, or the word is missing because it is not one you need to know now.

	NOUNS	VERBS	ADJECTIVES	ADVERBS
1.	appreciation	appreciate	appreciative	appreciatively
2.	compassion	—	compassionate	compassionately
3.	controversy	—	controversial	—
4.	deception	deceive	deceptive	deceptively
5.	deliberation	deliberate	deliberate	deliberately
6.	infection	infect	infected infectious	—
7.	isolation	isolate	isolated	—
8.	rationalization	rationalize	—	—
9.	scandal	scandalize	scandalous	scandalously
10.	threat	threaten	threatened threatening	threateningly

For each item, look at the row in the chart above with the same number. Choose the word that correctly completes the sentence; be sure it is in the correct form.

1. The students showed their _____ for their teacher by having a party in his honor.

2. When chimpanzees are treated _____ they usually cooperate with researchers.

3. There has been a lot of _____ over the safety of some drugs. The way drugs are approved is a _____ issue.

4. It doesn't pay to use _____ practices in advertising. If you _____ customers they will take their business elsewhere.

5. Elaine made a _____ decision to give Troy's money to the woman in the car, but she didn't have to _____ long.

6. It's easy to pick up an _____ disease in the closed environment of an airplane.

7. The doctors _____ the man until they knew what kind of infection he had.

8. When you do something wrong, it is often easier to _____ your behavior than to admit the truth.

9. Politicians are sometimes forced out of office because of _____ behavior.

10. "I don't like it when people _____ me," she said, as she shook her finger at me _____.

Collocations

One way to improve your vocabulary is to learn new collocations for words. Using correct collocations makes you sound more like a native speaker.

alleviate (v.)	**alleviate** pain, poverty, stress, suffering, tension, unemployment
annoying (adj.)	**annoying** behavior, background music, noise, person, situation, sound
confine to (v.)	**confine to** bed, prison, the house, a cage, a hospital, a wheelchair
frantically (adv.)	call, clean, dig, search, shout, try, wave
miserable (adj.)	**miserable** animal, conditions, feeling, person, weather
nature (n.)	**the nature of** chimpanzees, politics, the conversation, the crime, the game, the problem, the proposal
*raise** (v.)	**raise** the prospect of . . . , doubts, issues, points, (serious ethical) questions
stimulating (adj.)	**stimulating** environment, activity, conversation, discussion, group of people
stimulate (v.)	**stimulate** business, discussion, growth, ideas, interest, participation, production, the brain, the economy, the imagination

*These collocations are given for only one meaning of *raise*, "bring to light."

institutions interact with the natural world. The goals of environmental science are to learn how nature works, how the environment affects us, how we affect the environment, and how we can live more sustainably without degrading our life support system.

Sustainability

*Sustainability, or **durability**, is built on the subthemes of **natural capital**, natural capital degradation, solutions, trade-offs, and how individuals matter.*

3 Sustainability, or durability, is the ability of Earth's various systems, including human cultural systems and economies, to survive and adapt to changing environmental conditions **indefinitely**.

4 . . . The first step [toward sustainability] is to understand the components and importance of natural capital—the natural resources and services that keep us and other species alive and support our economies.

indefinitely
a. forever
b. in the past

What Is Natural Capital?

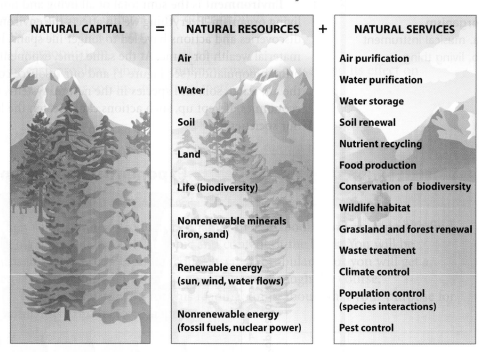

NATURAL CAPITAL	=	NATURAL RESOURCES	+	NATURAL SERVICES
		Air		Air purification
		Water		Water purification
		Soil		Water storage
		Land		Soil renewal
		Life (biodiversity)		Nutrient recycling
				Food production
		Nonrenewable minerals (iron, sand)		Conservation of biodiversity
				Wildlife habitat
		Renewable energy (sun, wind, water flows)		Grassland and forest renewal
				Waste treatment
		Nonrenewable energy (fossil fuels, nuclear power)		Climate control
				Population control (species interactions)
				Pest control

Figure 2

5 We can also think of energy from the sun as **solar capital** that warms the planet and supports photosynthesis, the process that plants use to provide food for themselves and for us and for other animals. This direct input of solar energy also produces indirect forms of renewable solar energy such as wind, flowing water, and fuels made from plants and plant residues (biofuels).

6 Natural capital is not fixed. It has changed over millions of years in response to environmental changes such as global warming and cooling and huge asteroids[1] hitting the earth. Forests have grown and disappeared, as have grasslands and deserts. Species **have become extinct** because of natural and human causes and new species have appeared. We have transformed many forests and grasslands into croplands—a more simplified form of natural capital created by humans.

have become extinct
a. died out
b. lived

---

[1]**asteroid** *a rocky object, a miniature planet that revolves around the sun*

7 The second step toward sustainability is to recognize that many human activities degrade natural capital by using normally renewable resources such as forests faster than nature can renew them. A key variable is the **rate** at which we are transforming parts of the earth to meet our needs and wants. Most natural environmental changes have taken place over thousands to hundreds of thousands of years. Humans are now making major changes in the earth's natural systems within 50 to 100 years. For example, in parts of the world we are clearing many mature forests much faster than nature can re-grow them.

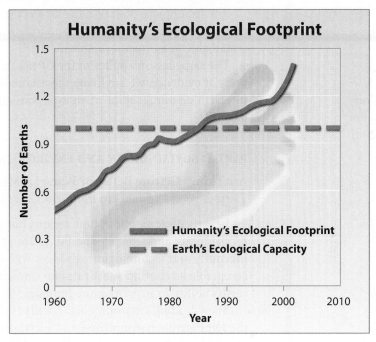

Figure 3

8 This leads us to search for workable solutions to these and other environmental problems. For example, one solution might be to stop cutting down diverse mature forests.

9 The search for solutions often involves conflicts, and resolving these conflicts requires us to make trade-offs, or compromises. To provide wood for making paper, for example, we can promote the planting of tree plantations in areas that have already been cleared or degraded.

10 In the search for solutions, individuals matter, whether they are working alone or in groups. For example, a scientist might find a way to make paper by using crop residues instead of cutting down trees. Or a group might work together to pass a law banning the clear-cutting of ancient forests while encouraging the planting of tree plantations in areas that have already been cleared or degraded. . . .

Environmentally Sustainable Societies: Protecting Natural Capital and Living Off Its Income

*An **environmentally sustainable society** meets the basic resource needs of its people in a just and equitable manner without degrading or depleting the natural capital that supplies these resources.*

11 The **ultimate** human goal on a path to sustainability or durability is an environmentally sustainable society—one that meets the current and future needs of its people for basic resources in a just and equitable manner without

compromising
a. promising
b. endangering

replenished
a. replaced
b. used often

squander
a. save
b. waste

accelerating
a. increasing
b. decreasing

ingenuity
a. stupidity
b. creativity

cite
a. mention
b. criticize

preserve
a. destroy
b. save

compromising the ability of future generations to meet their needs. Living sustainably means living off natural income **replenished** by soils, plants, air, and water and not depleting or degrading the earth's natural capital that supplies this income.

12   Imagine you win a million dollars in a lottery. If you invest this money and earn 10% interest per year, you will have a sustainable annual income of $100,000 without depleting your capital. If you spend $200,000 per year, your $1 million will be gone early in the seventh year. Even if you spend only $110,000 per year, you will be bankrupt early in the eighteenth year.

13   The lesson here is an old one: Protect your capital and live off the income it provides. Deplete, waste, or **squander** your capital, and you will move from a sustainable to an unsustainable lifestyle.

14   The same lesson applies to the earth's natural capital. According to a growing body of evidence, we are living unsustainably by wasting, depleting, and degrading the earth's natural capital at an exponentially **accelerating** rate (see Figure 3 on page 191).

PART 2: SUSTAINBILITY AND ENVIRONMENTAL WORLDVIEWS

Are Things Getting Better or Worse? A Millennium Assessment
There is good and bad environmental news.

15   Experts disagree about how serious our population and environmental problems are and what we should do about them. Some suggest that human **ingenuity** and technological advances will allow us to clean up pollution to acceptable levels, find substitutes for any scarce resources, and keep expanding the earth's ability to support more humans.

16   Many leading environmental scientists disagree. They appreciate and applaud the significant environmental and social progress that we have made, but they also **cite** evidence that we are degrading and disrupting the earth's life-support systems in many parts of the world at an exponentially accelerating rate. They call for much more action to protect the natural capital that supports our economies and all life.

17   According to environmental expert Lester R. Brown, "We are entering a new world, one where the collisions between our demands and the earth's capacity to satisfy them are becoming daily events. Our global economy is outgrowing the capacity of the earth to support it. No economy, however technologically advanced, can survive the collapse of its environmental support systems."

18   In 2005, the UN's *Millennium Ecosystem Assessment* was released. According to this four-year study by 1,360 experts from 95 countries, human activities are degrading or using unsustainably about 60% of the world's free natural services that sustain life on the earth. In other words, we are living unsustainably.

19   This pioneering comprehensive examination of the health of the world's life-support systems is also a story of hope. It says we have the tools to **preserve** the planet's natural capital by 2050 and describes common sense strategies for doing this.

20   The most useful answer to the question of whether things are getting better or worse is *both*. Some things are getting better and some are getting worse.

21   Our challenge is to not get trapped into confusion and inaction by listening primarily to either of two groups of people. Technological optimists tend to overstate the situation by telling us to be happy and not to worry, because technological innovations and conventional economic growth and development

will lead to a wonder world for everyone. In contrast, environmental **pessimists** overstate the problems to the point where our environmental situation seems hopeless. The noted conservationist Aldo Leopold argued, "I have no hope for a conservation based on fear."

22   Many environmental scientists and leaders believe that we must and can make a **shift** toward a more sustainable economy and civilization during your lifetime. In 2006, Lester Brown said, "Sustaining our current global civilization now depends on shifting to a renewable energy-based and a reuse/recycle economy with a diversified transport system, employing a sustainable mix of light rails,[1] buses, bicycles, and cars. Making this transition requires (1) restructuring the global economy so that it can sustain civilization, (2) an all-out effort to **eradicate** poverty, stabilize population, and restore hope, and (3) a systematic effort to restore natural systems. With each wind farm, rooftop solar panel, paper recycling facility, bicycle path, and reforestation program, we move closer to an economy that can sustain economic progress."

Environmental Worldviews and Ethics
The way we view the seriousness of environmental problems and how to solve them depends on our environmental worldview and our environmental ethics.

23   Differing views about the seriousness of our environmental problems and what we should do about them arise mostly out of differing environmental worldviews and environmental ethics. Your environmental worldview is a set of assumptions and values about how you think the world works and what you think your role in the world should be. Environmental ethics is concerned with your beliefs about what is right and wrong with how we treat the environment.

24   . . . People with widely differing environmental worldviews and ethical and cultural beliefs can take the same data, be logically consistent, and arrive at quite different conclusions because they start with different assumptions and moral principles or values. . . .

25   Some people in today's industrial consumer societies have a **planetary management worldview**. This view holds that we are separate from nature, that nature exists mainly to meet our needs and increasing wants, and that we can use our ingenuity and technology to manage the earth's life-support systems, mostly for our benefit. It assumes that economic growth is unlimited.

26   A second environmental worldview, known as the **stewardship worldview**, holds that we can manage the earth for our benefit but that we have an ethical responsibility to be caring and responsible managers, or stewards, of the earth. It says we should encourage environmentally beneficial forms of economic growth and discourage environmentally harmful forms.

27   Another worldview is the **environmental wisdom worldview**. It holds that we are part of and totally dependent on nature and that nature exists for all species, not just for us. It also calls for encouraging earth-sustaining forms of economic growth and development and discouraging earth-degrading forms. According to this view, our success depends on learning how the earth sustains itself and integrating such environmental **wisdom** into the ways we think and act. . . .

28   . . . Using the four scientific principles of sustainability to guide our lifestyles and economies could result in an environmental revolution during your lifetime. Figure 4 lists some of the shifts involved in bringing about this new cultural revolution.

(continued)

---

[1]**light rails** *urban rail public transportation that generally has lower capacity and lower speed than heavy rail and metro systems*

witness

a. see

b. invent

29 Scientific evidence indicates that we have perhaps 50 years and no more than 100 years to make such a cultural change. You will **witness** a historical fork in the road[2] at which point we will choose a path toward sustainability or continue on our current unsustainable course. Everything you do or don't do will play a role in which path we take.

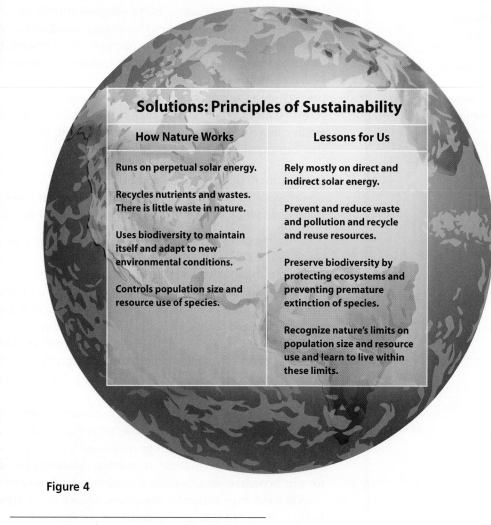

Solutions: Principles of Sustainability

How Nature Works	Lessons for Us
Runs on perpetual solar energy.	Rely mostly on direct and indirect solar energy.
Recycles nutrients and wastes. There is little waste in nature.	Prevent and reduce waste and pollution and recycle and reuse resources.
Uses biodiversity to maintain itself and adapt to new environmental conditions.	Preserve biodiversity by protecting ecosystems and preventing premature extinction of species.
Controls population size and resource use of species.	Recognize nature's limits on population size and resource use and learn to live within these limits.

Figure 4

_____

[2]**fork in the road** *place where the road divides into two parts*

COMPREHENSION CHECK

First Reading

PART 1

A. Complete the statements about the reading.

1. *Environment* is _____.

2. Everything we do, as living organisms _____.

3. *Environmental science* is a(an) _____ study that integrates information and ideas from both _____ sciences and _____ sciences.

4. The goal of environmental science is to:

   ____ a. learn about our relationship with our environment and how to live without destroying our life support system.

   ____ b. get governments to pass laws that protect the environment.

B. Check all of the answers that complete the statement correctly.

If the way we live is sustainable, it means that _____.

____ 1. we use our natural resources as we please

____ 2. we use renewable energy

____ 3. we cut down trees faster than nature can replace them

____ 4. we understand that uncontrolled population is impossible to support

____ 5. we replant forests when forests are cut down for wood or to make paper

____ 6. we preserve resources for future generations

____ 7. we can use anything we have enough money to buy

____ 8. the way individuals live can make a difference

PART 2

Answer the questions.

1. According to this textbook, are things getting better or worse?
2. What are three different ways of looking at our relationship with our environment?
3. How long do we have to change the way we live, according to this textbook?

Second Reading

Reread parts of the selection as needed to answer these questions. Mark the statements *T* (true) or *F* (false). Write the paragraph number(s) where you found evidence for each answer.

PART 1

1. T F Nature gives us resources and services that we could not live without. ¶____

2. T F The sun provides renewable energy including wind, the flow of water, and fuels from plants. ¶____

3. T F Earth's natural capital today is the same as it was millions of years ago. ¶____

4. T F Recent environmental changes are occurring at the same speed as they always have. ¶____

5. T F Solutions to environmental problems require compromises. ¶____

6. T F A sustainable society will deplete its natural capital. ¶____

7. T F There is more and more scientific evidence that societies today are depleting natural capital. ¶____

PART 2

1. T F Experts agree that human ingenuity will allow us to solve our environmental problems. ¶____

2. T F The UN's *Millennium Ecosystem Assessment* supports the view that we are living unsustainably. ¶____

3. T F The UN report offers no hope for solutions to our environmental problems. ¶____

4. T F Technological optimists and environmental pessimists both overstate their point of view in this discussion. ¶____

5. T F Humans are going to have to invest in restoring natural systems. ¶____

6. T F A person's environmental worldview is a set of ideas and values that the person assumes, that is believes, are true. ¶____

7. T F People with a stewardship worldview recognize that humans are an integral part of nature. ¶____

VOCABULARY

Vocabulary Building

Read the underlined word or expression in its context and match it with the correct meaning. Use a dictionary if necessary.

PART 1

____ 1. . . . increases in both the human population . . . and our resource consumption have <u>degraded</u> the air, water, soil, and species . . . (¶1)

____ 2. . . . how humans and their <u>institutions</u> interact with the natural world. (¶2)

____ 3. . . . made from plants and plant <u>residues</u> . . . (¶5)

____ 4. . . . resolving these conflicts . . . requires us to make trade-offs, or <u>compromises</u>. (¶9)

____ 5. Or a group might work together to pass a law <u>banning</u> the clear-cutting of ancient forests . . . (¶10)

____ 6. . . . without degrading or <u>depleting</u> the natural capital that supplies these resources. (third subhead)

____ 7. . . . you will be <u>bankrupt</u> early in the eighteenth year. (¶12)

a. reducing, using up too much of

b. agreements in which all sides accept less than what they want

c. unable to pay your debts

d. organizations, established systems

e. leftovers

f. lowered the quality of

g. saying that something must not be done, prohibiting

_____ 8. . . . and keep <u>expanding</u> the earth's ability to support more humans. (¶15)

_____ 9. ". . . a new world, one where the collisions between our <u>demands</u> and the earth's capacity to satisfy them . . . are becoming daily events. . . ." (¶17)

_____ 10. This pioneering <u>comprehensive</u> examination of the health of the world's life-support systems . . . (¶19)

_____ 11. . . . and a reuse/recycle economy with a <u>diversified</u> transport system . . . (¶22)

_____ 12. . . . an all-out effort to eradicate poverty, <u>stabilize</u> population, and restore hope, . . . (¶22)

_____ 13. Your environmental worldview is a set of <u>assumptions</u> and values . . . (¶23)

h. varied, with different types

i. stop from growing

j. things you think are true although you have no proof

k. complete, all-inclusive

l. needs or desires

m. making larger, increasing

Word Analysis

Recognizing parts of words can help you to:

- figure out the meaning of an unfamiliar word
- remember the meaning of words
- expand your vocabulary

These word parts will help you figure out what the words mean in the exercise on page 178.

inter- (Latin *between*) interact,* interdisciplinary,* international, intermarry, interface, interfaith, intermission

sub- (Latin *below*) subtheme,* submarine, subheading, subgroup, subhuman

equi/equa- (Latin *equal*) equitable,* equate, equation, equinox, equidistant

ultim- (Latin *last*) ultimate,* ultimatum

rupt- (Latin *break*) bankrupt,* disrupt,* erupt, interrupt

nov- (Latin *new*) innovate/innovations,* novice, novel (adj), novelty, renovate

*These words are in the reading selection.

Work with a partner. Analyze the underlined words and explain the meaning in your own words.

1. a. . . . how we <u>interact</u> with the earth . . . (1st subhead)

   b. . . . environmental science: an <u>interdisciplinary</u> study . . . (¶2)

   c. I attended an <u>interfaith</u> meeting of people who are interested in the environment.

2. a. Sustainability, or durability, is built on the <u>subthemes</u> of natural capital, natural capital degradation . . . (2nd subhead)

   b. The navy officers took us on a tour of their <u>submarine</u>.

3. a. An environmentally sustainable society meets the basic resource needs of its people in a just and <u>equitable</u> manner . . . (3rd subhead)

   b. We should not <u>equate</u> having more things with being happy.

   c. Our house is <u>equidistant</u> from my husband's and my work.

4. a. The <u>ultimate</u> human goal on a path to sustainability or durability is . . . (¶11)

   b. I gave my kids an <u>ultimatum</u>. Help me clean this house or I won't have time to drive you anywhere.

5. a. . . . you will be <u>bankrupt</u> early in the eighteenth year. (¶12)

   b. . . . we are degrading and <u>disrupting</u> the earth's life-support systems . . . (¶16)

   c. Please don't <u>interrupt</u> while I am speaking.

6. a. . . . technological <u>innovations</u> and conventional economic growth and development will lead to a wonder world for everyone. (¶21)

   b. I'm really a <u>novice</u> when it comes to using computers. My kids know more than I do.

   c. Well, that's a <u>novel</u> idea. I've never heard that one before.

Vocabulary Review

Complete the following statements about the reading selection with the correct words from the list below. Use each word only once.

PART 1

banning	indefinitely	rate
compromises	squander	replenish

1. Humans are using renewable resources faster than nature can

   _____ them and accelerating the natural

   _____ of change. If we want to live sustainably, we

   cannot _____ natural capital to satisfy our immediate

   wants.

2. As we search for solutions to environmental problems, we will have to resolve conflicts and make trade-offs, or _____.

3. Individuals, working alone or in groups, will decide our future. We will find some solutions in technological innovations, but we will probably have to make laws _____ some practices that waste and destroy our natural capital.

4. If we use our natural resources wisely, life on Earth can survive and adapt to changing environmental conditions _____.

PART 2

depleting	innovations	stabilize	wisdom
ingenuity	preserve	unsustainably	witness

1. Optimists say that human _____ and technological _____ will allow us to clean up pollution, find substitutes for scarce resources, and expand the earth's ability to support more humans.

2. Environmental experts and the *UN's Millennium Ecosystem Assessment* disagree, saying that we are living _____. We are wasting, degrading, and _____ natural capital at a rate that is leading to the collapse of our environmental support systems.

3. However, the UN report contains hope. We have the tools to _____ civilization as we know it. One of the things we must do is _____ population growth and switch to renewable energy sources.

4. We must develop a worldview that is based on environmental _____, that sees humans as part of and totally dependent on nature.

5. If we do not want to _____ catastrophic effects, scientific evidence indicates that we have 50–100 years to solve our environmental problems.

Using an Analogy to Illustrate a Concept

> Teachers and textbook writers often explain complicated ideas with an analogy, that is with a comparison to something they think students will already understand. This reading explains the concept of living sustainably by comparing it to winning the lottery and how you handle the money you win.

Reread paragraphs 12–14 and answer the questions.

1. In this comparison, what is the environmental equivalent of the million dollars?
2. What is the environmental equivalent of spending $100,000 a year?
3. What is the environmental equivalent of spending more than $100,000 a year?
4. Complete this sentence in your own words referring to the lottery example:

   Living unsustainably is like _____.

RESPONDING TO READING

Discuss these questions.

1. What is your environmental worldview?

2. What difficulties will humans have in learning each of the lessons for sustainable living in Figure 4?

3. Why do scientists say we must control or stabilize the human population?

4. What signs do you see that we are at the fork in the road right now, that societies now realize that a change in the way we view our environment is essential? What signs do you see that we are not there yet?

ABOUT THE READING

"Islands of Green" was published in the *Utne Reader,* September–October 2005.

**BEFORE
YOU READ**

Thinking about the Topic

You know what the color green is, but that meaning has been broadened in recent years when people discuss environmental issues.

1. What does the expression to "go green" mean? What do you think a "green building" is? What do you think a "green city" is?
2. What kinds of activities do governments and businesses get involved in when they go green?

Previewing

Preview the selection appropriately. Then answer these questions.

1. In the title, what does *green* mean?
2. What do the boldfaced headings suggest the "islands" are?
3. What do you think this article is going to be about?

Before you read, turn to Comprehension Check, First Reading on page 183. Your purpose for the first reading is to answer those questions.

READ

Islands of Green *By Leif Utne*

glimpse
a. remember
b. look quickly at

contention
a. claim, idea
b. meeting

as a drain
a. as something positive
b. as something negative

1   The model green city of the future already exists, but you can't yet find it on a map. It remains in pieces, scattered in urban areas around the world. As novelist William Gibson quipped, "The future is already here. It's just not evenly distributed yet." If you want to **glimpse** the future of the sustainable city today, these projects are good places to start.

PORTLAND

2   According to data released in June, Portland, Oregon, is the first U.S. city to meet the Kyoto Protocol's[1] target of reducing carbon emissions to below 1990 levels by 2012, with seven years to spare. Contrary to President Bush's **contention** that "Kyoto would have wrecked our economy," Portland's leaders say the city has benefited from better public transit, lower energy costs, more green space, and valuable expertise in energy efficiency and green building that is helping local firms win business around the globe. "People have looked at it the wrong way, **as a drain**," Mayor Tom Potter told *The New York Times.* "Actually, it's something

[1]**Kyoto Protocol** *an international agreement to reduce greenhouse gas emissions, signed in 1997*

that attracts people," he said of the effort to lower emissions. "It's economical; it makes sense in dollars."

LOS ANGELES

3   This desert city that epitomizes car-dependent sprawl is dying of thirst under a layer of concrete. "The rainfall we lose to runoff could provide up to half the water Los Angeles needs," says Andy Lipkis, head of the group TreePeople, in the Canadian ethical business magazine *Corporate Knights* (Winter 2005). Lipkis is working with the Los Angeles County government to transform the city from a sea of impermeable pavement into a porous tree-lined sieve that naturally **captures**, treats, and reuses rainfall. New street drains empty into gravel pits[2] that recharge the water table and prevent flooding, while surface trees absorb floodwater, sequester carbon,[3] and beautify the city.

PITTSBURGH

4   Drawing on the region's Amish and [Pennsylvania] Dutch[4] agricultural heritage, this Rust Belt[5] metropolis puts every other U.S. city to shame in the category of local food systems, according to a recent ranking of America's greenest cities by the group SustainLane. The Burgh boasts seven farmers' markets,[6] all of which accept food stamps,[7] and a whopping 188 community gardens—one for every 3,000 inhabitants and almost four times as many as runner-up Seattle.

BOGOTÁ, COLOMBIA

5   "Anything you do to make a city more friendly to cars makes it less friendly to people," says Enrique Peñalosa, former mayor of Colombia's capital city. In office from 1998 to 2001, Peñalosa led a massive effort to transform Bogota's infrastructure, including restricting car travel; building numerous parks, bikeways, and pedestrian zones; and creating a high-tech bus rapid transit (BRT) system. Inspired by the BRT in Curitiba, Brazil, Bogota's BRT cost one-twentieth of an equivalent light rail system. Peñalosa and the city used the savings to build new schools and libraries and extended the transit system into poorer **outlying** areas. In 2000, voters approved referenda declaring an annual car-free day and a ban on all private car traffic during rush hour by 2015.

RIO DE JANEIRO, BRAZIL

6   Built around a **cluster** of forested hills too steep to develop, the city of Rio contains Tijuca National Park, a remarkably well preserved **tract** of rainforest that is rich in wildlife—richer, in fact, than anything within many miles of the city. Now the city government is working with the state and landowners to create wildlife corridors to bring some of the city's biodiversity back out into the surrounding countryside.

GRONINGEN, NETHERLANDS

7   The Netherlands has done more than any country to promote car-free zones in its cities and towns. Every Dutch city of over 50,000 people has a car-free shopping district, all new towns must incorporate amenities for pedestrians and cyclists, and employers must locate new facilities near transit stops. But the closest thing to a

---

captures
a. catches
b. loses

outlying
a. in the city center
b. outside the city center

cluster
a. river
b. group

tract
a. piece
b. railroad

---

[2]**gravel** *small rocks which filter water*
[3]**sequester carbon** *capture carbon; trees and other plants use carbon in the process of photosynthesis*
[4]**Amish and [Pennsylvania] Dutch** *18th century immigrants to Pennsylvania who lived simple, agricultural lives. Dutch is a mispronunciation of Deutsch (German).*
[5]**Rust Belt** *area including U.S. states Ohio, Michigan, and Pennsylvania, where there was once a lot of heavy industry, which disappeared in the 1960s, 1970s, and 1980s, leaving old machinery to rust in the moist northern climate*
[6]**farmers' market** *central place where farmers bring their produce to sell directly to the public*
[7]**food stamps** *US government program, now call Supplemental Nutritional Assistance Program (SNAP) that helps low-income people and families buy the food they need for good health*

car-free utopia[8] is the university town of Groningen, reports Jay Walljasper in *E Magazine* (March/April 2005). The city leads the way with 47 percent of all urban trips made by bike, 26 percent on foot, and just 23 percent by car.

JOHANNESBURG, SOUTH AFRICA AND PEABODY, ENGLAND

8 If everyone lived the way Americans do, we'd need a total of five Earths to sustain ourselves. In an effort to reduce humanity's ecological footprint, the British-based One Planet Living project is promoting large-scale residential developments around the globe that allow residents to use only their fair share of Earth's resources. **Demonstration** OPL projects have been completed in Ivory Park Township, near Johannesburg, South Africa, and Peabody, England—home of the Beddington Zero-Energy Development (BedZED), the world's largest sustainable housing project.

CHINA'S NEW CITIES

9 Already home to one-sixth of humanity, China is planning to build housing for 400 million people in the next 12 years. This will require raising a slew of new cities from scratch, and pioneering green architect William McDonough is helping the Chinese government to design seven of them. In a *Newsweek* interview (May 16, 2005), he explains how to compensate for farmland lost to urbanization, "we'll move farms onto rooftops. . . . The farmers can live downstairs. And when you look at the city from a distance, it will look like part of the landscape."

demonstration
a. model, exemplary
b. old, out-of-date

---

[8]**utopia** *an imaginary, perfect world*

COMPREHENSION CHECK

First Reading

Answer these questions.

1. What changes has Portland made? What surprising result occurred?
2. What was L.A. losing that it couldn't afford to lose? Why was it losing it? What solution has been found?
3. In what area is Pittsburgh a leader?
4. In what area is Bogotá a leader?
5. What is there in the center of Rio de Janeiro that you would not expect in a big city? How do city and state governments plan to use this to benefit areas outside the city?
6. What is Groningen doing that is similar to what Bogotá is doing?
7. What type of project are the cities of Johannesburg, South Africa and Peabody, England, working on?
8. In what area does China have a huge need? What is one solution they are considering?

Second Reading

Read each statement. If it is a reasonable inference, circle *R*; if unreasonable, circle *U*. Write any evidence you can find for your choice on the line. For some items, the inference could be either reasonable or unreasonable.

1. (R) U Most cities in the world are not going green.

   An article with examples of green projects in only a few cities

   suggests that most cities are not going green yet.

2. R U The city government of Portland has some independent thinkers and risk-takers in it.

   _____

   _____

3. R U At some times of the year, Los Angeles gets rain.

   _____

   _____

4. R U Los Angeles has excellent mass transit to serve its large area.

   _____

   _____

5. R U Pittsburgh is in a desert.

   _____

   _____

6. R U The people of Bogotá agree with what Mayor Peñalosa accomplished.

   _____

   _____

7. R U Groningen has a good mass transit system.

   _____

   _____

8. R U New ideas for housing can do a lot to reduce humanity's ecological footprint.

   _____

   _____

9. R U China's existing cities are, on average, very large.

   _____

   _____

Vocabulary Building

Read the underlined word or expression in its context and match it with the correct meaning. Use a dictionary if necessary.

PART 1

_____ 1. It [The green city] remains in pieces, <u>scattered</u> in urban areas around the world (¶1)

_____ 2. ... "Kyoto would have <u>wrecked</u> our economy ..." (¶2)

_____ 3. This desert city that <u>epitomizes</u> car-dependent sprawl ... (¶3)

_____ 4. This desert city that epitomizes car-dependent <u>sprawl</u> ... (¶3)

_____ 5. Lipkis is working ... to transform the city from a sea of <u>impermeable</u> pavement ... (¶3)

_____ 6. ... to transform the city ... into a <u>porous</u> tree-lined sieve ... (¶3)

a. surfaces (concrete, asphalt) that water cannot go through

b. development spread out over a large area

c. having holes so water can go through

d. destroyed

e. spread over a wide area, in an irregular way

f. is the perfect example of

PART 2

_____ 7. ... to transform the city ... into a porous tree-lined <u>sieve</u> ... (¶3)

_____ 8. New street <u>drains</u> empty into gravel pits ... (¶3)

_____ 9. The Burgh <u>boasts</u> seven farmers' markets ... (¶4)

_____ 10. ... Peñalosa led a massive effort to transform Bogota's <u>infrastructure</u> ... (¶5)

_____ 11. ... all new towns must incorporate <u>amenities</u> for pedestrians and cyclists ... (¶7)

_____ 12. ... he explains how, to <u>compensate</u> for farmland lost to urbanization ... (¶9)

g. attractive, useful facilities

h. the basic systems of a country or city such as roads, sewers, and communications

i. kitchen equipment with holes that water goes through, a strainer

j. reduce or balance the bad effect of something

k. has something very good, has something to be proud of

l. pipes or holes that waste water flows into

Multiword Expressions

For each definition, scan the paragraph and find an equivalent multiword expression and write it on the line.

1. time before something had to happen (¶2) _____

2. all over the world (¶2, 8) _____

3. is reasonable, is intelligent (¶2) _____

(continued)

4. be really thirsty, not have enough water (¶3) _____

5. be so much better than someone or something else; make another look bad or ordinary (¶4) _____

6. the one who places second in a competition (¶4) _____

7. areas where people walk, no cars are permitted (¶5) _____

8. time when there is a lot of traffic and streets are crowded (¶5)

    _____

9. is first in something (¶7) _____

10. one's just or rightful part (¶8) _____

11. many (¶9) _____

12. from the beginning (¶9) _____

Vocabulary Review

Complete the following statements about the reading selection with the correct words or expressions from the list below. Use each word only once.

amenities	fair share	pedestrian zones
capture	infrastructure	scattered
carbon emissions	makes sense	wreck

1. A truly green city does not yet exist, but there are cities
    _____ around the globe that can give us an idea of what a truly green city of the future will be like.

2. Cities of the future will be less friendly to cars and more friendly to people; they will have _____, bike trails, and other
    _____.

3. If Portland, Oregon, is any example, reducing _____ by having more buses and fewer cars will not _____ the economy; on the contrary it will help improve it.

4. Desert cities like Los Angeles can _____ rainwater and recycle it.

5. Cities will need to invest in _____, especially in good mass transit systems like those in Bogotá, Colombia and Groningen, the Netherlands.

6. We are going to have to build housing that allows people to live comfortably without using more than their _____ of the world's resources.

7. When we begin new projects from scratch, it _____ to plan them so they are truly green.

TEXT ANALYSIS

Applying Knowledge of Text Organization, Format, and Writer's Purpose

Answer the questions.

1. In what ways is the organization of this article different from IBC organization?
2. What do you notice about the format of the main part of this article?
3. What do you think the author's purpose in writing this article was? What is the relationship between his purpose and the format?
4. What is the article's main idea? Where is it expressed?

RESPONDING TO READING

Discuss these questions.

1. Which of the ideas you read about in this article seem easier to implement, that is, more likely to be done, on a large scale? Explain what makes the ideas easier or more difficult to implement.

2. Which ideas appeal to you the most and the least? Why?

3. What innovations might make your city or area a greener place?

There are two selections in this chapter. The first, "Think You Can Be a Meat-Eating Environmentalist? Think Again!" is a flyer from People for the Ethical Treatment of Animals (PETA), an animal rights organization. The second, "It's a Plastic World" is from the book, *50 Simple Things You Can Do to Save the Earth*, published in 2008.

BEFORE YOU READ

Thinking about the Topic

Discuss these questions.

1. What are some things individuals can do to live more sustainably? Are these things easy or difficult to do? Are most people willing to change?
2. Where does the meat you buy in a store come from? What is a vegetarian? What does eating meat have to do with the environment?
3. What are the most common uses of plastics that you are familiar with? What happens to the plastic we throw away?

Previewing

Preview both selections appropriately. Then answer these questions.

1. What do these two selections have in common?
2. Which one seems more surprising to you?

Choose Part 1 or Part 2. Before you read, turn to Comprehension Check, First Reading on pages 191–192. Your purpose for the first reading is to answer those questions.

READ

Part 1: Think You Can Be a Meat-Eating Environmentalist? Think Again!

If you care about the planet, go vegetarian.

"If anyone wants to save the planet, all they have to do is stop eating meat. That's the single most important thing you can do." —*Sir Paul McCartney*

"[The meat industry is] one of the top two or three most significant contributors to the most serious environmental problems, at every **scale** from local to global." —*The United Nations*

scale
a. level
b. weight

Did You Know?

1   *Global Warming:* A 2006 U.N. report found that the meat industry is responsible for more greenhouse-gas emissions than all the cars, trucks, planes, and ships in the world combined. Researchers at the University of Chicago have determined that going vegetarian is more effective in countering global warming than switching from a standard American car to a hybrid.

2   *Pollution:* Animals raised for food in the U.S. produce 130 times more excrement[1] than the entire human population of the U.S.! According to the Environmental Protection Agency, the runoff from factory farms[2] pollutes our rivers and lakes more than all other industrial sources combined.

3   *Land Use:* More than 260 million acres[3] of U.S. forest have been cleared for grazing and for growing grain to feed farmed animals. More than 90 percent of all Amazon rainforest land cleared since 1970 is used for meat production. Many times more land is required to feed a meat-eater than a vegetarian.

4   *Water Use:* Livestock production accounts for half of all water used in the U.S. A vegetarian uses only 300 gallons of water per day, while a meat-eater uses more than 4,000.

5   *Energy Use:* The meat industry uses more than one-third of all the fossil fuels consumed in the U.S.

6   *Oceans:* Commercial fishing nets often scrape the ocean floor clear of all life and destroy coral reefs; they also kill porpoises,[4] birds, sea lions,[5] and other "bycatch"[6] animals. Coastal fish farms release massive amounts of feces, antibiotics,[7] parasites,[8] and **non-native** fish into sensitive **marine** ecosystems.

7   *Animals:* Chickens, pigs, turkeys, fish, and cows are intelligent, social animals who feel pain, just as humans, dogs, and cats do. More than 27 billion animals are mutilated, confined, and killed in ways that would horrify any compassionate person.

8   You can find great-tasting, protein-packed vegetarian foods—like veggie burgers, meatless barbecue ribs, and mock chicken—at practically any grocery store. Considering the proven health benefits of a vegetarian diet (the American Dietetic Association states that vegetarians have a reduced risk of obesity, heart disease, and various types of cancer), there's no excuse for eating meat.

non-native
a. normal to the area
b. not normal to the area

marine
a. military
b. related to oceans

---

[1]**excrement (and feces in ¶6)** *solid waste from animals and humans, a source of methane (CH$_4$), a greenhouse gas that contributes to global warming*

[2]**factory farms** *agribusiness has converted traditional farms to Concentrated Animal Feeding Operations (CAFO) where animals are strictly confined and deprived of their natural lifestyle*

[3]**acre** *a unit for measuring land area, 4,840 square yards (approx 4,047 square meters)*

[4]**porpoises** *(see top picture at right)*

[5]**sea lions** *(see bottom picture at right)*

[6]**bycatch** *species that are caught incidentally along with targeted species; they are usually thrown away*

[7]**antibiotics** *drugs used to kill bacteria and cure infections*

[8]**parasites** *plants or animals that live in or on other plants or animals and get food and protection from them without giving anything to their hosts*

Part 2: It's a Plastic World

By John Javna, Sophie Javna, and Jesse Javna

Americans throw away 2.5 million plastic bottles every hour.

practically
a. almost
b. hopefully

miracle
a. wonderful
b. natural

concept
a. food
b. idea

1 **BACKGROUND**

Take a look around your home and try counting the things made of plastic. It could take you all day—plastic is used in **practically** everything we buy.

2 Plastic is a **miracle** material, but it has serious environmental drawbacks: It's made of nonrenewable fossil fuels; manufacturing it creates pollution and toxic waste; and it's not biodegradable. On top of that, we throw most of it away.

3 Clearly, we need to cut down on "disposable" plastic. But we also need to change the way plastic is made, and the materials it's made from. That's why people are working on *bioplastic,* which is biodegradable, compostable, made from renewable and sustainably harvested materials . . . and works as well as "normal" plastic.

4 **DID YOU KNOW?**

- "Bioplastic—plastic made from plants instead of fossil fuels—isn't a new **concept.** The very first synthesized plastic, created in 1845, was a cotton-derived material called *celluloid.* By the 1870s, it was used widely for dental plates, combs, and toothbrushes.
- Today, manufacturers make an estimated 200 million tons of plastic a year. Less than 3.5% is recycled . . . which means that every year, we add 193 million tons of plastic to the world—permanently. About 25% of our landfill space is taken up by plastics.
- Not all of the plastic winds up in landfills. In a part of the Pacific Ocean known informally as the *Pacific Garbage Vortex,* there's a bigger mass of plastic than there is of plankton.[1]
- Consumer alert: Bioplastic isn't automatically good for the environment just because it's made from plants. Some bioplastic is made from GE[2] crops, some doesn't biodegrade, and some has toxic additives; some interferes with recycling and some contains engineered nanoparticles, particles so small they can pass in and out of our cells. It takes some research to tell the difference.

5 **WHAT YOU CAN DO**

Your Partner: The Institute for Local Self-Reliance has been "working to strengthen communities through the smart utilization of local resources" since 1974. One current focus: creating sustainable bioplastics. Get acquainted: *ilsr.org* and *sustainableplastics.org*

Your Goal: Cut down on disposable plastics and help make sustainable bioplastics a viable alternative.

6 **Start Simple**

- "Choose durability over single-use disposable plastics," says Brenda Platt of ILSR. "Can you use a travel mug instead of a polystyrene cup, reusable shopping bags instead of plastic or paper? After we reduce consumption, we can move on to choosing better materials."
- So . . . pick a few disposable plastic items you use, and dispose of them—permanently. For suggestions: *50 simplethings.com/plastic*

---

[1]**plankton** *drifting organisms in bodies of water, important food supply for aquatic life*
[2]**GE** *genetically engineered*

7 **Steps for Success**

    Step 1: Become a plastics expert. Read about the different polymers in the *Plastics Guide* you'll find at *50simplethings.com/plastic.* And read about bioplastics at ILSR's *sustainableplastics.org*

    Step 2: Spread the word. Let's assume the world isn't going to quit using disposable plastic items **overnight**. One way to get the word out is to substitute new bioplastics for the worst of the fossil-fuel-based stuff. Get your PTA[3] or congregation[4] to switch to potato- or corn-based compostable forks, spoons, and cups to replace polystyrene.

    Step 3: Lobby businesses and institutions to switch their takeout containers and utensils to compostable natural fibers. Start with sympathetic people: natural food stores, green restaurants, coffee shops. Then target local schools, public events, and festivals.

    Step 4: Start composting. Compostable plastics don't make sense unless they're composted. When they're landfilled, they give off methane, a powerful greenhouse gas.

    Step 5: For the ambitious: Get the most harmful and wasteful plastics banned locally. Oakland, San Francisco, and two dozen other cities are already banning polystyrene takeout containers and encouraging the use of alternatives. Push your local government to do the same. Get more info at *50simplethings.com/plastic*

---

overnight
a. immediately
b. during the night

> *Interesting Facts*
>
> - It's estimated that every three years, the amount of plastic in the ocean doubles.
> - According to the *Wall Street Journal:* Americans use 100 billion plastic shopping bags each year.

---

[3]**PTA** *Parent Teacher Association*
[4]**congregation** *group of people who go to the same church, synagogue, or mosque*

COMPREHENSION CHECK

First Reading

Reread parts of the selection as needed. Circle *T* (true) or *F* (false). Write the paragraph number(s) where you found evidence for each answer.

PART 1

1. T F Raising animals for food contributes to global warming. ¶___

2. T F In the United States, farm animals create more waste than humans. ¶___

3. T F Other industries are responsible for more water pollution than the meat industry. ¶___

4. T F It takes more land to produce meat than to grow plants for food. ¶___

5. T F Meat eaters are responsible for much more consumption of water than vegetarians. ¶___

6. T F Unlike raising meat, raising fish does not pollute the environment. ¶___

(continued)

7. T F Animals are not sentient beings, so it doesn't matter how we treat them ¶___

8. T F Vegetarians have a higher risk of heart disease than meat eaters. ¶___

PART 2

1. T F Bioplastic is a recent invention. ¶___

2. T F Very little plastic is recycled. ¶___

3. T F Not all plastic that is thrown away goes to garbage dumps; a lot goes into the ocean. ¶___

4. T F All bioplastic is biodegradable and compostable. ¶___

5. T F The authors recommend that we reduce our use of disposable plastic products and influence others to do the same. ¶___

6. T F Even compostable plastics can be a source of greenhouse gases if they are not composted. ¶___

7. T F The ultimate goal is to get the fossil-fuel-based plastics banned and use only sustainable bioplastics. ¶___

Second Reading

Read each statement. If it is a reasonable inference, circle *R*; if unreasonable, circle *U*. Jot down on a separate piece of paper any evidence you can find to support your choice. For some items, the inference could be either reasonable or unreasonable.

PART 1

1. R U Paul McCartney is a vegetarian.

2. R U Meat production today is not a sustainable process.

3. R U The pollution caused by factory farms is local.

4. R U It is not economical to grow grain to feed animals to produce meat for people.

5. R U The author would recommend eating fish because it is healthy.

6. R U Porpoises and sea lions are hunted by humans for food.

7. R U Shipping meat within a country consumes fossil fuel and contributes to global warming.

8. R U A significant number of people are eating vegetarian substitutes for meat.

PART 2

1. R U People are recycling enough plastic to make a real difference.

2. R U The authors would recommend drinking bottled water.

3. R U Polystyrene is among the bad plastics.

4. R U The authors would be likely to eat in fast-food restaurants.

5. R U The authors would favor the government playing a role in regulating the types of plastic that may or may not be used.

6. R U Composting biodegradable plastic is preferable to putting it in a landfill.

Vocabulary Building

Read the underlined word or expression in its context and match it with the correct meaning. Use a dictionary if necessary.

VOCABULARY

PART 1

_____ 1. . . . the meat industry is responsible for more greenhouse-gas <u>emissions</u> than all cars, trucks, planes, and ships in the world combined. (¶1)

_____ 2. . . . going vegetarian is more effective in <u>countering</u> global warming than switching from a standard American car to a hybrid. (¶1)

_____ 3. More than 260 million acres . . . have been cleared for <u>grazing</u> and for growing grain to feed farmed animals. (¶3)

_____ 4. <u>Livestock</u> production accounts for half of all water used in the U.S. (¶4)

_____ 5. Commercial fishing nets often <u>scrape</u> the ocean floor <u>clear of</u> all life and destroy coral reefs . . . (¶6)

_____ 6. More than 27 billion animals are <u>mutilated</u> . . .every year (¶7)

_____ 7. . . . killed in <u>horrible</u> ways . . . (¶7)

_____ 8. . . . <u>mock</u> chicken . . . . (¶8)

a. severely and violently hurt or damaged

b. farm animals

c. terrible, frightening, upsetting

d. reducing the bad effects of

e. not real, imitation

f. animals eating grass

g. substances sent out into the air

h. remove

PART 2

_____ 1. . . . it [plastic] has serious environmental <u>drawbacks</u> . . . (¶2)

_____ 2. . . . we need to <u>cut down on</u> "disposable" plastic. (¶3)

_____ 3. . . . we need to cut down on "<u>disposable</u>" plastic. (¶3)

_____ 4. . . . bioplastic, which is . . . made from renewable and sustainably <u>harvested</u> materials . . . (¶3)

_____ 5. About 25% of our landfill space is <u>taken up</u> by plastics. (¶4)

_____ 6. Not all of the plastic <u>winds up in</u> landfills. (¶4)

_____ 7. Bioplastic isn't <u>automatically</u> good for the environment . . . (¶4)

_____ 8. . . . help make sustainable bioplastics a <u>viable</u> alternative. (¶5)

_____ 9. "Choose <u>durability</u> over single-use disposable plastics" . . . (¶6)

_____ 10. Then <u>target</u> local schools . . . (¶7)

a. aim at, direct message to

b. certain to be

c. filled, occupied

d. quality that makes something last for a long time

e. intended to be used once and thrown away

f. workable

g. reduce the use of

h. goes to, ends up in

i. disadvantages

j. gathered, collected

Vocabulary Review

Complete the following statements about the reading selection with the correct word or expression from the list below. Use each word or expression only once.

PART 1

counter	horrible	marine
emissions	livestock	scale

1. Human consumption of meat and fish is not an efficient use of our natural capital for several reasons. Raising both _____ and fish contributes to environmental problems.

2. Methane _____ from animal waste contribute more to global warming than all the vehicles in the world!

3. Coastal fish farms are also bad for the environment and seriously damage _____ ecosystems.

4. Furthermore, there is an ethical problem. Animals in factory farms are deprived of a normal lifestyle by being confined in small spaces. They are also killed in _____ ways that would upset a compassionate person.

5. People who reduce their consumption of meat and fish will help
_____ global warming and other damage to the
environment, showing that each person, on a small _____,
can help save the planet.

PART 2

concept	drawbacks	overnight
cut down on	durability	wind up
disposable		

1. Plastic is very useful, but if it is not biodegradable, it has serious
_____.

2. First of all, plastic is meant to be _____, so lots of it is
thrown away.

3. In addition, because of its _____, it lasts a long time,
taking up space in landfills and polluting the oceans.

4. Some plastics are recyclable, but not everyone has caught on to the
_____ of recycling, and tons of plastic
_____ in landfills.

5. The solution has at least two parts: _____ the amount of
plastic we use, and switch or convert to biodegradable, compostable
bioplastics.

6. The problem won't be solved _____, but individuals have
an important role in bringing about change.

TEXT ANALYSIS   *Lists*

Answer these questions about lists.

1. What kinds of lists do you find in these selections? How are they formatted?
   How are they ordered?
2. Why do you suppose writers use lists?
3. Do you prefer lists to paragraphs? Why or why not?
4. Which of the two selections uses lists more effectively? Explain.

RESPONDING TO READING   **Discuss these questions.**

1. Which of the changes suggested in these readings have you already made or
   would you be willing to make? Why or why not?

2. If you were to write a similar reading, what other environmental problems
   would you write about? What suggestions would you make for ways that
   individuals can lessen their footprints?

3. What are some problems with getting humans to make the necessary changes
   to reduce their negative impact on the environment?

CHAPTER 24

"Prayer for the Great Family" appeared in *Turtle Island,* the collection that won the Pulitzer Prize for poetry in 1975. The poem is based on a Native American prayer from the Mohawk tribe. Gary Snyder is one of the most important American poets of the second half of the twentieth century. A strong connection with nature during his childhood in the Pacific Northwest developed into his interest in Native Americans, Buddhism, and environmental activism.

BEFORE YOU READ

Thinking about the Topic

Discuss these questions.

1. What is the purpose of prayers?
2. Who might the Great Family be? What kind of prayer could this be?

READ

Prayer for the Great Family

By Gary Snyder

1   Gratitude[1] to Mother Earth, sailing through night and day—
and to her soil: rich, rare, and sweet
in our minds so be it.[2]

2   Gratitude to Plants, the sun-facing light-changing leaf
and fine root-hairs; standing still through wind
and rain; their dance is in the flowing spiral grain
in our minds so be it.

3   Gratitude to Air, bearing the soaring Swift[3] and the silent
Owl[4] at dawn.[5] Breath of our song
clear spirit breeze[6]
in our minds so be it.

4   Gratitude to Wild Beings, our brothers, teaching secrets,
freedoms, and ways; who share with us their milk;
self-complete, brave, and aware
in our minds so be it.

5   Gratitude to Water: clouds, lakes, rivers, glaciers;[7]
holding or releasing; streaming through all
our bodies salty seas
in our minds so be it.

---

[1] **gratitude** *thanks*
[2] **so be it** *like amen, a typical ending for a prayer*
[3] **swift** *a type of bird, related to the hummingbird*
[4] **owl** *a bird that hunts at night*
[5] **dawn** *daybreak, the beginning of day when light first appears*
[6] **breeze** *gentle wind*
[7] **glaciers** *large masses of ice that move slowly over land*

6   Gratitude to the Sun: blinding pulsing[8] light through
     trunks of trees, through mists,[9] warming caves where
     bears and snakes sleep—he who wakes us—
     in our minds so be it.

7   Gratitude to the Great Sky
     who holds billions of stars—and goes yet beyond that—
     beyond all powers, and thoughts
     and yet is within us—
     Grandfather Space.
     The Mind is his Wife.
     so be it.

                    (after a Mohawk prayer)

_____

[8]**pulsing** *on and off, flickering*
[9]**mists** *air filled with drops of water*

COMPREHENSION CHECK

First Reading

Answer these questions.

1. What aspect of the environment is dealt with in each stanza?
2. What do you think Snyder means by "the Great Family"?

Second Reading

Read the poem at least one more time. Then answer the questions. Support your answers with evidence from the poem.

1. What details about nature does the poet mention? What images do they create? What senses, (sight, smell, taste, touch) do these images appeal to?
2. How does each stanza relate to "natural capital" as defined in Chapter 21?
3. What does Snyder suggest should be humans' attitude toward Mother Earth and the Great Sky?
4. What connection is suggested between humans and the Great Sky?

RESPONDING TO READING

Read the quotes* and discuss the questions.

"Instead of making the world safer for humankind, the foolish tinkering with the powers of life and death by the occidental scientist-engineer-ruler puts the whole planet on the brink of degradation."

" . . . there can be no health for humans and cities that bypasses the rest of nature."

1. What is the worldview of the occidental scientist-engineer-ruler referred to in the first quote?

*From *The Practice of the Wild* by Gary Snyder, pages 19 and 181, respectively.

2. Given the content of the poem and the quotes from Snyder's essays that follow it, which worldview do you think Snyder follows: the planetary management worldview, the stewardship worldview, or the environmental wisdom worldview? Explain.

3. Why do you think Snyder chose to express his ideas in the form of a prayer?

4. Go back and reread the quotes on the opening page of this unit (page 167). How is your reaction to them different from what it was before reading the selections in this unit?

5. How do you think Synder might interpret the quotes on the opening page of this unit?

UNIT WRAP-UP

Extending Your Vocabulary

Word Families

Study the chart below to learn other forms of some of the words in this unit. If a box is blank, either there is no word to fill it, or the word is missing because it is not one you need to know now.

	NOUNS	VERBS	ADJECTIVES	ADVERBS
1.	compensation	compensate	compensatory	—
2.	disposal	dispose	disposable	—
3.	diversity	diversify	diversified diverse	—
4.	durability	endure	durable	—
5.	gratitude	—	grateful	gratefully
6.	miracle	—	miraculous	miraculously
7.	pollution	pollute	polluted unpolluted	—
8.	sustainability	sustain	sustainable unsustainable	sustainably unsustainably
9.	wisdom	—	wise	wisely

For each item, look at the row in the chart above with the same number. Choose the word that correctly completes the sentence; be sure it is in the correct form.

1. Courts often award _____ for injuries people suffer on the job.

2. A lot of _____ diapers wind up in landfills.

3. It is important to preserve the _____ of life forms as well as cultures.

4. Plastic made from fossil fuels is _____; it is not biodegradable or compostable.

5. We should be _____ for all that nature has given us.

6. Mr. Chang was in a very serious car accident. It is a _____ that he survived.

7. Hopefully, _____ of our waterways will be eliminated and children in the future will be able to swim in _____ lakes and rivers.

8. Nature will _____ us if we use her gifts wisely.

9. Do you think it is a _____ decision to buy a hybrid car?

Polysemous Words

Read each sentence. Match the underlined word with the correct meaning. In some cases, you will use the same answer twice. An asterisk indicates a meaning that was used in this unit.

1. ___ "People have looked at it [the effort to lower emissions] the wrong way, as a drain.*"

   ___ New street drains* empty into gravel pits . . .

   ___ That purchase was a mistake. That was money down the drain.

   ___ Drain the spaghetti and run a little cold water on it.

   ___ Working six days a week drains all my energy.

   a. hole or pipe to catch water
   b. wasted, lost
   c. remove, take away
   d. something negative, a burden
   e. remove liquid from

2. ___ Runoff* from factory farms pollutes our waterways.

   ___ None of the candidates won the election, so there will be a runoff.

   a. second election
   b. water that flows over land into waterways

3. ___ Plastic takes up* a lot of space in landfills.

   ___ I don't want to take up too much of your time.

   ___ Let's take up this ugly carpet; I prefer the bare floor.

   ___ Nilda is planning to take up a new sport; she needs to do more exercise.

   a. remove
   b. occupy, use
   c. become interested in, start

(continued)

4. ___ . . . [a] sieve that naturally <u>treats</u>*
and reuses rainfall.

   ___ My parents <u>treat</u> me like a child.

   ___ Let me <u>treat</u> you to dinner.

   ___ How is the doctor <u>treating</u> your
condition?

   ___ Our boss <u>treats</u> us with respect.

a. deal with, behave towards

b. try to cure, give medical help

c. pay for someone else

d. cleans or processes

5. ___ The meat industry is one of the
<u>top</u>* . . . contributors . . .

   ___ [. . . plastic is not biodegradable.]
<u>On top of</u> that,* we throw most
of it away.

   ___ Our apartment is on the <u>top</u> floor
of the building.

   ___ He went to a <u>top</u> college.

   ___ Where's the <u>top</u> of the jar?

   ___ The children played with <u>tops</u> at
the party.

   ___ The table has a glass <u>top</u>.

a. one of the best

b. the lid, cover

c. the highest

d. the upper surface

e. in addititon to, what's more

f. a toy that spins

g. one of the largest

6. ___ A lot of plastic <u>winds up</u>* in
landfills and in the ocean.

   ___ We hope to <u>wind</u> the meeting <u>up</u>
by 5 P.M.

a. end an activity

b. go somewhere without
intending to, end up

WRITING

**Choose one of the suggestions for writing below. Talk about what you plan to
write with a classmate who chose the same topic. Then follow the instructions
for writing.**

Personal Writing

1. Individuals, alone or in a group, make a difference. Make a list of resolutions
or goals (things you can do) to help the environment. Write several paragraphs
about what you will do.

Academic Writing

2. Write about something that is being done to help the environment in your
area. What is being done? Where? What is the goal? How well is it working?

If you do not have knowledge of such a project, search for information by typing
the name of your town and the words "act locally" into an Internet search engine.
You might also want to put in the name of your state and the words "solutions
environmental problems."

Creative Writing

3. Prayers often use rhythm and repetition. Write a prayer-like poem that reflects your philosophy or view of something important.

Try to use some of the following vocabulary, as well as the words in the glossary, in writing about the topic you choose: *accelerate, ban, comprehensive, compromise, cut down on, deadline, disposable, diversify, dramatically, drawback, emissions, extinct, horrible, indefinitely, lobby, miracle, on top of that, overnight, preserve, rate, squander, stabilize, wisdom, witness.*

Glossary

biodegradable capable of being broken down by living organisms; things from plant or animal sources are biodegradable

biodiversity the number and variety of different plants, animals, and other living things in a particular place

bioplastic plastic made from renewable sources rather than petroleum; may lack water resistance and durability

carbon dioxide (CO_2) the most important greenhouse gas produced by human activities, primarily through the burning of fossil fuels

celluloid thermoplastic first created in 1856 (though first called *celluloid* in 1870); thermoplastics are flammable and decompose easily

compost aerobically decomposed organic matter that holds moisture and minerals and thus helps plants grow; **compostable** will decompose like plant matter

ecological footprint (also **carbon footprint**) amount of land and water needed 1) to supply a population with the renewable resources it uses and 2) to absorb or dispose of the wastes from use of such resources

ecosystem a community of living things interacting with each other and the environment in which they live

emissions gases, particles, and materials released or emitted into the environment, commonly from combustion or burning

footprint See Ecological footprint

fossil fuels mineral fuels from fossil sources; they are hydrocarbons found in the top layer of the Earth's crust and include coal, oil, natural gas, and methane; burning them emits carbon dioxide, a greenhouse gas

global warming the increase in the average temperature on Earth because of increases in greenhouse gases in the atmosphere, primarily because of human activities

green (a green city, green building, green architect) environmentally friendly, doing things in a way that is good for the environment

greenhouse gases gases in the atmosphere that block loss of heat into space and thus contribute to global warming; the most common are carbon dioxide (CO_2) and methane (CH_4)

hybrids cars that run on a combination of electricity and gasoline, reducing emissions and increasing gas mileage

landfill place where waste material is disposed of by burial; a garbage dump

methane (CH_4) a fossil fuel and greenhouse gas emitted by animal waste and decomposition of organic matter, as well as by defrosting permafrost

natural capital the natural resources and natural services that keep us and other species alive and support our economies; it is not fixed—in other words, we can degrade or destroy it or use it up

(continued)

permafrost soil that stays at or below the freezing point of water (0°C or 32°F) for two or more years

pollution unclean, unhealthy conditions in the environment caused by contaminants (e.g., air pollution, water pollution)

polymer a substance composed of molecules with repeating structural units connected by chemical bonds; plastics, DNA and proteins, shellac, nylon, PVC (polyvinyl chloride), and polystyrene are polymers

polystyrene a polymer made from a liquid hydrocarbon that is commercially manufactured from petroleum by the chemical industry

rainforest a forest characterized by heavy rainfall, on average 68–78 inches per year

resource anything obtained from the environment to meet our needs and wants; **perpetual resource** a resource that is renewed continuously—for example, solar energy, which is expected to last as long as the sun lasts (at least 6 billion years); **renewable resource** a resource that can be replenished fairly rapidly through natural processes as long as it is not used up faster than it is replaced—for example, forests, grasslands, wild animals, fresh water, fresh air, and fertile soil; **non-renewable resource** a resource that takes millions of years to form, such as petroleum

reuse using a resource over and over in the same form, for example, glass bottles can be collected, washed, and refilled many times; this takes less energy, fewer resources, and produces less pollution and environmental degradation than recycling

recycling collecting waste materials, processing them into new materials, and selling these new products (e.g., discarded aluminum cans can be crushed and melted to make new aluminum cans or other aluminum items that consumers can buy); this takes less energy, water, and other resources, and produces much less pollution and environmental degradation than making new aluminum products

runoff water that flows over land; may contain and/or pick up contaminants

sustainability the ability of Earth's various systems, including human cultural systems and economies, to survive and adapt to changing environmental conditions indefinitely

sustainable yield the highest rate at which a renewable resource can be used indefinitely without reducing its available supply

toxic waste poisonous material that is thrown away that can cause death or injury to living creatures

water table the level below the surface of the ground where there is water

wildlife corridor an area of habitat connecting wildlife populations separated by human activities

Word List

CHAPTER 1
blind with rage
broaden
depressed* (adj.)
disparity
enhance*
enliven
enrich
expose*
furthermore*
gratification
intensity*
intimate
intrusive
mentor (n.)
mutual* aid*
obligation
ongoing*
overweight
pinched (adj.)
reassurance
routinely intersect
silverware
unequal

CHAPTER 2
a lifetime's worth of
apologize
back out of
beat up
break up with
bulk*
bullying (n.)
cautious
core* (n.)
deny*
desperately
enlarge
fabulous
forever
gossip (n.)
hang out with
just as good as
keep in touch with
keep up (with)
link* (v.)
look over
outlet
pose* as
profile (n.)
quarrel (n.)
realm

take over
tremendous

CHAPTER 3
a good deal of
chances are
contradict*
critical
evoke
exposure*
folk wisdom
frankness
keep confidences
peer (n.)
physical* attractiveness
promote*
proximity
reciprocity
respondent*
sense of humor
similarity*
stem from
trait
verdict
virtually*

CHAPTER 4
all the way
amazed (adj.)
blush (v.)
delighted (adj.)
desperate haste
despise
frighten
funny
get along all right
know intimately
on the way home
scare (v.)
startled (adj.)
sullen
try (someone/something) out
utterly

CHAPTER 5
accomplish
authoritarian
authoritative*
bolster (v.)
burst (v.)
bursting (adj.)

cheer (v.)
chore
commute (v.)
devoted to (adj.)
disengaged (adj.)
eventually*
exhausted (adj.)
flatter
gaze out
hectic
hustle (v.)
indomitable
infectious
insignificant*
inspire
isolated* (adj.)
landmark
limp (n.)
manage to
nurture
parenting styles*
permissive
point out
portrait
potential* (n.)
put your mind to
puzzled (adj.)
radiant
recount (v.)
reflect on
rummage through
shortcoming
spy (v.)
stare (v.)
stumble
tangible
thrive
urge
with a jolt
wobbly

CHAPTER 6
accurately*
annoyance
annoyed (adj.)
articulate (adj.)
ashamed (adj.)
bear (v.)
beyond (one's) grasp
blur (v.)
bulbous
clutch

consequently*
console
dumb
exhaustion
fascinating (adj.)
fling (flung, flung)
frustrated (adj.)
frustration
furious
fury
glance (v.)
grab
guilt
guilty
hatred
herd (v.)
hero
humble
humiliated (adj.)
humiliation
ignorance*
illiterate
lawn
leering (adj.)
multisyllabic
painstaking
proficient
resent
resentment
restrain*
scribbles (n.)
shame (n.)
sheepishly
smirk (n.)
solemn
squinty
squirm
stagger
stomp
stumble
swelling (adj.)
throb
twist away
weep (wept, wept)
wistful
yell (v.)

CHAPTER 7
convince*
day off
drawn (adj.)
envy (v.)

*Words with an asterisk can be found on the Academic Word List used by the Classic Vocabulary Profiler at the Compleat Lexical Tutor site.

frown (v.)
hire (v.)
make up (his) mind
nod (v.)
prune (v.)
show up
shrug
unequivocally
visa

CHAPTER 8
brief*
craziness
fog (n.)
grunt (v.)
imply*
mull over
panorama
ponder
pursue*
rage (n.)
terrified (adj.)
vow (v.)
wanderings
wonder (v.)

CHAPTER 9
acute stress*
alarm reaction*
bored (adj.)
boring (adj.)
chronic stress*
close call
come up with
commit*
confrontation
cooperation*
cope with
crisis (pl. crises)
deal with
deplete
excited (adj.)
exciting (adj.)
exhausted (adj.)
exhausting (adj.)
feel sorry for
flush (v.)
frustrated (adj.)
frustrating (adj.)
get out of hand
give and take
irritable
irritated (adj.)
irritating (adj.)
minimize* (the) impact*
on your way to
overwhelmed (adj.)
overwhelming (adj.)
pace (n.)
perspiration

prolonged (adj.)
relaxed* (adj.)
relaxing* (adj.)
release* (v.)
relieve that uptight feeling
resistance
rush-hour traffic
strain (n.)
strategy*
strive
take it easy
tension*
tranquility
tune out
turmoil

CHAPTER 10
alert
assess*
boost
brisk
currently under way
ensure*
eventually*
fatigue
impressive
keep your posture erect
lecture* (n.)
moderately
pick-me-up
rate (v.)
sedative
stubborn
subsequently*
subtle
tip (n.)
to a small degree

CHAPTER 11
abnormality
adage
adrenaline and dopamine
cardiac symptom
catecholamine
cease*
circulate
clogged (adj.)
dispute (n.)
estimate* (v.)
excess
haggard
immunity
impaired (adj.)
impede
massive
mend
mononucleocytes
play a role*
provocative
rather

recover*
recruit (v.)
resemble
sample (n.)
spasm
speculate
spouse
stabilize*
stimulate
striking (adj.)
telomerase
telomere
toxic
trigger* (v.)
underpinnings
upcoming
whittle down to nubs

CHAPTER 12
arresting (adj.)
bait (n.)
come to with a start
commotion
crawl (v.)
emerge*
era
exclaim
forfeit
impulse
make for
outgrow
scream
sober (v.)
spacious
spirited (adj.)
stone image*
strike (v.)
summon
whisper (v.)

CHAPTER 13
abhorrent
bewildered (adj.)
blueprint (= plan)
connotation
constitute*
crystallize
devilish
feminine companionship
gait
heritage
impressive
in a huff
incest taboo
indignation
infancy
instinct
legacy
mate
mode*

nonrational
pelt (n.)
potentiality
query
rear (v.)
reminiscent of
remote
restrict*
selfish
standardized unreason
trace* descent
undergo*
undesirous

CHAPTER 14
accuse
aloofness
avert one's eyes
code* (n.)
collide
confront
dilemma
famine-stricken
finger-crunching handshake
ignore*
innocuous
invade
jam (v.)
jerk (v.)
law suit
linger
misconstrue
molestation
on behalf* of
protest (n.)
quintessential
reject* (v.)
retreat (v.)
ritual
row (n. = commotion)
sexual* harassment
somewhat*
steely resolve
stunned (adj.)
unanimous
unhesitatingly
untoward
uproar

CHAPTER 15
acquit
anchor (n.)
assimilate
bias*
compliance
fortress (v.)
get along
grief
make ends meet
neglect

plaintively
preconceived notion*
prejudice (n.)
racial harmony
rationalize*
restore*
riot (n.)
stereotype (n.)
surmise
trend*
vulnerable

CHAPTER 16
alike
a trifle
accomplished (adj.)
apiece
assorted
at your disposal
bargain (v.)
bonus
dawdle
dye
exclusively*
exquisite
extract* (v.)
fertile
go astray
go insane
grasp (v.)
highest bidder
ignore*
inhabitant
in stock
lend (someone) a hand
marvel (n.)
mission
nasty
oversight
pass away
peasant
peddle (v.)
sake (n.) / for their own sake
sinful
starve to death
the salt of the earth
utter despair
vagrant (n.)
venture into (v.)
wares
weave

CHAPTER 17
airtight
alternative*
appreciate*
bring out into the open
confess
controversial*
cover all the bases

cut a deal
deceive
deliberate on
expel
figure out
find out
frantically
get away with
get caught
grim
hack into
horrified (adj.)
impact* (n.)
implicate*
manipulate*
reflect on
rumor
scandal
shed light on
the nature of (something)
trade places
virtue

CHAPTER 18
assert
betray
burn (= reproduce)
commit* the resources*
copyright
dead-end (v.)
distribute*
establish* a following
get it right
get signed
grant* (v.)
keep yourself afloat
livelihood
make a living
penalty
rehearsal time
resources*
soul
stiff
stifle
strive
threaten
turn a profit
undertaking* (n.)
up-and-coming
victimless crime
well-being
wholesale . . . theft

CHAPTER 19
affectionate
alleviate
altruistic
anguish
begrudge
bleak

bond* (n.)
callous
captive
cognitive
come down with
compassionate
compatible*
condone
confine*
cure (n.)
deleterious
despair (n.)
embrace (v.)
empathy
emulate
gamboling
gene
haunt (v.) / be haunted by
humane
infect
infringe on
insane
isolation* chamber
justified* (adj.)
lot (n.) (= condition)
mandatory
miserable
mockery
natural habitat
pick up (= learn)
prey to
primate
privilege
prone to
replicate
sensory deprivation
sterile
stimulating (adj.)
sustain*
vaccine

CHAPTER 20
annoying (adj.)
awkward small talk
bitter and bold
bleary
cramped (adj.)
deliberately
gash
grip (v.)
hold up
lecherous
lingering (adj.)
maid
pocked with rust
retrieve
roar (v.)
screech (v.)
shift* (n.)
splotched (adj.)
stare (n.)

stool
surreptitiously
swollen (v. swell, swelled, swollen)

CHAPTER 21
accelerating (adj.)
assumption*
ban (v.)
bankrupt (adj.)
become extinct
cite*
comprehensive*
compromise
degrade
demand
deplete
disrupt
diversified* (adj.)
equitable
eradicate
expand*
indefinitely*
ingenuity
innovation*
institution*
integrate*
interdisciplinary
organism
pessimist
pollution
preserve
rate (n.)
replenish
residue
shift* (v.)
squander
stabilize*
subtheme
ultimate*
wisdom
witness

CHAPTER 22
a slew of
amenities
around the globe*
boast (v.)
capture (v.)
cluster (n.)
compensate* for
contention
demonstration*
drain (n.)
dying of thirst
epitomize
fair share
from scratch
glimpse (v.)
go green

impermeable pavement
infrastructure*
lead the way
make sense
outlying
pedestrian zone
porous
put (someone) to shame
runner up
rush hour
scatter

sprawl (n.)
(time, money) to spare
tract
wreck (v.)

CHAPTER 23
automatically*
concept*
counter (v.)
cut down on

disposable*
drawback
durability
emissions
graze
harvested (adj.)
horrible
livestock
marine (adj.)
miracle
mock (adj.)

mutilate
non-native
overnight (immediately)
practically
scale (n.)
scrape (something) clear of
take up
targeted* (adj.)
viable
wind up

Map of North America

RUSSIA

Chukchi Sea

GREENLAND

ICELAND

Beaufort Sea

Baffin Bay

Bering Sea

Alaska (USA)

Labrador Sea

Gulf of Alaska

Yukon Territory

Northwest Territories

Nunavut

Hudson Bay

Newfoundland

PACIFIC OCEAN

British Columbia

Alberta

CANADA

Manitoba

Quebec

Prince Edward Island

Saskatchewan

Ontario

New Brunswick

Nova Scotia

Maine

Washington

Montana

North Dakota

Minnesota

Wisconsin

Michigan

New York

Vermont

New Hampshire

Massachusetts

Rhode Island

Connecticut

Oregon

Idaho

Wyoming

South Dakota

Nebraska

Iowa

Illinois

Indiana

Ohio

Pennsylvania

New Jersey

Delaware

Maryland

Bermuda (U.K.)

UNITED STATES OF AMERICA

West Virginia

Virginia

Nevada

Utah

Colorado

Kansas

Missouri

Kentucky

North Carolina

ATLANTIC OCEAN

California

Tennessee

South Carolina

Arizona

New Mexico

Oklahoma

Arkansas

Alabama

Georgia

Mississippi

Texas

Louisiana

Florida

THE BAHAMAS

Hawaii (USA)

MEXICO

Gulf of Mexico

CUBA

HAITI

Map of the World

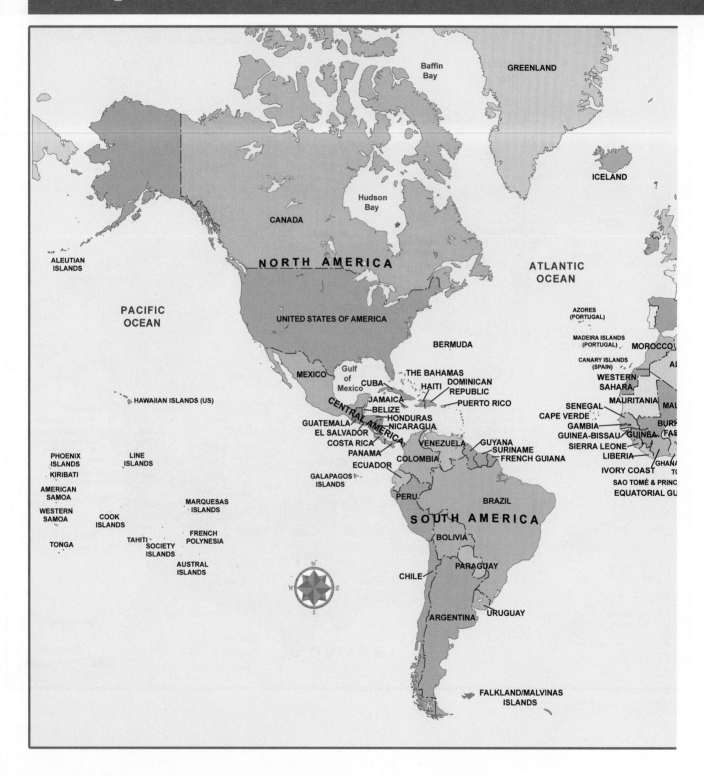

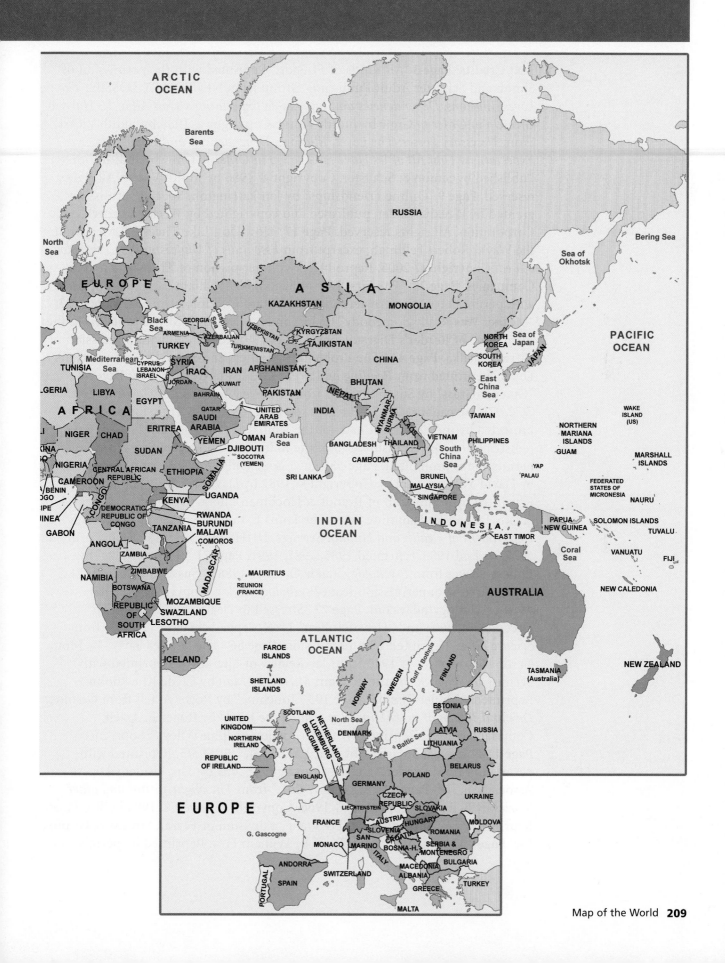

ARCTIC
OCEAN

Barents
Sea

RUSSIA

Bering Sea

North
Sea

Sea of
Okhotsk

EUROPE

ASIA

PACIFIC
OCEAN

KAZAKHSTAN

MONGOLIA

Black
Sea

GEORGIA

Caspian Sea

NORTH
KOREA

Sea of
Japan

UZBEKISTAN

KYRGYZSTAN

ARMENIA

AZERBAIJAN

SOUTH
KOREA

JAPAN

TURKEY

TURKMENISTAN

TAJIKISTAN

CHINA

East
China
Sea

Mediterranean
Sea

CYPRUS

SYRIA

TUNISIA

LEBANON

ISRAEL

IRAQ

JORDAN

IRAN

AFGHANISTAN

BHUTAN

ALGERIA

LIBYA

EGYPT

BAHRAIN

KUWAIT

PAKISTAN

NEPAL

TAIWAN

WAKE
ISLAND
(US)

AFRICA

QATAR

SAUDI
ARABIA

UNITED
ARAB
EMIRATES

INDIA

MYANMAR
BURMA

NORTHERN
MARIANA
ISLANDS

NIGER

CHAD

ERITREA

YEMEN

OMAN

Arabian
Sea

LAOS

VIETNAM

GUAM

MARSHALL
ISLANDS

SUDAN

DJIBOUTI

SOCOTRA
(YEMEN)

BANGLADESH

THAILAND

South
China
Sea

PHILIPPINES

NIGERIA

CENTRAL AFRICAN
REPUBLIC

ETHIOPIA

SOMALIA

SRI LANKA

CAMBODIA

YAP

PALAU

FEDERATED
STATES OF
MICRONESIA

NAURU

CAMEROON

BENIN

TOGO

KENYA

UGANDA

BRUNEI

MALAYSIA

GUINEA

CONGO

DEMOCRATIC
REPUBLIC OF
CONGO

RWANDA

BURUNDI

MALAWI

TANZANIA

SINGAPORE

INDONESIA

PAPUA
NEW GUINEA

SOLOMON ISLANDS

TUVALU

GABON

COMOROS

INDIAN
OCEAN

EAST TIMOR

VANUATU

FIJI

ANGOLA

ZAMBIA

MADAGASCAR

ZIMBABWE

Coral
Sea

NEW CALEDONIA

NAMIBIA

MAURITIUS

BOTSWANA

REUNION
(FRANCE)

AUSTRALIA

REPUBLIC
OF
SOUTH
AFRICA

MOZAMBIQUE

SWAZILAND

LESOTHO

NEW ZEALAND

ICELAND

FAROE
ISLANDS

ATLANTIC
OCEAN

TASMANIA
(Australia)

SHETLAND
ISLANDS

NORWAY

SWEDEN

Gulf of Bothnia

FINLAND

ESTONIA

SCOTLAND

North Sea

RUSSIA

UNITED
KINGDOM

NETHERLANDS

LUXEMBURG

BELGIUM

DENMARK

LATVIA

NORTHERN
IRELAND

Baltic Sea

LITHUANIA

REPUBLIC
OF IRELAND

ENGLAND

GERMANY

POLAND

BELARUS

EUROPE

CZECH
REPUBLIC

UKRAINE

LIECHTENSTEIN

SLOVAKIA

FRANCE

AUSTRIA

HUNGARY

MOLDOVA

G. Gascogne

SLOVENIA

SAN
MARINO

CROATIA

ROMANIA

MONACO

BOSNIA-H.

SERBIA &
MONTENEGRO

ANDORRA

ITALY

MACEDONIA

BULGARIA

PORTUGAL

SPAIN

SWITZERLAND

ALBANIA

GREECE

TURKEY

MALTA

Credits

from the Author. **Page 140** Why you shouldn't do it? www.musicunited.org. **Page 148** "A Plea for the Chimpanzees" by Jane Goodall. Reprinted with permission from *The New York Times*. Copyright © 1987. **Page 159** "The Wallet" by Andrew McCuaig. Copyright © 2006. First published by *Beloit Fiction Journal* in the Spring of 2003, in addition to the Flash Forward Anthology. Reprinted by permission. **Page 169** MILLER Living in the environment, 15E, "Humans and Sustainability." Copyright © 2007 Brooks/Cole, a part of Cengage Learning, Inc. Reproduced by permission. www.cengage.com/permissions. **Page 181** "Islands of Green" by Leif Utne. Reprinted from Utne Reader (Sept.–Oct. 2005), the digest of the alternative press; www.utne.com. Copyright © 2005 Ogden Publications, Inc. **Page 188** "Think You Can Be a Meat-Eating Environmentalist? Think Again!" Reprinted with permission of People for the Ethical Treatment of Animals. Copyright © 2006. **Page 190** "It's a Plastic World" from the book *50 Simple Things You Can Do to Save the Earth* by John Javna. Copyright © 2008 by John Javna. Reprinted by permission of Hyperion. All rights reserved. **Page 196** "Prayer for the Great Family" by Gary Snyder, from *Turtle Island*. Copyright © 1974 by Gary Snyder. Reprinted by permission of New Directions Publishing Corp.

Photo credits: Cover (top left) Stephen Maka/Photex/Zefa/Corbis, (center right) Dave King/Dorling/Kindersley; **Unit and chapter opener** (background) Reginald Wickham; **Page 1** Shutterstock; **Page 9** (top left) © Corbis, (top right) © Fred de Noyelle/Godong/Corbis; **Page 31** (top left) © Fly Fernandez/Zefa/ Corbis, (top right) © Kevin Doge/Corbis, (top bottom) © Kevin Doge/Corbis; **Page 62** © Timothy Tadder/Corbis; **Page 72** © ML Sinibaldi/Corbis; **Page 94** © Gideon Mendel/Corbis; **Page 131** Shutterstock © Rafael Ramirez Lee; **Page 140** Getty Images; **Page 149** © Nigel J. Dennis; Gallo Images/Corbis; **Page 150** Y.F. Wong/Shutterstock **Page 167** © Corbis